I am a Warrior and a member of a team.
I serve the people of the United States and live the Army Values.

I will always place the mission first.

I will never accept defeat.

I will never quit.

I will never leave a fallen comrade.

I am disciplined, physically and mentally tough, trained, and
proficient in my warrior tasks and drills.
I always maintain my arms, my equipment, and myself.

I am an expert and I am a professional.

I stand ready to deploy, engage, and destroy
the enemies of the United States of America
in close combat.

I am a guardian of freedom and
the American way of life.

I am an American Soldier.

This publication is available at
Army Knowledge Online
(https://armypubs.us.army.mil/doctrine/index.html)

*STP 21-1-SMCT

Soldier Training Publication
No. 21-1-SMCT

Headquarters
Department of the Army
Washington, D.C., 11 September 2012

Contents

Preface v

Chapter 1 Introduction to the SMCT System 1-1

Chapter 2 Training Guide 2-1

Chapter 3 Warrior Skills Level 1 Tasks 3-1

Appendix A Battle Drills A-1

Appendix B Proponent School or Agency Codes B-1

Glossary Glossary-1

Subject Area 1: Shoot/Maintain, Employ, and Engage with
Assigned Weapon System 3-1
071-100-0032 Maintain an M16 series Rifle/M4 series rifle carbine
.... 3-1
071-COM-0029 Perform a Function Check on an M-16 Series
Rifle/ M4 Series Carbine 3-9
071-COM-0028 Load an M16 Series Rifle/M4 Series Carbine. 3-11
071-COM-0027 Unload an M16 Series Rifle/M4 Series
Carbine 3-13
071-COM-0030 Engage Targets with an M16 Series Rifle/M4
Series Carbine 3-15
071-COM-0033 Correct Malfunctions on an M-16 Series Rifle/M4
Series Carbine 3-18
071-COM-0031 Zero an M-16 Series Rifle/M4 Series Carbine 3-20
071-COM-4401 Perform Safety Checks on Hand Grenades 3-24
071-COM-4407 Employ Hand Grenades 3-29

Subject Area 2: Move..3-33
071-COM-0501 Move as a Member of a Team.......................3-33
071-COM-0541 Perform Exterior Movement Techniques During
an Urban Operation 3-36
071-COM-1000 Identify Topographic Symbols on a Military
Map 3-42
071-COM-1001 Identify Terrain Features on a Map 3-46
071-COM-1008 Measure Distance on a Map 3-53
071-COM-1002 Determine the Grid Coordinates of a Point on a
Military Map 3-57
071-COM-1005 Determine a Location on the Ground by Terrain
Association...3-65
071-COM-1012 Orient a Map to the Ground by Map-Terrain
Association...3-67
071-COM-1011 Orient a Map Using a Lensatic Compass 3-69
071-COM-1003 Determine a Magnetic Azimuth Using a Lensatic
Compass 3-75
071-COM-1006 Navigate from One Point on the Ground to
Another Point While Dismounted...3-80
071-COM-1030 Navigate from One Point on the Ground to
Another Point While Mounted 3-82
113-610-2005 Navigate Using the Defense Advanced Global
Positioning System (GPS) Receiver (DAGR) 3-85
071-COM-0502 Move Under Direct Fire 3-87
071-COM-0503 Move Over, Through, or Around Obstacles
(Except Minefields)..3-91
071 COM-0510 React to Indirect Fire while Dismounted........3-94
071-COM-3002 React to Indirect Fire while Mounted.............3-95
071-COM-0513 Select Temporary Fighting Positions 3-97

Subject Area 3: Communicate..3-99
113-587-2070 Operate SINCGARS Single-Channel (SC) 3-99
113-571-1022 Perform Voice Communications 3-101
081-COM-0101 Request Medical Evacuation 3-103
171-COM-4079 Send a Situation Report (SITREP) 3-106
071-COM-4080 Send a Spot Report (SPOTREP) 3-108
071-COM-0608 Use Visual Signaling Techniques.................3-111

Subject Area 4: Survive 3-154
031-COM-1036 Maintain Your Assigned Protective Mask.....3-154
031-COM-1035 Protect Yourself from Chemical and Biological
(CB) Contamination Using Your Assigned Protective Mask ..3-157
031-COM-1019 React to Chemical or Biological (CB)
Hazard/Attack 3-164
031-COM-1040 Protect Yourself from CBRN
Injury/Contamination with the JSLIST Chemical-Protective
Ensemble 3-168
031-COM-1013 Decontaminate Yourself and Individual
Equipment Using Chemical Decontaminating Kits 3-173
031-COM-1037 Detect Chemical Agents Using M8 or M9 Detector
Paper..3-179
031-COM-1021 Mark CBRN-Contaminated Areas................3-182
081-COM-1001 Evaluate a Casualty (Tactical Combat Casualty
Care) 3-185
081-COM-1003 Perform First Aid to Clear an Object Stuck in the
Throat of a Conscious Casualty 3-193
081-COM-1005 Perform First Aid to Prevent or Control Shock
....3-195
081-COM-1023 Perform First Aid to Restore Breathing and/or
Pulse 3-197
081-COM-1032 Perform First Aid for Bleeding and/or Severed
Extremity...3-20 3
081-831-1051 Transport a Casualty Using a Military Vehicle 3-206
081-COM-1046 Transport a Casualty.....................................3-210
081-COM-1007 Perform First Aid for Burns 3-217
052-192-1270 React to Possible Improvised Explosive Device
(IED)
(Located at https://www.us.army.mil/suite/doc/23838478) 3-220
052-192-1271 Identify Visual Indicators of an Implosive Device
(IED)
(Located at https://www.us.army.mil/suite/doc/23838510) 3-220
093-89D-1264 Search Suspect Vehicle for Improvised Device
(IED) 3-220
301-371-1000 Report Intelligence Information 3-222
071-COM-0804 Perform Surveillance without the Aid of
Electronic Device 3-225

301-348-1050 Report Information of Potential Intelligence Value **3-230**
071-COM-0006 React to Man-to-Man Contact **3-234**

Subject Area 5: Adapt **3-249**
171-COM-0011 Employ Progressive Levels of Individual Force When Confronting Civilians **3-249**
181-105-1001 Conduct operations According to the Law of War **3-252**
191-376-5148 Search an Individual **3-254**
301-CAT-1001 See Yourself Culturally **3-259**
150-SRT-0001 Develop Professionally **3-261**
150-SRT-0002 Develop in the Five Dimensions of Comprehensive Soldier Fitness **3-264**
071-COM-0801 Challenge Persons Entering Your Area.........**3-266**
071-COM-0815 Practice Noise, Light, and Litter Discipline ..**3-269**
191-376-5216 Search a vehicle for Explosive Devices or Prohibited Items at an Installation Access Control Point **3-271**
191-405-0087 Search a Vehicle **3-277**

Preface

This manual is one of a series of soldier training publications (STPs) that support individual training. Commanders, trainers, and Soldiers will use this manual and STP 21-24-SMCT to plan, conduct, sustain, and evaluate individual training of warrior tasks and battle drills in units.

This manual includes the Army Warrior Training plan for warrior skills level (SL) 1 and task summaries for SL 1 critical common tasks that support unit wartime missions. This manual is the only authorized source for these common tasks. Task summaries in this manual supersede any common tasks appearing in military occupational specialty (MOS)-specific Soldier manuals.

Training support information, such as reference materials, is also included. Trainers and first-line supervisors will ensure that SL 1 Soldiers have access to this publication in their work areas, unit learning centers, and unit libraries.

This manual applies to the Active Army, the Army National Guard/Army National Guard of the United States, and the United States Army Reserve unless otherwise stated.

The proponent of this publication is the United States Army Training and Doctrine Command (TRADOC), with the United States Army Training Support Center (ATSC) designated as the principle publishing, printing, and distribution agency. Proponents for the specific tasks are the Army schools and agencies as identified by the school code, listed in appendix A. This code consists of the first three digits of the task identification number.

Record any comments or questions regarding the task summaries contained in this manual on a DA Form 2028 (*Recommended Changes to Publications and Blank Forms*) and send it to the respective task proponent with information copies forwarded to—

> • Commander, U.S. Army Training and Doctrine Command,
> ATTN: ATCG-MT,
> Fort Eustis, VA 23604-5701.
>
> • Commander, U.S. Army Training Support Center,
> ATTN: ATIC-APR,
> Fort Eustis, VA 23604-5166.

This page intentionally left blank.

CHAPTER 1

Introduction to the SMCT System

1-1. GENERAL

The Army's basic mission is to train and prepare Soldiers, leaders, and units to fight and win in combat. As explained in the Army's capstone training doctrine (ADP 7-0), units do not have the time or the resources to achieve and sustain proficiency with every possible training task. Therefore, commanders must identify the tasks that are the units' critical wartime tasks. These tasks then become the unit's mission essential task list (METL). Commanders use the METL to develop their unit-training plan. Noncommissioned officers (NCOs) plan the individual training that Soldiers need to become warriors and to accomplish the METL. The STPs, also known as Soldier's manuals (SMs), provide the critical individual tasks for each military occupational specialty (MOS) that support all of the unit's missions. The NCO leadership uses the tasks in the SMs to train the Soldiers and measure the Soldiers' proficiency with these unit-critical tasks. The manuals provide task performance and evaluation criteria and are the basis for individual training and evaluation in the unit and for task-based evaluation during resident training.

The Army identified warrior tasks and battle drills (WTBD) that enhance a Soldier's readiness to fight on the battlefield. Warrior tasks are a collection of individual Soldier skills known to be critical to Soldier survival. Examples include weapons training, tactical communications, urban operations, and first aid. Battle drills are group skills designed to teach a unit to react and survive in common combat situations. Examples included react to ambush, react to chemical attack, and evacuate injured personnel from a vehicle. WTBD increases the relevance of training to current combat requirements and enhance the rigor in training. The driving force behind the change comes from lessons learned. Standards remain constant but commanders must be aware that the enemy adapts at once and Soldier training will change sooner because of current operational environments.

Note: If a task identified in the SMCT is not current refer to "DTMS", or the Central Army Registry (CAR) https://atiam.train.army.mil/catalog/catalog/search.html, all tasks are reviewed annually and may change before the SMCT is updated.

1-2. PURPOSE

This Soldier's Manual of Common Tasks (SMCT), Warrior Skill Level (SL) 1, contains the individual tasks that are essential to the Army's ability to win on the modern battlefield. In an operational environment, regardless of job or individual MOS, each Soldier risks exposure to hostile actions. This manual contains the warrior skills that Soldiers must be able to perform to fight, survive, and win in combat.

This SMCT gives the commander, NCO trainer, first-line supervisor, and individual Soldiers the information necessary to support integration and sustainment training in their units. This information allows trainers to plan, prepare, train, evaluate, and monitor individual training of warrior tasks. Using the appropriate mission-training plan (MTP), military occupational specialty (MOS)-specific Soldier's training publication (STP), and this manual help provide the foundation for an effective unit-training plan.

1-3. COMMANDER'S RESPONSIBILITIES

The commander at each level develops a unit METL in consultation with the command sergeant major and subordinate commanders. Using the training planning process described in ADP 7-0, the commander develops the METL and then determines the level of training needed to attain and maintain proficiency. WTBD in chapter 4 supports an Army at war and becomes the key element in Army Warrior Training (AWT). Commanders use the unit METL and AWT to determine the necessary training for the unit and develop a strategy to accomplish the required training throughout the fiscal year (FY). The commander also gives the NCO leadership the guidance they need to carry out this strategy. Each commander must design a unit training plan that prepares the unit for the full spectrum of operations. Soldiers must develop and sustain proficiency in the critical tasks for their MOS and skill level. The commander's unit training program should provide individual training for all Soldiers assigned to the unit and evaluate Soldier proficiency by routine. The leader's assessment and the AWT are two tools that give the NCO leadership and commander information about the status of training for individuals and for the unit, which should be integrated with collective training such as the MTPs, crew drills, and battle drills.

Chapter 2 provides information about where tasks are trained to standard and how often tasks are trained to maintain proficiency.

Based on the commander's guidance, individual training in the unit is the responsibility of the NCO trainers. The commander must give the NCO trainer the priorities, resources, and directions needed to carry out training. He or she must also assess the training results of the MTP and other training events, and adjust the unit training plan as a result. To develop a training program, use the following seven-step approach:

Step 1. Set the objectives for training.

Step 2. Plan the resources (personnel, time, funds, facilities, devices, and training aids).

Step 3. Train the trainers.

Step 4. Provide the resources.

Step 5. Manage risks, environmental and safety concerns.

Step 6. Conduct the training.

Step 7. Evaluate the results.

1-4. TRAINER'S RESPONSIBILITIES

Trainers must use the following steps to plan and evaluate training:

a. *Identify individual training requirements.* The NCO determines which tasks Soldiers need to train based on the commander's training strategy. The unit's training plan, METL, MTP, and the AWT plan (chapter 2) are sources for helping the trainer define the individual training needed.

b. *Plan the training.* Plan individual training based on the unit's training plan. Be prepared to take advantage of opportunities to conduct individual training ("hip pocket" training).

c. *Gather the training references and materials.* The task summaries list references that can assist the trainer in preparing for the training of that task. The Reimer Digital Library provides current training materials.

d. *Manage risks and environmental and safety concerns.* Assess the risks involved with training a specific task regarding the conditions current at the time of training and, if necessary, implement controls to reduce the risk level. Ensure that training preparation takes into account those cautions, warnings, and dangers associated with each task as well as environmental and safety concerns (FM 5-19).

e. *Train each Soldier.* Demonstrate to the Soldier how to do the task with standard proficiency and explain (step by step) how to do the task. Give each Soldier the opportunity to practice the task step by step.

f. *Check each Soldier.* Evaluate how well each Soldier performs the tasks in this manual. Conduct these evaluations during individual training sessions or while evaluating individual proficiencies when conducting unit collective tasks. This manual provides a training and evaluation guide for each task to enhance the NCO's ability to conduct year-round, hands-on evaluations of tasks critical to the unit's mission. Use the information in the AWT plan (chapter 2) as a guide to determine how often to train Soldiers using each task to maintain proficiency.

g. *Record the results.* Use the leader book referred to in FM 7-1 to record task performance. This gives the leader total flexibility with the methods of recording training tasks. The trainer may use DA Form 5164-R (*Hands-on Evaluation*) and DA Form 5165-R (*Field Expedient Squad Book*) as part of the leader book. These forms are optional and reproducible anywhere.

h. *Retrain and evaluate.* Work with each Soldier until he/she performs the task to standard. Well-planned, integrated training increases the professional competence of each Soldier and contributes to the development of an efficient unit. The NCO or first-line supervisor is a vital link to the conduct of training.

1-5. SOLDIER'S RESPONSIBILITIES

Each Soldier must be able to perform the individual tasks that the first-line supervisor has identified based on the unit's METL. The Soldier must perform the task to the standard listed in this SMCT. If a Soldier has a question about how to do a task, or which tasks in this manual he or she must perform, it is the Soldier's responsibility to go to the first-line supervisor for clarification. The first-line supervisor knows how to perform each task or can direct the Soldier to the appropriate training materials. In addition, each Soldier should—

a. Know the training steps for both the WTBD and the MOS-specific critical tasks for his or her skill level. A list of the critical tasks is found in chapter 2 of this manual and the STP for the specific MOS (MOS-specific tasks).

b. Check the Reimer Digital Library for new training materials to support self-development with maintaining earlier trained tasks or to learn new tasks.

1-6. TASK SUMMARIES

Task summaries document the performance requirements of a critical warrior task. They provide the Soldier and the trainer with the information necessary to evaluate critical tasks. The formats for the task summaries are—

a. *Task title.* The task title identifies the action to perform.

b. *Task number.* The task number is a 10-digit number that identifies each task. The first three digits of the number represent the proponent code for that task. (Appendix A provides a list of proponent codes.) Include the entire 10-digit task number, along with the task title, in any correspondence relating to the task.

c. *Conditions.* The task conditions identify all the equipment, tools, materials, references, job aids, and supporting personnel that the Soldier needs to perform the task. This section identifies any environmental conditions that can alter task performance such as visibility, temperature, or wind. This section also identifies any specific cues or events (for example, a chemical attack or identification of an unexploded ordnance hazard) that trigger task performance.

d. *Standards.* A task standard specifies the requirements for task performance by indicating how well, complete, or accurate a product must be produced, a process must be performed, or both. Standards are described in terms of accuracy, tolerances, completeness, format, clarity, number of errors, quantity, sequence, or speed of performance.

e. *Training and evaluation guide.* This section has two parts. The first part, Performance Steps, lists the individual steps that the Soldier must complete to perform the task. The second part is the Performance Evaluation guide. This provides guidance about how to evaluate a Soldier's performance of the task. It is composed of three subsections. The *Evaluation Preparation* subsection identifies special setup procedures and, if required, instructions for evaluating the task performance. Sometimes the conditions and standards must be modified so that the task can be evaluated in a situation that does not, without approximation, duplicate actual field performance. The *Performance Measures* subsection identifies the criteria for acceptable task performance. The Soldier is rated (GO/NO GO) on how well he or she performs specific actions or produces specific products. As indicated in *Evaluation Guidance*, a Soldier must score a GO on all or specified performance measures to receive a GO on the task in order to be considered trained.

f. *References.* This section identifies references that provide more detailed and thorough explanations of task performance requirements than that given in the task summary description. This section identifies resources the Soldier can use to improve or maintain performance.

g. In addition, task summaries can include safety statements, environmental considerations, and notes. Safety statements (danger, warning, and caution) alert users to the possibility of immediate death, personal injury, or damage to equipment. Notes provide additional information to support task performance.

1-7. TRAINING TIPS FOR NCO LEADERS

a. Prepare yourself.

(1) Get training guidance from your chain of command about when to train, which Soldiers to train, availability of resources, and a training site.

(2) Get task, conditions and standards from the task summary in this manual. Ensure that you can do the task. Review the task summary and the references in the reference section. Practice doing the task or, if necessary, have someone train you how to perform the task.

b. Prepare the resources.

(1) Obtain the required resources as identified in the conditions statement for each task and/or modified in the training and evaluation guide.

(2) Gather the equipment and ensure that it is operational.

(3) Prepare a training outline consisting of informal notes about what you want to cover during your training session.

(4) Practice your training presentation.

(5) Coordinate for the use of training aids and devices.

(6) Prepare the training site using the conditions statement as modified in the training and evaluation guide.

c. Train the Soldiers.

    (1) Tell the Soldier what task to do and how well it must be done. Refer to the task standards and the performance measures for the task, as appropriate.

    (2) Caution Soldiers about safety, environment, and security considerations.

    (3) Demonstrate how to do the task to the standard level. Have the Soldiers study the appropriate training materials.

    (4) Provide any necessary training involving basic skills Soldiers must have before they can be proficient with the task.

    (5) Have the Soldiers practice the task until they can perform it to standard levels.

    (6) Provide critical information to those Soldiers who fail to perform at task standard levels, and have them continue to practice until they can perform at standard levels.

    (7) Combine training involving the individual tasks contained in this manual with the collective tasks contained in the MTP. Ensure that the necessary safety equipment and clothing needed for proper performance of the job are on hand at the training site.

d. Record the results: First-line supervisors record the results and report information to the unit leadership.

1-8. TRAINING SUPPORT

Appendix A lists the task proponents and agency codes (first three digits of the task number) with addresses for submitting comments concerning specific tasks in this manual.

1-9. EVALUATING TASK PERFORMANCE

Trainers need to keep the following points in mind when preparing to evaluate their Soldiers:

a. Review the performance measures to become familiar with the criteria about which you will score the Soldier.

b. Ensure that all necessary equipment and clothing needed for proper performance of the job are on hand at the training site. Remember to include safety equipment.

c. Prepare the test site according to the conditions section of the task summary. Some tasks contain special evaluation preparation instructions. These instructions tell the trainer what modifications must be made concerning job conditions to evaluate the task. Reset the site to its original condition after evaluating each Soldier to ensure that the conditions are the same for each Soldier.

d. Advise each Soldier about any special guidance that appears in the evaluation preparation section of the task summary before evaluating.

e. Score each Soldier regarding the information in the performance measures and evaluation guidance. Record the date of training and task performance score (GO/NO GO) in the sections training records for each Soldier.

(1) When applicable, conduct an exercise after-action review to allow training participants to discover for themselves what happened, why it happened, and how it can be done better. Once all key points are discussed and linked to future training, the evaluator will make the appropriate notes for inclusion into the score.

(2) Score the Soldier GO if all performance measures pass. Score the Soldier NO GO if the Soldier fails any step. If the Soldier fails, show the Soldier what they did wrong and allow the Soldiers to take the test again.

This page intentionally left blank.

CHAPTER 2

Training Guide

2-1. THE ARMY WARRIOR TRAINING PLAN

a. Army Warrior Training focuses on training Soldiers warrior tasks, battle drills, and tasks from a unit's METL. This chapter and chapter 4 provides information identifying individual tasks to train and assist in the trainer's planning, preparation, training assessment, and monitoring of individual training in units. It lists by general subject area, and skill level, the critical warrior tasks Soldiers must perform, the initial training location, and a suggested expertise of training.

b. The training location column uses brevity codes to indicate where the task is first taught to standard levels. If the task is taught in the unit, the word "UNIT" appears in this column. If the task is trained by a self-development media, "SD" appears in this column. If the task is taught in the training base, the brevity code (BCT, OSUT, and AIT) of the resident course appears. Brevity codes and resident courses are listed below.

Brevity Codes	
BCT	Basic Combat Training
OSUT	One Station Unit Training
AIT	Advanced Individual Training
UNIT	Trained in/by the Unit
SD	Self-Development Training

c. The sustainment-training column lists how often (frequency) Soldiers should train with the task to ensure they maintain their proficiency. This information is a guide for commanders to develop a comprehensive unit training plan. The commander, in conjunction with the unit trainers, is in the best position to determine which tasks, and how often Soldiers should train to maintain unit readiness. (See chapter 4 for a list of individual tasks that support the WTBD to be trained in each Army unit.)

Frequency Codes	
AN	Annually
SA	Semiannually
QT	Quarterly

Army Warrior Training Plan			
Task Number	Title	Training Location	Sustainment Training Frequency
Warrior Skill Level 1			
Subject Area 1: Shoot/Maintain, Employ, and Engage with Assigned Weapon System:			
071-COM-0032	Maintain an M16 Series Rifle/M4 Series Rifle Carbine	BCT/OSUT	AN
071-COM-0029	Perform a Function Check on an M16-Series Rifle/M4 Series Carbine	BCT/OSUT	QT
071-COM-0028	Load an M16- Series/M4 Series Carbine	BCT/OSUT	SA
071-COM-0027	Unload an M16- Series Rifle/M4Series Carbine	BCT/OSUT	SA
071-COM-0030	Engage Targets with an M16-Series Rifle/ M4 Series Carbine	BCT/OSUT	SA
071-COM-0033	Correct Malfunctions of an M16-Series Rifle /M4 Series Carbine	BCT/OSUT	QT
071-COM-0031	Zero an M16-Series Rifle/M4 Series Carbine	BCT/OSUT	SA
Subject Area 2: Shoot/Employ Hand Grenades:			
071-COM-4401	Perform Safety Checks on Hand Grenades	BCT/OSUT	AN
071-COM-4407	Employ Hand Grenades	BCT/OSUT	AN
Subject Area 3: Move/ Perform Individual Movement Techniques:			
071-COM-0501	Move as a Member of a Team	BCT/OSUT	SA
071-COM-0541	Perform Exterior Movement Techniques	BCT/OSUT	AN
Subject Area 4: Move/ Navigate From One Point To Another:			
071-COM-1000	Identify Topographic Symbols on a Military Map	BCT/OSUT	AN
071-COM-1001	Identify Terrain Features on a Map	BCT/OSUT	AN
071-COM-1008	Measure distance on a Map	BCT/OSUT	AN

Army Warrior Training Plan			
Task Number	*Title*	*Training Location*	*Sustainment Training Frequency*
071-COM-1002	Determine the Grid Coordinates of a Point on a Military Map	BCT/OSUT	AN
071-COM-1005	Determine a Location on the Ground by Terrain Association	Unit	AN
071-COM-1012	Orient a Map to the Ground by Map-Terrain Association	BCT/OSUT	AN
071-COM-1011	Orient a Map Using a Lensatic Compass	BCT/OSUT	AN
071-COM-1003	Determine a Magnetic Azimuth Using a Lensatic Compass	BCT/OSUT	AN
071-COM-1006	Navigate from One Point on the Ground to Another Point While Dismounted	BCT/OSUT	SA
071-COM-1030	Navigate from One Point on the Ground to Another Point While Mounted	Unit	SA
113-610-2005	Navigate using the Defense Advanced Global Positioning System (GPS) Receiver (DAGR)	Unit	SA
Subject Area 5: Move/ Move under Fire:			
071-COM-0502	Move Under Direct Fire	BCT/OSUT	SA
071-326-0503	Move Over, Through, or Around Obstacles (Except Minefields)	BCT/OSUT	SA
071-COM-0510	React to Indirect Fire While Dismounted	BCT/OSUT	SA
071-326-3002	React to Indirect Fire While Mounted	BCT/OSUT	SA
071-COM-0513	Select Temporary Fighting Positions	BCT/OSUT	SA
Subject Area 6: Communicate/ Perform Voice Communications (SITREP/SPOTREP/9-Line MEDEVAC)			
113-587-2070	Operate SINCGARS Single-Channel (SC)	BCT/OSUT	SA
113-571-1022	Perform Voice Communications	BCT/OSUT	AN
081-COM-0101	Request Medical Evacuation	BCT/OSUT	AN

Army Warrior Training Plan			
Task Number	*Title*	*Training Location*	*Sustainment Training Frequency*
171-COM-4079	Send a Situation Report (SITREP)	BCT/OSUT	AN
071-COM-4080	Send a Spot Report (SPOTREP)	BCT/OSUT	AN
Subject Area 7: Communicate/ Visual Signaling Techniques:			
071-326-0608	Use Visual Signaling Techniques	BCT/OSUT	SA
Subject Area 8: Survive/ React to Chemical, Biological, Radiological, and Nuclear (CBRN) Attack/Hazard			
031-COM-1036	Maintain Your Assigned Protective Mask	BCT/OSUT	AN
031-COM-1035	Protect Yourself from Chemical and Biological (CB) Contamination Using Your Assigned Protective Mask	BCT/OSUT	AN
031-COM-1019	React to Chemical or Biological (CB) Hazard/Attack	BCT/OSUT	AN
031-COM-1040	Protect Yourself from CBRN Injury/Contamination with the JSLIST Chemical-Protective Ensemble	BCT/OSUT	SA
031-COM-1013	Decontaminate Yourself and Individual Equipment Using Chemical Decontaminating Kits	BCT/OSUT	AN
031-COM-1037	Detect Chemical Agents Using M8 or M9 Detector paper	BCT/OSUT	AN
031-COM-1021	Mark CBRN-Contaminated Areas	Unit	AN
Subject Area 9: Survive/ Perform Immediate Lifesaving Measures:			
081-COM-1001	Evaluate a Casualty (Tactical Combat Casualty Care)	BCT/OSUT	AN
081-COM-1003	Perform First Aid to Clear an Object Stuck in the Throat of a Conscious Casualty	BCT/OSUT	AN
081-COM-1005	Perform First Aid to Prevent or Control Shock	BCT/OSUT	AN

Army Warrior Training Plan			
Task Number	Title	Training Location	Sustainment Training Frequency
081-COM-1023	Perform First Aid to Restore Breathing and/or Pulse	BCT/OSUT	AN
081-COM-1032	Perform First Aid for a Bleeding and/or Severed Extremity	BCT/OSUT	AN
081-831-1051	Transport a Casualty using a Military Vehicle	Unit	AN
081-COM-1046	Transport a Casualty	BCT/OSUT	AN
081-COM-1007	Perform First Aid for Burns	BCT/OSUT	AN
Subject Area 10: Survive/Perform Counter IED:			
052-192-1270	React to possible Improvised Explosive Device (IED)	BCT/OSUT	AN
052-192-1271	Identify Visual Indicators of an Improvised Device (IED)	BCT/OSUT	AN
093-89D-1264	Search Suspect Vehicle for Improvised Device (IED)	Unit	AN
Subject Area 11: Survive/ Maintain Situational Awareness/Every Soldier as Sensor:			
301-371-1000	Report Intelligence Information	BCT/OSUT	AN
071-331-0804	Perform Surveillance without the Aid of Electronic Device	Unit	SA
301-348-1050	Report Information of Potential Intelligence Value	BCT/OSUT	SA
Subject Area 12: Survive/Perform Combatives:			
071-COM-0006	React to Man-to-Man Contact	BCT/OSUT	SA
Subject Area 13: Adapt/ Assess and Respond to Threats (Escalation of Force):			
171-COM-0011	Employ Progressive Levels of Individual Force when Confronting Civilians	BCT/OSUT	AN
181-105-1001	Conduct operations According to the Law of War	BCT/OSUT	AN

Army Warrior Training Plan			
Task Number	Title	Training Location	Sustainment Training Frequency
191-376-5148	Search an Individual	BCT/OSUT	AN
Subject Area 14: Adapt/ Adapt to Changing Operational Environment:			
301-CAT-1001	See Yourself Culturally	BCT/OSUT	SA
Subject Area 15: Adapt/ Grow Professionally and Personally (Build Resilience):			
150-SRT-0001	Develop Professionally	BCT/OSUT	SA
150-SRT-0002	Develop in the Five Dimensions of Comprehensive Soldier Fitness	BCT/OSUT	SA
071-COM-0801	Challenge Persons Entering your Area	BCT/OSUT	AN
071-COM-0815	Practice Noise, Light, and Litter Discipline	BCT/OSUT	AN
191-376-5216	Search a Vehicle for Explosive Devices or Prohibited Items at an Installation Access Control Point	BCT/OSUT	AN
191-405-0087	Search a Vehicle	BCT/OSUT	AN
Subject Area 16: (Battle Drills) React to Contact:			
071-410-0002	React to Direct Fire While Mounted (Repeat)	BCT/OSUT	SA
071-COM-0513	Select Temporary Fighting Positions (Repeat)	BCT/OSUT	SA
071-100-0030	Engage Targets with an M16-Series Rifle/ M4 Series Carbine (Repeat)	BCT/OSUT	SA
071-326-0608	Use Visual Signaling Techniques (Repeat)	BCT/OSUT	AN
071-COM-0502	Move under Direct Fire (Repeat)	BCT/OSUT	SA
071-COM-0510	React to Indirect Fire While Dismounted (If Applicable) (Repeat)	BCT/OSUT	SA
071-326-3002	React to Indirect Fire While Mounted (If Applicable) (Repeat)	BCT/OSUT	SA
113-571-1022	Perform Voice Communications (Repeat)	BCT/OSUT	AN
071-COM-0501	Move as a member of a Team (Repeat)	BCT/OSUT	SA

Army Warrior Training Plan			
Task Number	*Title*	*Training Location*	*Sustainment Training Frequency*
071-COM-4407	Employ Hand Grenades (Repeat)	BCT/OSUT	AN
Subject Area 17: (Battle Drills) Establish Security:			
071-COM-0513	Select Fighting Positions (Repeat)	BCT/OSUT	SA
113-571-1022	Perform Voice Communications (Repeat)	BCT/OSUT	AN
071-COM-0801	Challenge Persons Entering Your Area	BCT/OSUT	AN
071-COM-1004	Perform Duty as a Guard	BCT/OSUT	AN
191-376-4114	Control Entry To and From a Restricted Area	BCT/OSUT	AN
191-376-5216	Search a vehicle for Explosive Devices or Prohibited Items as an Installation Access Control Point	BCT/OSUT	AN
071-COM-0815	Practice Noise, Light, and Litter Discipline (Repeat)	BCT/OSUT	AN
191-376-5151	Control Access to a Military Installation	Unit	AN
071-326-0608	Use Visual Signaling Techniques (Repeat)	BCT/OSUT	AN
Subject Area 18: (Battle Drills) Perform Actions as a member of a Mounted Patrol:			
551-001-1042	Dismount a Vehicle	Unit	SA
551-001-1043	React to a Vehicle Rollover	Unit	SA
551-001-1041	Establish Security while Mounted	BCT/OSUT	AN
551-001-1040	Perform 5/25/200 meter Scan	BCT/OSUT	SA
113-571-1022	Perform Voice Communications (Repeat)	BCT/OSUT	AN
551-88M-1658	Prepare Vehicle for Convoy Operations	Unit	SA
Subject Area 19: (Battle Drills) Evaluate a Casualty:			
081-COM-0101	Request Medical Evacuation (Repeat)	BCT/OSUT	SA
081-COM-1001	Evaluate a Casualty (Repeat)	BCT/OSUT	AN

Army Warrior Training Plan			
Task Number	*Title*	*Training Location*	*Sustainment Training Frequency*
081-COM-1003	Perform First Aid to Clear an Object Stuck in the Throat of a Conscious Casualty (Repeat)	BCT/OSUT	AN
081-COM-1005	Perform First Aid to Prevent or Control Shock (Repeat)	BCT/OSUT	AN
081-COM-1023	Perform First Aid to Restore Breathing and/or Pulse (Repeat)	BCT/OSUT	AN
081-COM-1032	Perform First Aid for Bleeding of an Extremity (Repeat)	BCT/OSUT	AN
081-831-1051	Transport a Casualty Mounted using a Military Vehicle (Repeat)	Unit	AN
081-COM-1046	Transport a Casualty (Repeat)	BCT/OSUT	AN
113-571-1022	Perform Voice Communications (Repeat)	BCT/OSUT	AN
Subject Area 20: React to Ambush (near/far)			
052-192-1271	Indentify Visual Indicators of an IED (Repeat)	BCT/OSUT	AN
052-192-3261	React to an IED Attack (Repeat)	BCT/OSUT	AN
071-COM-0006	React-to-man-to-man-contact (Repeat)	BCT/OSUT	AN
071-COM-0030	Engage Targets with M4/M16 Rifle (Repeat)	BCT/OSUT	SA
071-COM-4407	Employ Hand Grenades (Repeat)	BCT/OSUT	AN
071-COM-0501	Move as a member of a team (Repeat)	BCT/OSUT	AN
071-COM-0502	Move under direct fire (Repeat)	BCT/OSUT	AN
071-326-0513	Select temporary fighting positions (Repeat)	BCT/OSUT	AN
071-326-0608	Use visual Signaling Techniques (Repeat)	BCT/OSUT	AN
113-571-1022	Perform voice communication (Repeat)	BCT/OSUT	AN
React to Indirect Fire			

Army Warrior Training Plan			
Task Number	Title	Training Location	Sustainment Training Frequency
071-COM-0510	React to Indirect Fire Dismounted (Repeat)	BCT/OSUT	AN
071-326-0608	Use visual Signaling Techniques (Repeat)	BCT/OSUT	AN
113-571-1022	Perform voice communication (Repeat)	BCT/OSUT	AN
071-COM-0501	Move as a member of a team (Repeat)	BCT/OSUT	AN

This page intentionally left blank.

CHAPTER 3

Warrior Skills Level 1 Tasks

Subject Area 1: Shoot/Maintain, Employ, and Engage with Assigned Weapon System

071-100-0032

Maintain an M16 Series Rifle/M4 Series Rifle Carbine

WARNING
Do not squeeze the trigger until the weapon has been cleared. Inspect the chamber to ensure that it is empty and no ammunition is in position to be chambered. Failure to do so may lead to death or serius injury.

Conditions:
Given an M16 series rifle or M4 series carbine, a magazine, 5.56 ammunition, and small-arms accessory case with the following cleaning materials: clean wiping rags, bore brush, chamber brush, toothbrush, cleaning rod, small-arms patches, pipe cleaners, rifle bore cleaner (RBC), and cleaner, lubricant, and preservative (CLP).

Standards: Clear, disassemble, clean, inspect, lubricate, assemble, and perform a function check on the M16/M4. Maintain the magazine and ammunition.

Special Condition: This task is being superseded by 071-COM-0033, REFER TO DTMS OR CAR (https://atiam.train.army.mil/catalog/catalog/search.html) for the new task.

Special Standards: None

Special Equipment:

Cue: None

*Note:*None

Performance Steps

WARNING
Weapon must be cleared to be considered safe.

1. Clear the weapon.
   a. Point weapon in safe direction.

b. Attempt to place the selector lever on SAFE.

Note: If weapon is not cocked, lever can't be pointed toward safe.

c. Remove the magazine from the weapon, if present.

d. Lock the bolt open.

(1) Pull the charging handle rearward.

(2) Press the bottom of the bolt catch.

(3) Move the bolt forward until it engages the bolt catch.

(4) Return the charging handle to the forward position.

(5) Ensure the receiver and chamber are free of ammo.

e. Place the selector lever on safe.

f. Press the upper portion of the bolt catch to allow the bolt to go forward.

g. Place the selector lever from SAFE to SEMI.

h. Squeeze trigger.

i. Pull the charging handle fully rearward and release it, allowing the bolt to return to the full forward position.

j. Place the selector lever on SAFE.

2. Disassemble the weapon.

a. Remove the sling.

CAUTION

Do not use a screwdriver or any other tool when removing the handguards. Doing so may damage the handguards, slip ring, or both.

Do not bend or dent the gas tube while removing handguard.

---

b. Remove the handguards only if you can see dirt or corrosion through the vent holes.

Note: Hand guards on the M16A2 are interchangeable because they are identical. On the M16A4 the hand guards can be replaced by the M5 adapter rails. On the M4 carbine series, the hand guards can be replaced by the M4 adapter rails. The M4 and M5 adapter rails are marked with a T for top and B for bottom. The operator is only authorized to remove the lower adapter rail and rail covers for cleaning, lubrication, or attaching accessories.

(1) Place the weapon on the buttstock.

(2) Press down on the slip ring with both hands.

(3) Pull the handguards free.

c. Push the take down pin as far as it will go.

d. Pivot the upper receiver from the lower receiver.

e. Push the receiver pivot pin in as far as it will go.

f. Separate the upper and lower receivers.

g. Remove carrying handle, if applicable.

(1) Loosen the screws on the left side of the clamping bar.

(2) Lift the handle off once the clamping bar is loose.

h. Pull back the charging handle.

i. Remove the bolt carrier and bolt.

j. Remove the charging handle.

k. Disassemble the bolt carrier.

(1) Remove the firing pin retaining pin.

Note: Do not spread open or close split end of pin.

(2) Push in bolt assembly to locked position.

CAUTION

Do not drop or hit the firing pin. Damage to the pin may cause the weapon to malfunction.

---

(3) Drop firing pin out of rear of bolt carrier.

(4) Remove the bolt cam pin by turning it one-quarter of a turn and lifting it out.

(5) Remove bolt assembly from carrier.

(6) Press the rear of the extractor pin to check spring function.

Note: Any weak springs should be reported to the unit armor for replacement.

(7) Remove the extractor pin by pushing it out with the firing pin.

(8) Lift out the extractor and spring, taking care that the spring does not separate from the extractor.

l. Remove buffer and buffer spring from buttstock.

(1) Press in buffer depress retainer and release buffer.

(2) Remove buffer and action spring.

m. Remove the buttstock. (M4 series only)

(1) Extend the buttstock assembly to full open.

(2) Separate the buttstock assembly from the lower receiver extension.

(a) Grasp the lock lever in the area of the retaining nut.

(b) Pull downward.

(c) Slide the buttstock to the rear.

3. Clean the weapon.

Note: CLP is used to identify when lubricant is needed, however it can be replaced with LSA (weapons lubricant oil, semifluid), or LAW (lubricating oil, arctic weather) as applicable. Do not mix lubricants on the same weapon. The weapon must be thoroughly cleaned using dry cleaning solvent (SD) when changing from one lubricant to another.

a. Clean the bore.

Note: The bore of your weapon has lands and grooves called rifling. Rifling makes the bullet spin very fast as it moves down the bore and down range. Because it twists so quickly, it is difficult to push a new, stiff bore brush through the bore. You will find it easier to pull your bore brush through the bore. Also, because the brush will clean better if the bristles follow the grooves (called tracking), you want the bore brush to be allowed to turn as you pull it through.

(1) Attach three cleaning rod sections together.

(2) Swab out the bore with a patch moistened with CLP or RBC.

(3) Attach the bore brush.

Note: When using bore brush, don't reverse direction while in bore.

(4) Point muzzle down.

(5) Hold the upper receiver in one hand while inserting the end of the rod without the brush into the chamber.

(6) Let the rod fall straight through the bore.

Note: About 2 to 3 inches will be sticking out of the muzzle at this point.

(7) Attach the handle section of the cleaning rod to the end of the rod sticking out of the muzzle.

(8) Pull the brush through the bore and out of the muzzle.

(9) Take off the handle section.

(10) Run the brush through the bore again by repeating the process.

(11) Replace the bore brush with the rod tip.

(12) Attach a patch with CLP to the rod tip.

(13) Pull the patch through the bore.

b. Upper receiver group.

(1) Connect chamber brush to cleaning rod handle.

(2) Dip the chamber brush in CLP and insert in chamber and locking lugs.

(3) Push and twist to clean.

(4) Use a worn out bore brush to clean outside of gas tube.

Note: Gas tubes will discolor from heat. Do not attempt to remove discoloration.

(5) Clean the entire upper receiver by wiping it down.

c. Bolt carrier group.

(1) Clean carbon and oil from firing pin.

(2) Clean bolt carrier key with worn brush.

(3) Clean firing pin recess with pipe cleaner.

(4) Clean firing pin hole with pipe cleaner.

(5) Clean behind bolt rings and lip of extractor.

(6) Clean carbon deposits and dirt from locking lugs.

CAUTION

Do not use wire brush or any other type of abrasive material to clean aluminum surfaces. Damage to equipment may occur.

---

d. Lower receiver group.

(1) Wipe dirt from trigger with a patch.

(2) Use a patch dampened with CLP to clean powder fouling, corrosion, and dirt from outside parts of lower receiver and extension assembly.

(3) Use pipe cleaner to clean buttstock drain hole.

(4) Clean buffer assembly, spring, and inside with patch dampened with CLP.

(5) Wipe dry.

e. Clean the ejector.

WARNING

Do not use a live round to perform this process.

---

(1) Place a few drops of CLP on the ejector.

(2) Press the ejector in using a spent round casing or dummy round.

(3) Hook casing under extractor and rock back and forth against ejector.

(4) Repeat this process a few times adding lubricant until the action of the ejector is smooth and strong.

(5) Dry off excess CLP when process is completed.

WARNING

Do not interchange bolts between weapons.

---

4. Inspect the weapon for serviceability.

a. Upper receiver group.

(1) Check handguards or rails for cracks, broken tabs, proper installation, and loose heat shields.

(2) Check front sight post for straightness.

(3) Check depression of the front detent.

(4) Check compensator for looseness.

(5) Check barrel for straightness, cracks, burrs or looseness.

(6) Check charging handle for cracks, bends, or breaks.

(7) Check rear sight assembly for properly working windage and elevation adjustments.

(8) Ensure the short and long range sight spring holds the selected sight in place.

(9) Check gas tube for bends or retention to barrel.

b. Bolt carrier group.

(1) Inspect bolt cam pin for cracking or chipping.

(2) Inspect firing pin for bends, cracks, and sharp or blunted tip.

Note: Bolts that contain pits in the firing pin hole need replacing.

(3) Inspect for missing or broken gas rings.

(4) Inspect bolt cam pin area for cracking or chipping.

(5) Inspect locking lugs for cracking or chipping.

(6) Inspect extractor assembly for missing extractor spring assembly with insert and for chipped or broken edges on the lip which engages the cartridge rim.

(7) Inspect firing pin retaining pin to determine if bent or badly worn.

(8) Inspect bolt carrier for loose bolt carrier key.

(9) Inspect for cracking or chipping in cam pin hole area.

c. Lower receiver.

(1) Inspect buffer for cracks or damage.

(2) Inspect buffer spring for kinks.

(3) Inspect buttstock for broken buttplate or cracks.

(4) Inspect for bent or broken selector lever.

(5) Inspect rifle grips for cracks or damage.

(6) Inspect for broken or bent trigger.

(7) Visually inspect the inside parts of the lower receiver for broken or missing parts.

d. Turn in weapons with unserviceable parts for maintenance.

5. Lubricate the weapon.

Note: Under all but the coldest arctic conditions, CLP is the lubricant to use on the weapon. Temperature between +10 degrees fahrenheit and -10 degrees fahrenheit, use either CLP or LAW. For -35 degrees fahrenheit or lower, use LAW only. Lightly lube means apply a film of lubricant barely visible to the eye. Generously lube means apply the lubricant heavily enough so that it can be spread with the finger.

a. Upper receiver and carrying handle.

(1) Lightly lubricate inside of upper receiver, bore, chamber, front sight, outer surfaces of barrel, and under the handguards.

(2) Apply a drop or two of lubricant to the front sight detent.

(a) Depress and apply two or three drops of CLP to the front sight detent.

(b) Depress several times to work the lube into the spring.

(3) Apply a drop or two of lubricant to both threaded studs.

(a) Lightly lube the clamping bar and both round nuts.

(b) Lightly lube the mating surface.

(4) Apply one or two drops of lubricant to the adjustable rear sight.

(5) Ensure that the lubricant is spread evenly in the rear sight by rotating the following parts.

(a) Elevation screw shaft.

(b) Elevation knob.

(c) Windage knob.

(d) Windage screw.

b. Lower receiver group.

(1) Lightly lube the inside and outside lower receiver extension, buffer, and action spring.

(a) Lightly lube the inside buttstock assembly.

(b) Generously lube the buttstock lock-release lever and retaining pin.

(2) Generously lube the take down pin, pivot pin, detents, and all other moving parts and their pins.

c. Bolt carrier group.

(1) Lightly lube the charging handle and the inner and outer surfaces of the bolt carrier.

(2) Place one drop of CLP in the carrier key.

(3) Apply a light coat of CLP on the firing pin and firing pin recess in the bolt.

(4) Generously lube the outside of the bolt body, bolt rings, and cam pin area.

(5) Apply a light coat of CLP on the extractor and pin.

6. Assemble the weapon.

a. Install the buttstock assembly. (M4 series only)

(1) Align the buttstock assembly with the lower receiver extension.

(2) Pull downward on the lock release lever near the retaining pin.

(3) Slide the buttstock assembly onto the lower receiver extension.

b. Insert the action spring and buffer.

c. Assemble the bolt carrier.

(1) Insert the extractor and spring.

(2) Push in the extractor pin.

(3) Slide the bolt into the carrier.

DANGER

The cam pin must be installed in the bolt group. Failure to do so will cause weapon to explode when fired next. Injury or death may occur.

(4) Replace the bolt cam pin.

(5) Drop in and seat the firing pin.

(6) Pull the bolt back.

(7) Replace the retaining pin.

d. Engage and then push the charging handle in part of the way.

e. Slide in the bolt carrier assembly.

f. Push in the charging handle and the bolt carrier group together.

g. Join the upper and lower receivers.

h. Engage the receiver pivot pin.

i. Close the upper and lower receiver groups.

j. Push in the take down pin.

k. Replace the handguards.

l. Replace the carrying handle, if applicable.

m. Replace the sling.

7. Perform a function check on the weapon.

8. Maintain the magazine.

a. Disassemble magazine.

(1) Insert the nose of a cartridge into the hole in the base of the magazine.

(2) Raise the rear of the magazine until the indentation on the base is clear of the magazine.

(3) Slide the base forward until it is free of the tabs.

(4) Remove the magazine spring and follower (do not separate).

b. Clean all parts using a rag soaked with CLP.

c. Dry all parts.

d. Inspect parts for damage such as dents and corrosion.

Note: If any damage is found, turn in to maintenance.

e. Lightly lube the spring only.

(1) Insert the follower and spring into the magazine tube.

(2) Jiggle the spring to seat them in the magazine.

(3) Slide the base under all four tabs until it is fully seated.

(4) Make sure the printing is on the outside.

f. Assemble the magazine.

9. Maintain the ammunition.

a. Clean the ammunition with a clean dry rag.

b. Inspect for and turn in any ammunition with the following defects:

(1) Corrosion.

(2) Dented cartridges.

(3) Cartridges with loose bullets.

(4) Cartridges with the bullet pushed in.

Evaluation Preparation:

Setup: Provide the Soldier with the equipment and or materials described in the conditions statement.

Brief Soldier: Tell the Soldier what is expected of him by reviewing the task standards. Stress to the Soldier the importance of observing all cautions, warnings, and dangers to avoid injury to personnel and, if applicable, damage to equipment.

Performance Measures	GO	NO GO
1 Cleared the weapon.	_____	_____
2 Disassembled the weapon.	_____	_____
3 Cleaned the weapon.	_____	_____
4 Inspected the weapon for serviceability.	_____	_____
5 Lubricated the weapon.	_____	_____
6 Assembled the weapon.	_____	_____
7 Performed a function check on the weapon.	_____	_____
8 Maintained the magazine.	_____	_____
9 Maintained the ammunition.	_____	_____

Evaluation Guidance: Refer to chapter 1, paragraph 1-9e, (1) and (2).

References
Required: FM 3-22.9
Related:

071-COM-0029

Perform a Function Check on an M16-Series Rifle/M4-Series Carbine

WARNING
Before starting functional check, be sure to clear the weapon. DO NOT squeeze the trigger until the weapon has been cleared. Inspect the chamber to ensure that it is empty and no ammunition is in position to be chambered.

Conditions: You are a member of a squad or team preparing for an tactical operation and must ensure the operability of your assigned M16-series rifle or M4-series carbine.

Standards: Conduct a function check and ensure that the weapon operates properly with the selector switch in each position.

Special Condition: None

Special Standards: None

Special Equipment:

Cue: None

*Note:*A function check is the final step of maintaining your weapon. It is also performed anytime the proper operation of a weapon is in question. Stop a function check at anytime the weapon does not function properly and turn in the malfunctioning weapon as per unit Standing Operating Procedures.

Performance Steps

1. Confirm the M16/M4 is clear.
2. Conduct a function check on the M16/M4.
   a. Place selector lever on SAFE.
   b. Pull charging handle to rear and release.
   c. Pull trigger.
Note: Hammer should not fall.
   d. Place selector lever on SEMI.
   e. Pull trigger.
Note: Hammer should fall.
   f. Hold trigger to the rear and charge the weapon.
   g. Release the trigger with a slow, smooth motion, until the trigger is fully forward.
Note: An audible click should be heard.
   h. Pull trigger.
Note: Hammer should fall.

i. Place selector lever on BURST (M16A2, M16A4, and M4 only).

j. Charge weapon one time.

k. Squeeze trigger.

Note: Hammer should fall.

l. Hold trigger to the rear.

m. Charge weapon three times.

n. Release trigger.

o. Squeeze trigger.

Note: Hammer should fall.

p. Place the selector switch on AUTO (M16A3 and M4A1 only).

q. Pull the charging handle to the rear, charging the weapon.

r. Squeeze the trigger.

Note: Hammer should fall.

s. Hold the trigger to the rear.

t. Cock the weapon again.

u. Fully release the trigger then squeeze it again.

Note: The hammer should not fall because it should have fallen when the bolt was allowed to move forward during the chambering and locking sequences.

Evaluation Preparation:

Setup: Provide the Soldier with the equipment and/or materials described in the conditions statement.

Brief Soldier: Tell the Soldier what is expected by reviewing the task standards. Stress to the Soldier the importance of observing all cautions, warnings, and dangers to avoid injury to personnel and, if applicable, damage to equipment.

Performance Measures	GO	NO GO
1 Confirmed the M16/M4 was clear.	_____	_____
2 Conducted a function check on the M16/M4.	_____	_____

Evaluation Guidance: Refer to chapter 1, paragraph 1-9e, (1) and (2).

References
Required:
Related: FM 3-22.9, TM 9-1005-319-10

071-100-0028

Load an M16-Series Rifle/M4-Series Carbine

Conditions: Given an M4 or M4A1 carbine with magazines loaded with 5.56-mm ammunition. You must load the M16-series/M4-series carbine so that a round is chambered.

Standards: Ensure the weapon is loaded for the appropriate mode. A magazine is inserted, a round is chambered and the selector lever is place on SAFE if the weapon is not to be immediately fired.

Special Condition: This task is being superseded by 071-COM-0028, refer to DTMS or CAR (https://atiam.train.army.mil.catalog/catalog/search.html) for the new task.

Special Standards: None

Special Equipment:

Cue: None

Note: None

1. Determine the mode in which the weapon will be operated.
   a. Semiautomatic mode.
   b. Automatic mode for M16A1, M16A3, and M4A1.
   c. Burst mode for M16A2, M16A4, M4, and M4 - modular weapon system (MWS).
2. Point the weapon in a safe direction.
3. Cock the weapon.
   a. Pull the charging handle to the rear.
   b. Check the chamber to ensure it is clear.
Note: The chamber can be checked either by locking the bolt to the rear or by holding the bolt to the rear and then observing the chamber area.
   c. Return the charging handle to the forward position.
4. Place the selector lever on :
   a. SAFE for semiautomatic or automatic fire modes.
   b. BURST for burst fire mode.
5. Select BURST fire mode.
Note: Step 5 should only be performed if you have selected to fire the M16A2, M16A4, M4, or the M4 - MWS in the burst mode. For all other modes and weapons proceed to step 6.
   a. Rotate the BURST cam to the BURST position.
   b. Ensure the bolt is forward and the selector level is on BURST.

c. Squeeze the trigger and hold it in the rear position.

d. Pull the charging handle to the rear and release three times.

e. Pull the charging handle to the rear one more time and hold it to the rear.

f. Release the trigger.

g. Lock the bolt open by pressing the bottom portion of the bolt catch.

h. Return the charging handle to the forward position.

i. Place the selector lever on SAFE.

6. Insert the magazine.

a. Push the magazine upwards until the magazine catch engages.

b. Tap upward on the bottom of the magazine to ensure the magazine is seated.

7. Chamber a round.

Note: A round may be chambered with the bolt assembly open or closed.

a. With the bolt open:

(1) Press the upper portion of the bolt catch allowing the bolt to go forward.

(2) Tap the forward assist to ensure that the bolt is fully forward and locked.

b. With the bolt closed—

(1) Pull the charging handle to the rear as far as it will go.

(2) Release the charging handle.

Note: The charging handle should not be rode forward.

```
WARNING
The weapon is now loaded and should be pointed in a safe direction.
```

(3) Tap the forward assist to ensure that the bolt is fully forward and locked.

8. Place selector lever on SAFE and close the ejection port cover if the weapon is not to be fired immediately.

Evaluation Preparation:

Setup: Have Soldiers use their assigned weapons and magazines. Provide blank or dummy ammunition.

Brief Soldier: Tell the Soldier to load the carbine.

Performance Measures	GO	NO GO
1 Determined the mode in which the weapon will be operated.	_____	_____
2 Pointed the weapon in a safe direction.	_____	_____
3 Cocked the weapon.	_____	_____
4 Placed the selector lever on the desired mode.	_____	_____
5 Rotated the burst cam to the burst position for the BURST mode only.	_____	_____
6 Inserted the magazine.	_____	_____
7 Chambered a round.	_____	_____
8 Placed selector lever on SAFE and closed the ejection port cover if the weapon was not to be fired immediately.	_____	_____

Evaluation Guidance: Refer to chapter 1, paragraph 1-9e, (1) and (2).

References
Required: FM 3-22.9 and TM 9-1005-319-10

071-100-0027

Unload an M16-Series Rifle/M4-Series Carbine

Conditions: Given a loaded M16-series rifle or M4-series carbine. You must unload the M16-series rifle or M4-series carbine.

Standards: Unload the M16-series rifle or M4-series carbine so that the magazine and all ammunition are removed from the weapon.

Special Condition: This task is being superseded by 071-COM-0027, refer to DTMS or CAR (https://atiam.train.army.mil/catalog/catalog/search.html) for the new task.

Special Standards: None

Special Equipment:

Cue: None

Note: None

Performance Steps

1. Point the weapon muzzle in a safe direction.
2. Place the selector lever on SAFE.
Note: If the weapon is not cocked, you cannot place the selector lever on SAFE.
3. Remove the magazine.
4. Lock the bolt open.
    a. Pull the charging handle to the rear.
    b. Press the bottom portion of the bolt catch, locking the bolt open.
    c. Return the charging handle to the forward position.
    d. Place the selector lever on SAFE.
Note: If the weapon was cocked before locking the bolt open then the selector lever should already be on SAFE.
5. Remove any ammunition from the receiver and chamber.
6. Return the bolt to the closed position.
    a. Press the upper portion of the bolt catch allowing the bolt to go forward.
    b. Place selector lever on SEMI.
    c. Pull the trigger to release the pressure on the firing pin spring.
    d. Close the ejection port cover.

Evaluation Preparation:

Setup: At a test site, provide an M4 or M4A1 carbine loaded with dummy ammunition.

Brief Soldier: Tell the Soldier to unload the carbine.

Performance Measures	GO	NO GO
1 Pointed the weapon muzzle in a safe direction.	_____	_____
2 Placed the selector lever on SAFE.	_____	_____
3 Removed the magazine.	_____	_____
4 Locked the bolt open.	_____	_____
5 Removed any ammunition from the receiver and chamber.	_____	_____
6 Returned the bolt to the closed position.	_____	_____

Evaluation Guidance: Refer to chapter 1, paragraph 1-9e, (1) and (2).

References
Required: FM 3-22.9 and TM 9-1005-319-10

071-COM-0030
Engage Targets with an M16-Series Rifle/M4 Series Carbine

Conditions: Given a loaded M16/M4-series rifle/carbine, magazines, ammunition, individual combat equipment, and stationary or moving targets (personnel or equipment) at engageable ranges. Some iterations of this task should be performed in MOPP.

Standards: Detect, identify as threat, and determine range to targets in assigned sector of fire. Fire the M16-series rifle/M4-series carbine, while applying correct fundamentals of marksmanship and aiming and engagement techniques so that each target is hit or suppressed.

Performance Steps

1. Detect targets by using one of the following:

Note: Detection of targets depends on your position, your skill in scanning, and your ability to observe the are and recognize target indicators.

    a. Self preservation method.

b. 50-meter overlapping strip method.

c. Maintaining observation on the area .

2. Select Position.

Note: Your situation should affect your physical positioning and firing stance. Your position should protect you from enemy fire and observation, yet allow you to place effective fire on targets in your sector of fire. Your position may vary from a fixed location to a temporary location during movement.

3. Determine range to targets.

a. 100-meter unit of measure method.

b. Appearance of objects method.

c. Front sight post method.

4. Identify targets in your designated sector of fire.

5. Fire on targets using correct fundamentals of marksmanship and appropriate aiming and engagement techniques.

a. Apply the fundamentals of marksmanship.

(1) Steady position

(2) Aiming.

(3) Breath control.

(4) Trigger squeeze.

b. Use appropriate aiming and engagement techniques as needed.

(1) Combat fire techniques.

(2) Chemical, biological, radiological and nuclear (CBRN) firing.

(3) Night firing.

(4) Moving targets.

(5) Short-range marksmanship techniques.

c. Fire on the targets until they are destroyed, suppressed, or you receive an order to cease fire.

Evaluation Preparation: *Setup:* On a live-fire range, provide sufficient quantities of equipment and ammunition to support the number of Soldiers tested. Have each Soldier use his own rifle and magazine.

Brief Soldier: Tell Soldier that he/she is to detect and engage targets in his/her sector and, when asked, state the range to the target. Tell the Soldier to unload the carbine.

At a test site, provide an M4 or M4A1 carbine loaded with dummy ammunition.

Performance Measures	GO	NO GO
1 Detected targets by using one of the following methods.	____	____
2 Selected position.	____	____
3 Determined range to a target.	____	____
4 Identified targets in your designated sector of fire.	____	____
5 Fired on targets using correct fundamentals of marksmanship and appropriate aiming and engagement techniques.	____	____

Evaluation Guidance: Refer to chapter 1, paragraph 1-9e, (1) and (2).

References
Required: FM 3-21.75 (FM 21-75), FM 3-22.9, and TM 9-1005-319-10
Related:

071-100-0033

Correct Malfunctions of an M16-Series Rifle/M4-Series Carbine

Conditions: Given a loaded M16-series rifle/M4-series carbine that has stopped firing, magazine, a complete cleaning rod, and a pointed object. You must correct malfunctions on the M16-series rifle/M4-series carbine.

Standards: Eliminate the stoppage so that firing can be resumed.

Special Condition: This task is being superseded by 071-COM-0033, refer to DTMS or CAR (https://atiam.train.army.mil/catalog/catalog/search.html) for the new task.

Special Standards: None

Special Equipment:

Cue: None

Note: None

Performance Steps

1. Perform immediate action.
Note: The key word "SPORTS" will help you remember the steps for immediate action in sequence; slap, pull, observe, release, tap, shoot.

   a. Slap upward on the magazine to ensure it is fully seated and that the magazine follower is not jammed..
Note: When slapping up on the magazine, be careful not to knock a round out of the magazine into the line of the bolt carrier.

   b. Pull the charging handle fully to the rear.

   c. Observe the ejection of a live round or expended cartridge.
Note: If a weapon fails to eject a cartridge, perform remedial action.

   d. Release the charging handle; do not ride the charging handle.

   e. Tap the forward assist to ensure that the bolt is closed.

   f. Squeeze the trigger and try to fire the rifle.
Note: Apply immediate action only once for a stoppage. If the rifle fails to fire a second time for the same malfunction remedial action should be performed.

2. Perform remedial action.

   a. Correct an obstructed chamber.

      (1) Lock the charging handle to the rear.

      (2) Place the weapon on SAFE.

(3) Remove the magazine.

(4) Visually inspect the chamber.

(5) Remove obstructions from the chamber by:

(a) Angling the ejection port downward and shaking the rifle to remove single rounds.

(b) Using a pointed object to lessen jammed rounds then shake out when loose.

(c) Using a cleaning rod to push out a round or cartridge case stuck in the chamber.

b. Correct a mechanical malfunction.

(1) Clear the weapon.

(2) Disassemble the weapon.

(3) Inspect for dirty, corroded, missing, or broken parts.

(4) Clean dirty or corroded parts.

(5) Replace missing or broken parts.

(6) Assemble the weapon.

(7) Perform a function check.

Evaluation Preparation:

Setup: Provide an M4 or M4A1 carbine loaded with dummy ammunition.

Brief Soldier: Tell the Soldier that the rifle has stopped firing. Tell the Soldier that the weapon is cool and that he/she is to perform the immediate or remedial actions on the rifle. All steps must be performed in the proper sequence.

Performance Measures	GO	NO GO
1 Performed immediate action.	_____	_____
2 Performed remedial action.	_____	_____

Evaluation Guidance: Refer to chapter 1, paragraph 1-9e, (1) and (2).

References
Required: FM 3-22.9 and TM 9-1005-319-10
Related:

071-100-0031
Zero an M16 Series Rifle/M4-Series Carbine

Conditions: Given an M16-series rifle/M4-series carbine, 18 rounds of 5.56-mm ammunition, the appropriate 25-meter zero target (300-meter for M16A2/M16A3/M16A4/M4/M4A1 or 250-meter for M16A1), sandbags for support, and a requirement to zero your weapon.

Standards: Fire the weapon and adjust the sights so that 5 out of 6 rounds in two consecutive shot groups strike within the 4-centimeter circle on the target using 18 rounds or less. Record your zero.

Special Condition: This task is being superseded by 071-COM-0031, refer to DTMS or CAR (https://atiam.train.army.mil/catalog/catalog/search.html) for the new task.

Special Standards: None

Special Equipment:

Cue: None

Note: None

Performance Steps

1. Set either the battlesight zero or mechanical zero on your weapon.
   a. Determine whether to set a mechanical zero or the battlesight zero.
      (1) Set a mechanical zero if—
         (a) The weapon sights have been serviced.
         (b) The weapon is newly assigned to the unit.
         (c) The current zero on the weapon is questionable.
      (2) Set a battlesight zero if a mechanical zero is not required.
   b. Set a mechanical zero on your weapon.
      (1) Adjust the front sight.
         (a) Move the front sightpost until the base of the front sightpost is flush with the front sightpost housing.
         (b) (M16A1 only) Move the front sightpost, from the flush position, 11 clicks in the direction of UP.
      (2) Adjust the rear sight (by weapon type).
         (a) (M16A1 only) Turn the rear sight windage drum left until it stops.
         (b) (M16A1 only) Turn the windage drum right 17 clicks to center it.
         (c) (M16A2/M16A3/M16A4/M4-series) Set rear apertures by

positioning the apertures so the unmarked aperture is up and the 0-200 meter aperture is down.

(d) (M16A2/M16A3/M16A4/M4-series) Set windage by turning the windage knob to align the index mark on the 0-200 meter aperture with the long center index line on the rear sight assembly.

(e) (M16A2/M16A3) Set the elevation of the M16A2/A3 by turning the elevation knob counterclockwise until the rear sight assembly rests flush with the carrying handle and the 8/3 marking is aligned with the index line on the left side of the carrying handle.

(f) (M16A4 only) Turn the elevation knob counterclockwise until the rear sight assembly rests flush with the carrying handle and the 6/3 marking is aligned with the index line on the left side of the carrying handle.

(g) (M4-series only) Turn the elevation knob counterclockwise until the rear sight assembly rests flush with the detachable carrying handle and the 6/3 marking is aligned with the index line on the left side of the carrying handle.

c. Set a battlesight zero on your weapon.

Note: No changes are made to the front sight when setting a battlesight zero.

(1) (M16A1 only) Adjust rear sight by flipping the aperture to ensure the aperture marked "L" is visible.

(2) (M16A2/M16A3/M16A4/M4-Series only) Adjust rear aperture by positioning the apertures so the unmarked aperture is up and the 0-200 meter aperture is down.

(3) (M16A2/M16A3/M16A4/M4-Series only) Adjust windage by turning the windage knob to align the index mark on the 0-200 meter aperture with the long center index line on the rear sight assembly.

(4) (M16A2/M16A3 only) Adjust elevation by—

(a) Turning the elevation knob counterclockwise until the rear sight assembly rests flush with the carrying handle and the 8/3 marking is aligned with the index line on the left side of the carrying handle.

(b) Turning the elevation knob one more click clockwise.

(5) (M16A4 only) Adjust elevation by—

(a) Turning the elevation knob counterclockwise until the rear sight assembly rests flush with the carrying handle and the 6/3 marking is aligned with the index line on the left side of the carrying handle.

(b) Turning the elevation knob two more clicks clockwise so the index line on the left side of the detachable carrying handle is aligned with the "Z" on the elevation knob.

(6) (M4-series only) Adjust elevation by turning the elevation knob counterclockwise until the rear sight assembly rests flush with the detachable carrying handle and the 6/3 marking is aligned with the index line on the left side of the carrying handle.

2. Establish a correct sight picture.

a. Confirm the correct 25-meter zero target is facing you.

b. Assume a prone supported firing position.

c. Align the sights.

(1) Center the top of the front sight post in the center of the rear sight.

(2) Visualize imaginary cross hairs in the center of the rear aperture so that the top of the front sight post touches the imaginary horizontal line and the front sight post bisects imaginary vertical line.

(3) Verify the sight picture.

d. Align the aiming point.

(1) Aim at target center.

(2) Position the top of the front sight post center mass of the scaled silhouette target.

(3) Confirm that an imaginary vertical line drawn through the center of the front sight post splits the target.

(4) Confirm that an imaginary horizontal line drawn through the top of the front sight post splits the target.

3. Establish a tight shot group.

Note: A tight shot group is three consecutive rounds within a 4 centimeter or less circle.

a. Fire a three-round shot group at the 25-meter zeroing target.

b. Identify the shot group on the target.

c. Repeat step 3a and step 3b until two consecutive three-round shot groups fall within a 4 centimeter or less circle.

Note: If a tight shot group is not obtained after 18 rounds then remedial training must be done.

4. Adjust sights (if required) to obtain a zero.

Note: Do not adjust the sights your just fired shot groups meet the standard.

a. Determine the necessary sight adjustments by identifying the center of the last fired shot group and identifying the adjustment to move this point to the center of the strike zone (zero offset).

Note: The numbered squares around the edges of the target each represent a click on the sight.

b. Adjust Elevation.

Note: One click clockwise moves the strike of the bullet down one square, while one click counterclockwise moves the strike of the bullet up one square.

(1) Find the horizontal line nearest the center of the shot group.

(2) Follow the line either left or right to the nearest edge of the target.

(3) Identify the number of clicks and the direction of adjustment shown at the edge of the target.

(4) Adjust the front sight in the indicated direction by the appropriate number of clicks.

(5) Record the adjustment made on the target.

c. Adjust Windage.

Note: Three clicks counterclockwise moves the strike of the bullet left one square, while three clicks clockwise moves the strike of the bullet right one square.

(1) Find the vertical line (up and down) nearest the center of the shot group.

(2) Follow the line either up or down to the nearest edge of the target.

(3) Identify the number of clicks and the direction of adjustment shown at the edge of the target.

(4) Adjust the rear sight in the indicated direction by the appropriate number of clicks.

(5) Record the adjustment made on the target.

5. Establish a zero.

a. Fire a three round shot group at the 25-meter zeroing target.

b. Identify the location of the shot group on the target.

(1) Return to step 4, if two of three rounds do not strike within the strike zone/zero offset.

(2) Proceed to step 6 if two of three rounds strike within the strike zone/zero offset.

6. Confirm the zero.

Note: A zero is confirmed when five of six rounds land within the center 4 centimeter center circle or the zero offset circle.

a. Fire a three-round shot group at the 25-meter zeroing target.

b. Identify the location of the shot group on the target.

(1) Return to step 4, if two of three rounds do not strike within the strike zone/zero offset.

(2) Cease fire if two of three rounds strike within the strike zone/zero offset (your zero is confirmed).

7. (M4-series only) Rotate the rear sight elevation knob counterclockwise (down) two clicks to the 300-meter setting.

8. Record your zero.

a. Compute your zero.

b. Write your zero on a piece of tape.

c. Attach the tape to your weapon.

Evaluation Preparation:

Setup: Provide the Soldier with the equipment and or materials described in the conditions statement.

Brief Soldier: Tell the Soldier what is expected of him by reviewing the task standards. Stress to the Soldier the importance of observing all cautions, warnings, and dangers to avoid injury to personnel and, if applicable, damage to equipment.

Performance Measures	GO	NO GO
1 Set either the mechanical zero or the battlesight zero on your weapon.	_____	_____
2 Established a correct sight picture.	_____	_____
3 Established a tight shot group.	_____	_____

Performance Measures	GO	NO GO
4 Adjusted sights (if required) to obtain a zero.	_____	_____
5 Established a zero.	_____	_____
7 (M4-series only) Rotated the rear sight elevation knob counterclockwise (down) two clicks to the 300-meter setting.	_____	_____
8 Recorded your zero.	_____	_____

Evaluation Guidance: Refer to chapter 1, paragraph 1-9e, (1) and (2).

References
Required: FM 3-22.9 and TM 9-1005-319-10

Conditions: Given any standard issue U.S. hand grenade, a shipping container, canister, and a load bearing vest (LBV), load bearing equipment (LBE), Modular, Lightweight, Load-bearing, Equipment (MOLLE) or Interceptor Body Armor (IBA); and a requirement to employ hand grenade(s).

071-325-4401

Perform Safety Checks on Hand Grenades

Standards: Inspect the shipping container, canister, and hand grenade for defects; report and turn in hand grenade that has defect(s) that cannot be corrected; secure hand grenade(s) properly to the LBV, LBE, MOLLE or IBA

Special Condition: This task is being superseded by 071-325-4401, refer to DTMS or CAR (https://atiam.train.army.mil/catalog/catalog/search.html) for the new task.

Special Standards: None

Special Equipment:

Cue: None

Note: If any discrepancies are found upon receipt of an issued shipping container, canister or hand grenade, personnel should return the shipping container, canister or hand grenade to the issuing person or dispose of it in accordance with the unit tactical standing operating procedures(TACSOP).

Performance Steps

1. Inspect hand grenade shipping container (Figure 071-325-4401-1), if applicable.

Figure 071-325-4401-1. Shipping container.

a. Shipping container is not damaged.

b. Inform supervisor if shipping container is damaged.

2. Inspect the grenade canister (Figure 071-325-4401-2), if applicable.

Figure 071-325-4401-2. Grenade canister.

    a. Inspect the canister for damage.

       (1) Check to see if seal on the canister has been tampered with or is missing.

       (2) Ensure canister is not dented or punctured.

       (3) Inform supervisor of any deficiencies found.

    b. Open the canister.

WARNING

Do not attempt to remove the grenade found upside down in its packing container.

---

       (1) Check to see if the grenade is upside down inside of the shipping canister.

         (a) Replace canister top and tape in place if grenade found upside down.

         (b) Report deficiencies to supervisor.

         (c) Return canister to ammunition disposal personnel.

       (2) Check to see if the safety pin is in proper position.

         (a) Ensure that safety pin is in place and undamaged.

         (b) Check that the legs of the safety pin have either angular spread or diamond crimp.

       (3) Ensure safety clip (when installed) is in place and undamaged.

   3. Inspect the hand grenade.

    a. Remove the packing material and the hand grenade from the canister.

       (1) Check for rust on the body or the fuze.

       (2) Ensure holes are not visible in the body or the fuze.

       (3) Check hand grenade for cracked body.

       (4) Place back in canister if any defect(s) are found, if applicable.

    b. Ensure the safety pin (1) is secured properly (Figure 071-325-4401-3).

Note: If not properly secured, carefully push it into place while holding the safety lever down.

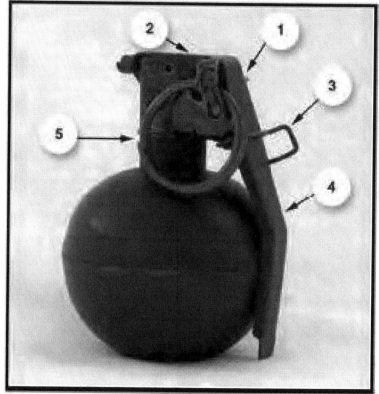

Figure 071-325-4401-3. Grenade components.

c. Ensure the confidence clip (2) is present and properly secured to the pull ring.

d. Ensure the safety clip (3) is present and properly secured to the safety lever (4).

Note: If not properly secured, carefully push it into place while holding the safety lever down.

WARNING
Never remove the fuze from a live grenade.

e. Check the hand grenade fuze assembly (5) for tightness.

f. Ensure the safety lever (4) is not bent or broken.

g. Turn in defective hand grenade, if applicable.

4. Secure the grenade.

> **WARNING**
>
> Never carry the grenades suspended by the safety pull ring or safety lever. Do not attach grenades to clothing or equipment by the pull ring. Do not tape hand grenades to Soldier's gear. Do not attempt to modify a grenade.

    a. Carry hand grenades using the proper procedures.
    b. Ensure that the grenade is fully inside the carrying pouch.
    c. Secure pouch flap.

Evaluation Preparation:

Setup: Provide the Soldier with the equipment and or materials described in the conditions statement.

Brief Soldier: Tell the Soldier what is expected of him by reviewing the task standards. Stress to the Soldier the importance of observing all cautions, warnings, and dangers to avoid injury to personnel and, if applicable, damage to equipment.

Performance Measures	GO	NO GO
1 Inspected hand grenade shipping container, if applicable.	_____	_____
2 Inspected the hand grenade canister, if applicable.	_____	_____
3 Inspected the hand grenade.	_____	_____
4 Secured the hand grenade.	_____	_____

Evaluation Guidance: Refer to chapter 1, paragraph 1-9e, (1) and (2).

References
Required: TM 9-1330-200-12
Related:

071-COM-4407

Employ Hand Grenades

Conditions: Given a fragmentation, concussion, riot control, smoke, or incendiary grenade with a time-delay fuse, a point or area target to engage, and load bearing vest (LBV), load bearing equipment (LBE), Modular, Lightweight, Load-bearing, Equipment (MOLLE) or Improved Outer Tactical Vest (IOTV).

Standards: Engage target with a hand grenade by: selecting appropriate hand grenade based on type target, determining throwing position, correctly gripping, preparing, and throwing the hand grenade so it is within the effective range of the target.

Special Condition: None

Special Standards: None

Special Equipment:

Cue: None

Note: None

Performance Steps

1. Select appropriate hand grenade based on type of target.
2. Select proper throwing position.

Note: You can use five positions to throw grenades - standing, prone-to-standing, kneeling, prone-to-kneeling, and alternate prone. However, If you can achieve more distance and accuracy using your own personal style, do so as long as your body is facing sideways and toward the enemy's position, and you throws the grenade overhand.

    a. Ensure you have a proper covered position.

    b. Determine the distance to the target.

    c. Align your body with the target.

3. Grip the hand grenade.

Note: Do not remove the safety clip or the safety pin until the grenade is about to be thrown.

    a. Place the hand grenade in the palm of the throwing hand with the safety lever placed between the first and second joints of the thumb.

Note: For left handed throwers the grenade is inverted with the top of the fuze facing downwards in the throwing hand.

    b. Keep the pull ring away from the palm of the throwing hand so that it can be easily removed by the index or middle finger of the free hand.

4. Prepare the hand grenade.

    a. Tilt the grenade forward to observe the safety clip.

b. Remove the safety clip by sweeping it away from the grenade with the thumb of the opposite hand.

c. Insert the index or middle finger of the nonthrowing hand in the pull ring until it reaches the knuckle of the finger (Figure 071-COM-4407-1).

Figure 071-COM-4407-1. Pull ring grip, right/left hand.

DANGER
If pressure on the safety lever is relaxed after the safety clip pin are removed, the striker can rotate and strike the primer while the thrower is still holding the grenade. Continuing to hold the grenade beyond this point can result in injury or death.

d. Ensure that you are holding the safety lever down firmly.

e. Twist the pull ring toward the body (away from the body for left handed throwers) to release the pull ring from the confidence clip.

CAUTION
Never attempt to reinsert a safety pin into a hand grenade during training. In combat, however, it may be necessary to reinsert a safety pin into a grenade. Take special care to replace the pin properly. If the tactical situation allows, it is safer to throw the grenade rather than to trust the reinserted pin.

f. Remove the safety pin by pulling the pull ring from the grenade (Figure 071-COM-4407-2 and Figure 071-COM-4407-3).

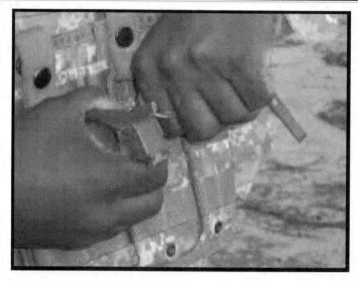

Figure 071-COM-4407-2. Right hand grip, pulling safety pin.

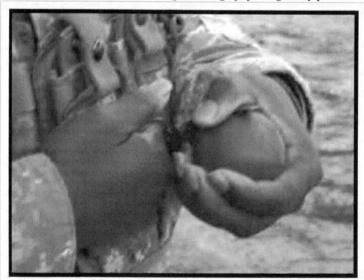

Figure 071-COM-4407-3. Left hand grip, pulling the safety pin.

5. Throw the hand grenade so it is within the effective range of the target.

    a. Observe the target to estimate the distance between the throwing position and the target area.

Note: In observing the target, minimize exposure time to the enemy (no more than 3 seconds).

WARNING

The flight path of the grenade must be checked to make sure no obstacles alter the flight of the grenade or cause it to bounce back toward you.

---

b. Ensure there are no obstacles that can alter or block the flight of the grenade when it is thrown.

c. Confirm body target alignment.

DANGER

Use cook-off procedures only in a combat environment. In training, never cook off live fragmentation hand grenades or offensive concussion grenades.

Never cook off the M84, stun grenade, or smoke grenades. These grenades have short fuze delays (1 to 2.3 seconds) and will cause serious personal injury if cook-off procedures are performed.

The grenade must be thrown immediately after count off.

---

d. Cook off the hand grenade. (Optional)

Note: Cooking off uses enough of the grenade's 4- to 5-second delay (about 2 seconds) to cause the grenade to detonate above ground or shortly after impact with the target.

(1) Release the safety lever.

(2) Count "One thousand one, one thousand two".

e. Throw the grenade overhand so that the grenade arcs, landing on or near the target.

Note: To be effective the target must be within the bursting radius of the grenade.

f. Allow the motion of the throwing arm to continue naturally once the grenade is released.

g. Seek cover to avoid being hit by fragments or direct enemy fire.

Note: If no cover is available, drop to the prone position with your protective head gear facing the direction of the grenade's detonation.

Evaluation Preparation:

Setup: Provide the Soldier with the equipment and or materials described in the conditions statement.

Brief Soldier: Tell the Soldier what is expected of him by reviewing the task standards. Stress to the Soldier the importance of observing all cautions, warnings, and dangers to avoid injury to personnel and, if applicable, damage to equipment.

Performance Measures	GO	NO GO
1 Selected the appropriate hand grenade based on type of target.	____	____
2 Selected appropriate throwing position.	____	____
3 Gripped the hand grenade.	____	____
4 Prepared the grenade.	____	____
5 Threw the hand grenade so it was within the effective range of the target.	____	____

Evaluation Guidance: Refer to chapter 1, paragraph 1-9e, (1) and (2).

References
Required:
Related: FM 3-23.30

Subject Area 2: Move

071-COM-0501

Move as a Member of a Team

Conditions:

You are a member of a dismounted team that is conducting tactical movement. You are not the team leader. You have your individual weapon and individual combat equipment.

Standards: Assume your position in the team's current formation, maintain proper distance between you and other team members, follow the team leader's example, and maintain security of your sector.

Special Condition: None

Special Standards: None

Special Equipment:

Cue: None

Note: The standard team is composed of four personnel - team leader (TL), automatic rifleman (AR), grenadier (G), and rifleman (R). The team leader designates positions based on the mission variables.

Performance Steps

1. Assume your position in the team's current formation.
Note: Specific positions vary based on the type of movement formation selected by the team leader.

a. Assume your position within the team wedge formation (Figure 071-COM-0501-1).
Note: This is the basic team formation. It is easy to control, is flexible, allows immediate fires in all directions, and offers all-round local security.

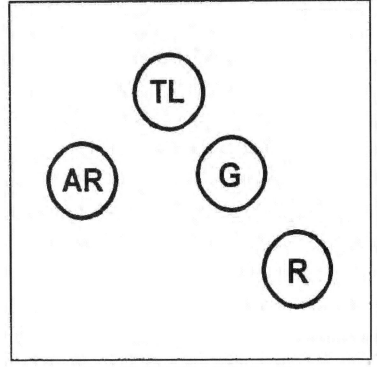

Figure 071-COM-0501-1. Wedge Formations

b. Assume your position within the team file formation (Figure 071-COM-0501-2).

Note: The file is used when employing the wedge is impractical. This formation is most often used in severely restrictive terrain, like inside a building; dense vegetation; limited visibility; and so forth. The distance between Soldiers changes due to constraints of the situation, particularly when in urban operations.

Figure 071-COM-0501-2. File Formation.

2. Maintain proper distance between you and other team members.

Note: The normal distance between Soldiers is 10 meters. When enemy contact is possible, the distance between teams should be about 50 meters. In open terrain such as desert, the interval may increase. The distance between individuals is determined by how much control the team leader can still exercise over his team members.

3. Maintain visual contact with your team leader.

Note: It is essential for all team members to maintain visual contact with the team leader.

4. Follow the team leader's example.

Note: When the team leader moves left, you move to the left. When the team leader gets down, you get down.

5. Adjust your position within the team as designated by the team leader.

6. Maintain security of your sector (i.e. to the flanks, front or rear of the team).

Evaluation Preparation:

Setup: Provide the Soldier with the equipment and or materials described in the conditions statement.

Brief Soldier: Tell the Soldier what is expected of him by reviewing the task standards. Stress to the Soldier the importance of observing all cautions, warnings, and dangers to avoid injury to personnel and, if applicable, damage to equipment.

Performance Measures	GO	NO GO
1 Assumed position in the team's current formation	___	___
2 Maintained proper distance from other team members.	___	___
3 Maintained visual contact with the team leader.	___	___
4 Followed the team leader's example.	___	___
5 Changed position within the team as designated by the team leader.	___	___
6 Maintained security of assigned sector.	___	___

Evaluation Guidance: Refer to chapter 1, paragraph 1-9e, (1) and (2).

References
Required:
Related: FM 3-21.75

071-COM-0541

Perform Exterior Movement Techniques During an Urban Operation

Conditions: Given an individual weapon with ammunition; individual protective equipment; and a requirement to move in urban terrain, with the enemy's location and strength uncertain.

Standards: Move within an urban area using proper urban movement techniques while minimizing exposure to enemy fire.

Special Condition: This task is being superseded by 071-COM-0541, refer to DTMS or CAR (https://atiam.train.army.mil/catalog/catalog/search.html) for the new task.

Special Standards: None

Special Equipment:

Cue: None

Note: Outdoor movement in urban terrain is best conducted as part of a buddy team, a fire team, or a squad. This ensures at least one Soldier is providing overwatch of another Soldier's movement, either from a stationary position or as both are moving, and prevents individual Soldiers from being isolated. This allows for a rapid engagement of any enemy that either exposes themselves (such as by leaning out of or by silhouetting themselves in a window) or by firing.

Performance Steps

1. Move across streets or open areas.

Note: Open areas include parks, plazas and large intersections as well as streets, open air buildings, and large rooms that are significantly exposed to exterior view. Ideally, avoid these open areas as they are potential killing zones for the enemy, especially crew-served weapons and snipers; however, operations often require movement across these areas. Cross these areas using the same basic techniques used to cross any danger area.

    a. Identify the far side position before moving with a clear understanding of how it will be occupied or cleared.

    b. Conduct a visual reconnaissance of all the dimensions of urban terrain to identify likely threat positions.

    c. Select a position on the far side that provides the best available cover.

    d. Select the best route to the far side position that minimizes the time exposed.

Note: Obscurants, such as smoke, are an option to conceal movement. However, thermal sighting systems can see through smoke and when smoke is thrown in an open area, an enemy may fire into the smoke cloud in anticipation of movement through or behind the smoke.

    e. Cross rapidly along the selected route to the selected position.

2. Move parallel to buildings.

Note: Moving parallel to buildings is the movement normally associated with moving down a roadway but also includes movement in plazas or other open areas that are between buildings. During contact, utilize smoke, suppressive fires, and individual movement techniques. In moving to adjacent buildings, team members should keep a distance of 3 to 5 meters between themselves, leapfrogging along each side of the street and from cover to cover.

    a. Soldier moves parallel to the side of a building.

    b. Use existing cover and concealment.

    c. Stay in the shadows.

    d. Present a low silhouette.

e. Use proper techniques to cross door and window openings

f. Move rapidly to the next position.

3. Move past building opening (windows and doors).

Note: The most common mistakes at windows are exposing the head in a first-floor window and not being aware of basement windows.

a. Move past an above-knee window.

(1) Stay near the side of the building.

(2) Stay below the level of the window.

(3) Avoid silhouetting self in window (Figure 071-COM-0541-1).

Figure 071-COM-0541-1. Soldier moving past window.

b. Move past a below-knee window (basement).

(1) Stay near the side of the building.

(2) Step or jump past the window without exposing legs (Figure 071-COM-0541-2).

Figure 071-COM-0541-2. Soldier moving past basement window.

c. Move past a full-height window (store type) or open door.

Note: A Soldier should not just walk past an adjacent full height window, as he presents a good target to an enemy inside the building.

(1) Identify a position on the far side of the window.

(2) Determine which technique to use to cross the opening.

(a) Run across the opening to the far side.

(b) Arc around the opening while covering the opening with your weapon while moving.

(3) Move rapidly to the far side position.

4. Move around corners.

Note: Before moving around a corner, the Solider must first observe around the corner. The most common two mistakes Soldier make at corners are exposing their head and upper body where it is expected and flagging their weapon.

a. Move around a corner by first observing around the corner.

(1) Lie flat on the ground, weapon at your side, ensuring that your weapon is not forward of the corner.

Note: DO not show your head below at the height an enemy would expect to see it.

(2) Expose your head (with Helmet) only enough to observe around the corner (Figure 071-COM-0541-3).

Note: When speed is required the Pie-ing method is applied.

Figure 071-COM-0541-3. Soldier looking around a corner.

(3) Continue movement around the corner, if clear.

b. Move around the corner by using the pie-ing method.

(1) Aim the weapon beyond the corner (without flagging) into the direction of travel.

(2) Side-step around the corner in a semi-circular fashion with the muzzle as the pivot point (Figure 071-COM-0541-4).

Figure 071-COM-0541-4. Soldier Pie-ing around a corner.

(3) Continue movement around the corner, if clear.

5. Cross a wall.

a. Reconnoiter the other side.

Note: The far side must be relatively safe from enemy fire, as once across the wall, the Soldier is fully exposed. Additionally, the immediate opposite side of the wall must be safe for landing; long drops and debris can cause injury.

b. Identify a far side position.

Note: Once across the wall, you will then move to this far side position. This position may be at the wall, near the wall, or away from the wall.

c. Crouch near the wall.

d. Hold your weapon with one hand while grabbing the top of the wall with the other hand

e. Pull with the hand on the wall while simultaneously swinging both legs over the wall, one right after the other.

f. Roll your whole body quickly over the wall while keeping a low silhouette (Figure 071-COM-0541-5).

Note: Speed of movement and a low silhouette deny the enemy a good target.

Figure 071-COM-0541-5. Soldier crossing a wall.

g. Move to you next position once on the far side.

Evaluation Preparation:

Setup: At the test site, provide all materials and equipment given in the task condition statement.

Brief Soldier: Tell the Soldier to move as a designated member of an assault element in urban terrain. The enemy strength and location are unknown.

Performance Measures	GO	NO GO
1 Moved across a street or open area.	_____	_____
2 Moved parallel to a building.	_____	_____
3 Moved passed a building opening (window or open door).	_____	_____

Performance Measures	GO	NO GO
4 Moved around a corner.	___	___
5 Crossed a wall.	___	___

Evaluation Guidance: Refer to chapter 1, paragraph 1-9e, (1) and (2).

References
Required: ATTP 3-06.11 and FM 3-21.75
Related:

071-COM-1000

Identify Topographic Symbols on a Military Map

Conditions: You are a member of a squad or team in a field environment and have been given; a 1:50,000 scale military map and a requirement to identify topographic symbols on the map.

Standards: Identify topographic symbols, colors, and marginal information on a military map.

Special Condition: None

Special Standards: None

Special Equipment:

Cue: None

Note: None

1. Identify the six basic colors on a military map (Figure 071-COM-1000-1).

COLORS	SYMBOLS
Black	Cultural (man-made) features other than roads
Blue	Water
Brown	All relief features - contour lines on old maps - cultivated land on red-light readable maps
Green	Vegetation
Red	Major roads, built-up areas, special features on old maps
Red-brown	All relief features and main roads on red-light readable maps

Figure 071-COM-1000-1. Colors

    a. Identify the features that the color black represents.

Note: Indicates cultural (manmade) features such as buildings and roads, surveyed spot elevations, and all labels.

    b. Identify the features that the color blue represents.

Note: Indicates hydrography or water features such as lakes, swamps, rivers, and drainage.

    c. Identify the features that the color green represents.

Note: Indicates vegetation with military significance such as woods, orchards, and vineyards.

    d. Identify the features that the color brown represents.

Note: Brown identifies all relief features and elevation such as contours on older edition maps and cultivated land on red light readable maps.

    e. Identify the features that the color red represents.

Note: Classifies cultural features, such as populated areas, main roads, and boundaries, on older maps.

    f. Identify the features that the color red-brown represents.

Note: These colors are combined to identify cultural features, all relief features, non surveyed spot elevations, and elevation such as contour lines on red light readable maps.

    g. Identify all other features and the colors they represent, if applicable.

Note: Other colors may be used to show special information. These are indicated in the marginal information as a rule.

2. Identify the symbols on a military map.

a. Use the legend, which should identify most of the symbols used on the map.

b. Identify each object by its shape on the map.

Note: For example, a black, solid square represents a building or a house; a round or irregular blue item is a lake or pond.

c. Use logic and color to identify each map feature.

Note: For example, blue represents water. If you see a symbol that is blue and has clumps of grass, this would be a swamp.

3. Identify the marginal information on a military map (Figure 071-COM-1000-2).

Figure 071-COM-1000-2. Topographical map.

a. Identify the sheet name (1).

b. Identify the sheet number (2).

c. Identify the series name (3).

d. Identify the scale (4).

e. Identify the series number (5).

f. Identify the edition number (6).
g. Identify the index to boundaries (7).
h. Identify the adjoining sheets diagram (8).
i. Identify the elevation guide (9).
j. Identify the declination diagram (10).
k. Identify the bar scales (11).
l. Identify the contour interval note (12).
m. Identify the spheroid note (13).
n. Identify the grid note (14).
o. Identify the projection note (15).
p. Identify the vertical datum note (16).
q. Identify the horizontal datum note (17).
r. Identify the control note (18).
s. Identify the preparation note (19).
t. Identify the printing note (20).
u. Identify the grid reference box (21).
v. Identify the unit imprint and symbol (22).
w. Identify the legend (23).

Evaluation Preparation:

Setup: Provide the Soldier with the equipment and or materials described in the conditions statement.

Brief Soldier: Tell the Soldier what is expected of him by reviewing the task standards. Stress to the Soldier the importance of observing all cautions, warnings, and dangers to avoid injury to personnel and, if applicable, damage to equipment.

Performance Measures	GO	NO GO
1 Identified the six basic colors on a military map.	⎯⎯	⎯⎯
2 Identified the symbols on a military map.	⎯⎯	⎯⎯
3 Identified the marginal information on a military map.	⎯⎯	⎯⎯

Evaluation Guidance: Refer to chapter 1, paragraph 1-9e, (1) and (2).

References
Required:
Related: FM 3-25.26

071-COM-1001

Identify Terrain Features on a Map

Conditions: You are a member of a squad or team in a field environment and have been directed to identify the terrain features on a map. You have been given a 1:50,000 scale military map.

Standards: Identify the five major, three minor, and two supplementary terrain features on a military map.

Special Condition: None

Special Standards: None

Special Equipment:

Cue: None

*Note:*All terrain features are derived from a complex landmass known as a mountain or ridgeline (Figure 071-COM-1001-1). The term ridgeline is not interchangeable with the term ridge. A ridgeline is a line of high ground, usually with changes in elevation along its top and low ground on all sides from which a total of 10 natural or man-made terrain features are classified.

Figure 071-COM-1001-1. Ridgeline.

1. Identify five major terrain features.

    a. Identify a hill (Figure 071-COM-1001-2).

Note: A hill is an area of high ground. From a hilltop, the ground slopes down in all directions. A hill is shown on a map by contour lines forming concentric circles. The inside of the smallest closed circle is the hilltop.

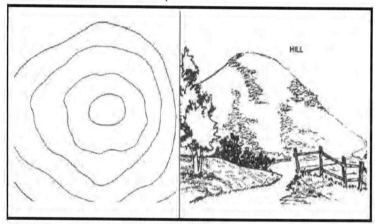

Figure 071-COM-1001-2. Hill.

    b. Identify a saddle (Figure 071-COM-1001-3).

Note: A saddle is a dip or low point between two areas of higher ground. A saddle is not necessarily the lower ground between two hilltops; it may be simply a dip or break along a level ridge crest. If you are in a saddle, there is high ground in two opposite directions and lower ground in the other two directions. A saddle is normally represented as an hourglass.

Figure 071-COM-1001-3. Saddle.

   c. Identify a valley (Figure 071-COM-1001-4).

Note: A valley is a stretched-out groove in the land, usually formed by streams or rivers. A valley begins with high ground on three sides and usually has a course of running water through it. If standing in a valley, three directions offer high ground, while the fourth direction offers low ground. Depending on its size and where a person is standing, it may not be obvious that there is high ground in the third direction, but water flows from higher to lower ground. Contour lines forming a valley are either U-shaped or V-shaped. To determine the direction water is flowing, look at the contour lines. The closed end of the contour line (U or V) always points upstream or toward high ground.

Figure 071-COM-1001-4. Valley.

   d. Identify a ridge (Figure 071-COM-1001-5).

Note: A ridge is a sloping line of high ground. If you are standing on the centerline of a ridge, you will normally have low ground in three directions and high ground in one direction with varying degrees of slope. If you cross a ridge at right angles, you will climb steeply to the crest and then descend steeply to the base. When you move along the path of the ridge, depending on the geographic location, there may be either an almost unnoticeable slope or a very obvious incline. Contour lines forming a ridge tend to be U-shaped or V-shaped. The closed end of the contour line points away from high ground.

Figure 071-COM-1001-5. Ridge.

e. Identify a depression (Figure 071-COM-1001-6).

Note: A depression is a low point in the ground or a sinkhole. It could be described as an area of low ground surrounded by higher ground in all directions, or simply a hole in the ground. Usually only depressions that are equal to or greater than the contour interval will be shown. On maps, depressions are represented by closed contour lines that have tick marks pointing toward low ground.

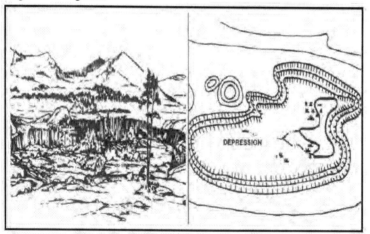

Figure 071-COM-1001-6. Depression.

2. Identify three minor terrain features.

a. Identify a draw (Figure 071-COM-1001-7).

Note: A draw is a stream course that is less developed than a valley. In a draw, there is essentially no level ground and, therefore, little or no maneuver room within its confines. If you are standing in a draw, the ground slopes upward in three directions and downward in the other direction. A draw could be considered as the initial formation of a valley. The contour lines depicting a draw are U-shaped or V-shaped, pointing toward high ground.

Figure 071-COM-1001-7. Draw.

b. Identify a spur (Figure 071-COM-1001-8).

Note: A spur is a short, continuous sloping line of higher ground, normally jutting out from the side of a ridge. A spur is often formed by two roughly parallel streams cutting draws down the side of a ridge. The ground will slope down in three directions and up in one. Contour lines on a map depict a spur with the U or V pointing away from high ground.

Figure 071-COM-1001-8. Spur.

c. Identify a cliff (Figure 071-COM-1001-9).

Note: A cliff is a vertical or near vertical feature; it is an abrupt change of the land. When a slope is so steep that the contour lines converge into one "carrying" contour of contours, this last contour line has tick marks pointing toward low ground. Cliffs re also shown by contour lines very close together and, in some instances, touching each other.

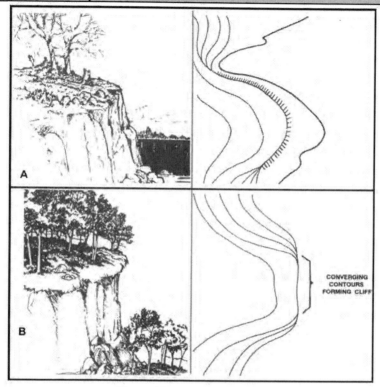

Figure 071-COM-1001-9. Cliff.

3. Identify two supplementary terrain features.

    a. Identify a cut (Figure 071-COM-1001-10).

Note: A cut is a man-made feature resulting from cutting through raised ground, usually to form a level bed for a road or railroad track. Cuts are shown on a map when they are at least 10 feet high, and they are drawn with a contour line along the cut line. This contour line extends the length of the cut and has tick marks that extend from the cut line to the roadbed, if the map scale permits this level of detail.

    b. Identify a fill (Figure 071-COM-1001-10).

Note: A fill is a man-made feature resulting from filling a low area, usually to form a level bed for a road or railroad track. Fills are shown on a map when they are at least 10 feet high, and they are drawn with a contour line along the fill line. This contour line extends the length of the filled area and has tick marks that point toward lower ground. If the map scale permits , the length of the fill tick marks are drawn to scale and extend from the base line of the fill symbol.

Figure 071-COM-1001-10. Cut and Fill.

Evaluation Preparation:

Setup: Provide the Soldier with the equipment and or materials described in the conditions statement.

Brief Soldier: Tell the Soldier what is expected of him by reviewing the task standards. Stress to the Soldier the importance of observing all cautions, warnings, and dangers to avoid injury to personnel and, if applicable, damage to equipment.

Performance Measures	GO	NO GO
1 Identified the five major terrain features.	_____	_____
2 Identified the three minor terrain features.	_____	_____
3 Identified the two supplementary terrain features.	_____	_____

Evaluation Guidance: Refer to chapter 1, paragraph 1-9e, (1) and (2).

References
Required:
Related: FM 3-25.26

071-COM-1008

Measure Distance on a Map

Conditions: You are a member of a squad or team in a field environment and have been directed to determine the distance between two known points. You have a 1:50,000 scale map, a strip of paper with a straight edge, and a pencil. You have been shown the beginning and ending points on the map.

Standards: Determine the straight-line distance between two points with no more than a 5 percent error and the road (curved line) distance between two points with no more than a 10 percent error.

Special Condition: None

Special Standards: None

Special Equipment:

Cue: None

Note: None

Performance Steps

1. Identify the graphic (bar) scale of the map.
2. Convert straight-line distance between two points on a map.

   a. Line up the straight edge of a strip of paper with the beginning and ending points on the map.

   b. Mark the beginning and ending points on the straight edge of the paper (Figure 071-COM-1008-1).

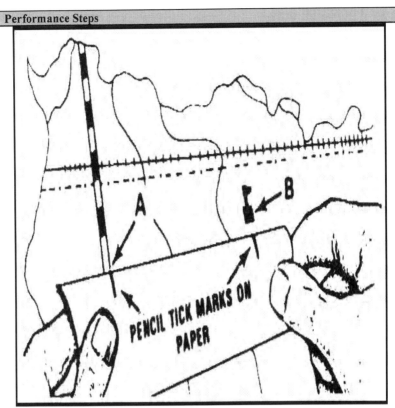

Figure 071-COM-1008-1. Beginning and Ending Points.

c. Place the starting point on the paper under the zero on the bar scale.

d. Measure off 4,000 meters and place a new tick mark on the paper.

e. Place the new tick mark under the zero on the bar scale.

f. Determine if the end point falls within the bar scale.

(1) Record the value on the scale of the end point, if the end point fits on the scale.

(2) Add 4,000 meters to this value (a) to get the total difference.

g. Determine if the end point falls outside the bar.

(1) Repeat steps 3d and 3e until the end point falls within the bar.

(2) Add 4,000 meters to the value you derived in step 3f(1) for each time you performed step 3d to achieve the total distance.

3. Convert map distance to ground distance.

a. Align the edge of a strip of paper with the beginning point and the point where the road makes the first curve on the map.

b. Mark on the straight edge of the paper the beginning and curve points.

c. Repeat steps 4a and b, each time using the point of the curve as the next beginning point, until you reach the end point.

d. Align the marks on the paper with the appropriate bar scale (Figure 071-COM-1008-2).

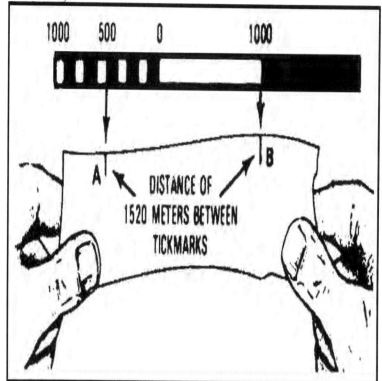

Figure 071-COM-1008-2. Distance between Beginning and Ending Points.

e. Determine the distance on the scale that compares to the distance on the paper.

4. Convert a road map distance to miles, meters or yards.

a. Align the edge of a strip of paper with the beginning point and the point where the road makes the first curve on the map.

b. Mark on the straight edge of the paper the beginning and curve points.

c. Repeat steps 5a and b, each time using the point of the curve as the next beginning point, until you reach the end point.

d. Place the starting point on the paper under the zero on the bar scale.

e. Measure off 4,000 meters and place a new tick mark on the paper.

f. Place the new tick mark under the zero on the bar scale.

g. Determine if the end point falls within the bar scale.

(1) Record the value on the scale of the end point, if the end point fits on the scale.

(2) Add 4,000 meters to this value (a) to get the total difference.

h. Determine if the end point falls outside the bar.
(1) Repeat steps 5d and 5e until the end point falls within the bar.
(2) Add 4,000 meters to the value you derived in step 5g(1) for each time you performed step 5d to achieve the total distance.

Evaluation Preparation:

Setup: Provide the Soldier with the equipment and or materials described in the conditions statement.

Brief Soldier: Tell the Soldier what is expected of him by reviewing the task standards. Stress to the Soldier the importance of observing all cautions, warnings, and dangers to avoid injury to personnel and, if applicable, damage to equipment.

Performance Measures	GO	NO GO
1 Identified the scale of the map.	_____	_____
2 Converted straight-line distance between two points on a map.	_____	_____
3 Converted map distance to ground distance.	_____	_____
4 Converted a road map distance to miles, meters, or yards.	_____	_____

Evaluation Guidance: Refer to chapter 1, paragraph 1-9e, (1) and (2).

References
Required:
Related: FM 3-25.26

Determine the Grid Coordinates of a Point on a Military Map

Conditions: You are a member of a squad or team in a field environment and have been directed to identify the grid coordinates of a point on a map. You have a 1:50,000 scale military map, a coordinate scale and protractor or plotting scale, a pencil, and paper. You have been shown the point on the map.

Standards: Determine the coordinates of the grid square, determine grid coordinates of a point with and without a coordinate scale and protractor or plotting scale. Identify the 100,000 meter square identifier to determine grid coordinate.

Special Condition: None

Special Standards: None

Special Equipment:

Cue: None

Note: None

1. Determine the coordinates of the grid square (Figure 071-COM-1002-1).

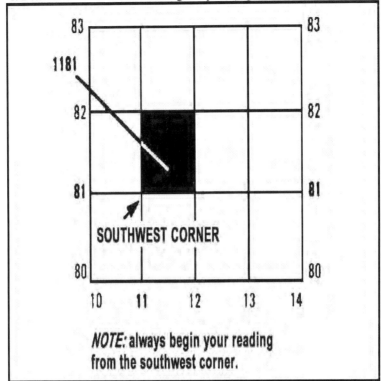

NOTE: always begin your reading from the southwest corner.

Figure 071-COM-1002-1. Identifying the Grid Square

a. Select the grid square that contains the identified point on the map (see Figure 071-COM-1002-1).

b. Read the north-south grid line that precedes the desired point (see Figure 071-COM-1002-1).

c. Record the number associated with that line.

d. Read the east-west grid line that precedes the desired point (see Figure071-COM-1002- 1).

e. Record the number associated with that line.

Note: The number of digits represents the degree of precision to which a point has been located and measured on a map the more digits the more precise the measurement. In the above example the four digits 1181 identify the 1,000 meter grid square to be used.

2. Determine point grid coordinates without a coordinate scale and protractor or plotting scale (Figure 071-COM-1002-2).

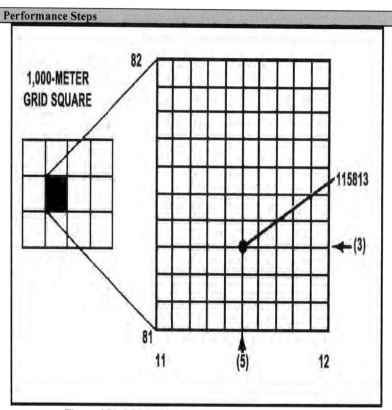

Figure 071-COM-1002-2. Grid Square 1181 Divided.

a. Allocate the grid square into a 10 by 10 grid.

b. Read right (from the lower left corner) to the imaginary gird line nearest the identified point.

Note: In the example the North-South imaginary line nearest the point is halfway or 5 lines out of a total of 10 lines. Therefore the first half of your grid coordinate is 115.

c. Read up (from the point reached in step 3b) to the imaginary gird line nearest the identified point.

Note: In the example the East-West imaginary line nearest the point is one third of the way up or 3 lines out of 10 lines. Therefore the second half of your grid coordinate is 813.

3. Determine point grid coordinates with coordinate scale and protractor or plotting scale (Figure 071-COM-1002-3).

Note: The most accurate way to determine the coordinates of a point on a map is with a coordinate scale. You need not imagine lines, because you can find the exact coordinates using the coordinate scale, protractor or the plotting scale. Each device actually includes two coordinate scales, 1:25,000 and 1:50,000 meters. Make sure that, regardless which device you use, you choose the correct scale.

Figure 071-COM-1002-3. Coordinate Scale and Protractor (Left) and Plotting scale (Right).

    a. Locate the grid square where the point is located (Example: Point A in Figure 071-COM-1002-4).

    b. Determine the coordinates of the grid square.

Note: The number of the vertical grid line on the left (west) side of the grid square gives the first and second digits of the coordinate. The number of the horizontal grid line on the bottom (south) side of the grid square gives the fourth and fifth digits of the coordinate.

    c. Determine the third and sixth digits of the coordinate.

        (1) Place a coordinate scale and protractor or a plotting scale on the bottom horizontal grid line of the grid square containing Point A.

        (2) Check to see that the zeros of the coordinate scale are in the lower left-hand (southwest) corner of the grid square where Point A is located (Figure 071-COM-1002-4).

NOTE: Slide scale to right and align Point A under vertical scale.

Figure 071-COM-1002-4. Placement of the Coordinate Scale.

(3) Slide the scale to the right, keeping the bottom of the scale on the bottom grid line until Point A is under the vertical (right-hand) scale (Figures 071-COM-1002-5 and 071-COM-1002-6).

Note: To determine the six-digit coordinate, look at the 100-meter mark on the bottom scale, which is nearest the vertical grid line. This mark is the third digit of the number 115. The 100-meter mark on the vertical scale nearest to Point A gives you the sixth digit of the number 813. The complete grid coordinate is 115813. Always read right, and then up.

Figure 071-COM-1002-5. Aligning the Coordinate Scale.

Figure 071-COM-1002-6. Aligning the Plotting Scale.

4. Add the two letter 100,000 meter square identifier to determined grid coordinate.

　　a. Identify the two letter 100,000 meter square identifier by looking at the grid reference box in the margin of the map (Figure 071-COM-1002-7).

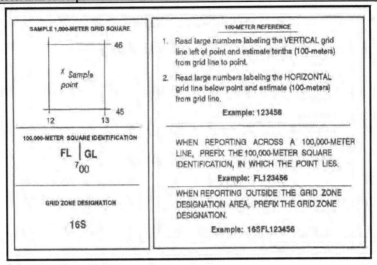

Figure 071-COM-1002-7. Grid Reference Box.

b. Place the 100,000 meter square identifier in front of the grid coordinate.

Note: In the example given the final grid coordinate becomes GL115813.

Evaluation Preparation:

Setup: Provide the Soldier with the equipment and or materials described in the conditions statement.

Brief Soldier: Tell the Soldier what is expected of him by reviewing the task standards. Stress to the Soldier the importance of observing all cautions, warnings, and dangers to avoid injury to personnel and, if applicable, damage to equipment.

Performance Measures	GO	NO GO
1 Determined the coordinates of the grid square.	_____	_____
2 Determined point grid coordinates without a coordinate scale and protractor or plotting scale.	_____	_____

Performance Measures	GO	NO GO
3 Determined point grid coordinates with coordinate scale and protractor or plotting scale.	___	___
4 Added the two letter 100,000 meter square identifier to the determined grid coordinate.	___	___

Evaluation Guidance: Refer to chapter 1, paragraph 1-9e, (1) and (2).

References
Required:
Related: FM 3-25.26

071-COM-1005

Determine a Location on the Ground by Terrain Association

Conditions: You are a member of a squad or team in a field environment and have been directed to determine your squad's/team's current location. You have a 1:50,000 scale military map, a compass, a coordinate scale and protractor or plotting scale, a pencil, and paper.

Standards: Determine the grid coordinates to your location to within 100 meters.

Special Condition: None

Special Standards: None

Special Equipment:

Cue: None

Note: None

Performance Steps

1. Orient the map.
Note: There are three ways to orient a map:
- Using a compass. The magnetic arrow of the compass points to magnetic north. As such, pay special attention to the declination diagram.
- Using terrain association. This method is typically used when a compass is not available or when the user has to make many quick references as he moves across country.
- Using Field-Expedient Methods. These methods are used when a compass is available and

there are no recognizable terrain features.

2. Identify the type of terrain feature on which you are located.
3. Identify the types of terrain features that surround your location.
4. Correlate the terrain features on the ground to those shown on the map.
5. Determine your location on the map.
6. Determine the six digit grid coordinate of your location.

Note: Grid coordinates of your location can be determined by using a coordinate scale and protractor, a plotting scale, or by visualizing a 10 by 10 grid box inside the appropriate grid square.

Evaluation Preparation:

Setup: Provide the Soldier with the equipment and or materials described in the conditions statement.

Brief Soldier: Tell the Soldier what is expected of him by reviewing the task standards. Stress to the Soldier the importance of observing all cautions, warnings, and dangers to avoid injury to personnel and, if applicable, damage to equipment.

Performance Measures	GO	NO GO
1 Oriented the map.	_____	_____
2 Identified the type of terrain feature on which you were located.	_____	_____
3 Identified the types of terrain features that surround your location.	_____	_____
4 Correlated the terrain features on the ground to those shown on the map.	_____	_____
5 Determined your location on the map.	_____	_____
6 Determined the six digit grid coordinate of your location.	_____	_____

References
Required:
Related: FM 3-25.26

071-COM-1012

Orient a Map to the Ground by Map-Terrain Association

Conditions: You are a member of a squad or team that is conducting movement in a field environment and you have been directed to orient a standard 1:50,000 scale military map to the ground. You do not have an operational compass.

Standards: Orient the map to within 30 degrees of magnetic north.

Special Condition: None

Special Standards: None

Special Equipment:

Cue: None

Note: A map can be oriented by terrain association when a compass is not available or when the user has to make many quick references as he moves across country. Using this method requires careful examination of the map and the ground, and the user must know his approximate location.

Performance Steps
   1. Hold the map in a horizontal position.
   2. Match terrain features appearing on your map with terrain features physically observable on the ground (Figure 071-COM-1012-1).

Figure 071-COM-1002-1. Terrain Association.
Align the map with the terrain features on the ground.

Evaluation Preparation:

Setup: Provide the Soldier with the equipment and or materials described in the conditions statement.

Brief Soldier: Tell the Soldier what is expected of him by reviewing the task standards. Stress to the Soldier the importance of observing all cautions, warnings, and dangers to avoid injury to personnel and, if applicable, damage to equipment.

Performance Measures	GO	NO GO
1 Held the map in a horizontal position.	____	____
2 Matched terrain features appearing on map with physical features on the ground.	____	____
3 Aligned the map with the terrain features on the ground to within 30 degrees of magnetic north.	____	____

Evaluation Guidance: Refer to chapter 1, paragraph 1-9e, (1) and (2).

References
Required:
Related: FM 3-25.26

071-COM-1011

Orient a Map Using a Lensatic Compass

Conditions: You are a member of a squad or team in a field environment and have been directed to orient a map in preparation for movement. You have a 1:50,000-scale topographic map of the area and a compass.

Standards: Orient the map to the ground using a compass.

Special Condition: None

Special Standards: None

Special Equipment:

Cue: None

Note: The first step for a navigator in the field is orienting the map. A map is oriented when it is in a horizontal position with its north and south corresponding to the north and south on the ground.

When orienting a map with a compass, remember that the compass measures magnetic azimuths. Since the magnetic arrow points to magnetic north, pay special attention to the declination diagram. Two techniques are used.

Special care should be taken when orienting your map with a compass. A small mistake can cause you to navigate in the wrong direction.

Once the map is oriented, magnetic azimuths are determined using the compass. Do not move the map from its oriented position since any change in its position moves it out of line with the magnetic north.

Performance Steps

1. Determine the direction of the declination and its value from the declination diagram on the map.
2. Lay the map in a horizontal position.
3. Use one of the two techniques to orient the map.
   a. Orient the map using the first technique.
      (1) Take the straightedge on the left side of the compass and place it alongside the north-south grid line with the cover of the compass pointing toward the top of the map.
Note: This procedure places the fixed black index line of the compass parallel to north-south grid lines of the map.
      (2) Keep the compass aligned as directed above while rotating the map and compass together until the magnetic arrow is below the fixed black index line on the compass.
Note: At this time, the map is close to being oriented.
      (3) Rotate the map and compass in the direction of the declination diagram.
      (4) Verify the G-M angle.
        (a) If the magnetic north arrow on the map is to the left of the grid north, check the compass reading to see if it equals the G-M angle given in the declination diagram (Figure 071-COM-1011-1).

Figure 071-COM-1011-1. Map oriented with 10 degrees west declination.

(b) If the magnetic north is to the right of grid north, check the compass reading to see if it equals 360 degrees minus the G-M angle (Figure 071-COM-1011-2).

Note: If the G-M angles are correct the map is oriented.

Figure 071-COM-1011-2. Map oriented with 21 degrees east declination.

b. Orient the map using the second technique.

(1) Draw a magnetic azimuth equal to the G-M angle given in the declination diagram with the protractor using any north-south grid line on the map as a base.

(2) If the declination is easterly (right), the drawn line is equal to the value of the G-M angle:

(a) Align the straightedge on the left side of the compass alongside the drawn line on the map.

(b) Rotate the map and compass until the magnetic arrow of the compass is below the fixed black index line (Figure 071-COM-1011-3).

Note: The map is now oriented.

MAGNETIC ARROW
ALIGNED WITH
BLACK INDEX LINE

TRUE NORTH
GRID NORTH
MAGNETIC NORTH

1975
G-M ANGLE
15°(260 MILS)

Figure 071-COM-1011-3. Map oriented with 15 degrees east declination.

(3) If the declination is westerly (left), the drawn line will equal 360 degrees minus the value of the G-M angle:

(a) Align the straightedge on the left side of the compass alongside the drawn line on the map.

(b) Rotate the map and compass until the magnetic arrow of the compass is below the fixed black index line.

Note: The map is now oriented.

Figure 071-COM-1011-4. Map oriented with 10 degrees west declination.

Evaluation Preparation:

Setup: Provide the Soldier with the equipment and or materials described in the conditions statement.

Brief Soldier: Tell the Soldier what is expected of him by reviewing the task standards. Stress to the Soldier the importance of observing all cautions, warnings, and dangers to avoid injury to personnel and, if applicable, damage to equipment.

Performance Measures	GO	NO GO
1 Determined the direction of the declination and its value from the declination diagram.	_____	_____
2 Laid the map in a horizontal position.	_____	_____
3 Used one of the two techniques to orient the map.	_____	_____

Evaluation Guidance: Refer to chapter 1, paragraph 1-9e, (1) and (2).

References
Required:
Related: FM 3-25.26

071-COM-1003

Determine a Magnetic Azimuth Using a Lensatic Compass

Conditions: You are a member of a squad or team in a field environment and have been directed to determine a magnetic azimuth. You have a compass and a designated point on the ground.

Standards: Determine the correct magnetic azimuth to the designated point within 3 degrees using the compass-to-cheek method, and within 10 degrees using the center-hold method.

Special Condition: None

Special Standards: None

Special Equipment:

Cue: None

Note: None

1. Inspect the compass (Figure 071-COM-1003-1).

Figure 071-COM-1003-1. Lensatic compass.

    a. Ensure floating dial, which contains the magnetic needle moves freely and does not stick.

    b. Ensure the sighting wire is straight.

    c. Ensure glass and crystal parts are not broken.

    d. Ensure numbers on the dial are readable.

2. Determine direction (Figure 071-COM-1003-2).

Figure 071-COM-1003-2. Lensatic compass floating dial.

 a. Align the compass to the direction you want to go or want to determine.

 b. Locate the scale beneath the index line on the outer glass cover.

 c. Determine to the nearest degree, or 10 mils, the position of the index line over the red or black scale.

Note: Effects of Metal and Electricity. Metal objects and electrical sources can affect the performance of a compass. However, nonmagnetic metals and alloys do not affect compass readings. The following separation distances are suggested to ensure proper functioning of a compass:

High-tension power lines .... 55 meters.
Field gun, truck, or tank... 18 meters.
Telegraph or telephone wires and barbed wire....... 10 meters.
Machine gun .... 2 meters.
Steel helmet or rifle.. 1/2 meter.

 3. Determine an azimuth with the compass-to-cheek method (Figure 071-COM-1003-3).

Figure 071-COM-1003-3. Compass-to-cheek method.

a. Open the cover to a 90-degree angle to the base.

b. Position the eyepiece at a 45-degree angle to the base.

c. Place your thumb through the thumb loop.

d. Establish a steady base with your third and fourth fingers.

e. Extend your index finger along the side of the compass base.

f. Place the hand holding the compass into the palm of the other hand.

g. Move both hands up to your face.

h. Position the thumb that is through the thumb loop against the cheekbone.

i. Move the eyepiece up or down until the dial is in focus.

j. Align the sighting slot of the eyepiece with the sighting wire in the cover on the desired point.

k. Read the azimuth under the index line.

4. Determine an azimuth with the center-hold method (Figure 071-COM-1003-4).

Note: This method offers the following advantages over the sighting technique:

  -It is faster and easier to use.

  -It can be used under all conditions of visibility.

-It can be used when navigating over any type of terrain.

-It can be used without putting down the rifle; however, the rifle must be slung well back over either shoulder.

-It can be used without removing eyeglasses

Figure 071-COM-1003-4. Centerhold technique.

a. Open the compass so that the cover forms a straight edge with the base.

b. Position the eyepiece lens to the full upright position.

c. Place your thumb through the loop.

d. Establish a steady base with your third and fourth fingers.

e. Extend your index finger along the side of the compass.

f. Place the thumb of your other hand between the eyepiece and lens.

g. Extend the index finger along the remaining side of the compass.

h. Secure the remaining fingers around the fingers of the other hand.

i. Place your elbows firmly into your side.

Note: This will place the compass between your chin and your belt.

j. Turn your entire body toward the object.

k. Align the compass cover directly at the object.

l. Read the azimuth from beneath the fixed black index line.

Evaluation Preparation:

Setup: Provide the Soldier with the equipment and or materials described in the conditions statement.

Brief Soldier: Tell the Soldier what is expected of him by reviewing the task standards. Stress to the Soldier the importance of observing all cautions, warnings, and dangers to avoid injury to personnel and, if applicable, damage to equipment.

Performance Measures	GO	NO GO
1 Inspected the compass.	_____	_____
2 Determined direction.	_____	_____
3 Determined an azimuth using the compass-to-cheek method.	_____	_____
4 Determined an azimuth using the center-hold method.	_____	_____

Evaluation Guidance: Refer to chapter 1, paragraph 1-9e, (1) and (2).

References
Required:
Related: FM 3-25.26

071-COM-1006

Navigate from One Point on the Ground to Another Point while Dismounted

Conditions: You are a member of a squad or team in a field environment and have been directed to conduct movement to a designated point. You have a 1:50,000-scale topographic map of the area, a coordinate scale, a protractor, and a magnetic compass.

Standards: Navigate to the designated point using terrain association, dead reckoning, or a combination of the two.

Special Condition: None

Special Standards: None

Special Equipment:

Note: None

Performance Steps

1. Navigate using terrain association.
   a. Identify the start point and destination point on the map.
   b. Analyze the terrain between these two points for both movement and tactical purposes.
   c. Identify terrain features that can be recognized during movement, such as hilltops, roads, rivers, etc.
   d. Plan the best route, including checkpoints, if needed.
   e. Determine the map distances between identified checkpoints and the total distance to be traveled.
   f. Determine the actual ground distance by adding 20 percent to the map distance.
Note: Twenty percent is a general rule of thumb for cross country terrain - road movement and flat terrain do not require this 20 percent increase.
   g. Move to the designated end point (or intermediate point) using identified terrain features as aiming points or handrails.
Note: Handrails are linear features like roads or highways, railroads, power transmission lines, ridgelines, or streams that run roughly parallel to your direction of travel.
2. Navigate using dead reckoning.
Note: The use of steering marks is recommended when navigating by dead reckoning. A steering mark is a distant feature visible along one's route that is used as distant aiming point that one moves towards. Once reached another steering point is identified until a change of direction or the final destination is reached.
   a. Identify the start point and destination point on the map.
   b. Analyze the terrain between these two points for both movement and tactical purposes.
   c. Plan the best route, including checkpoints, if needed.
   d. Determine the grid azimuths between identified checkpoints (if any) and the final point.
   e. Convert the grid azimuth(s) taken from the map to a magnetic azimuth(s).
   f. Determine the map distances between identified checkpoints and the total distance to be traveled.
   g. Determine the direction of movement using the compass.
   h. Move in the identified direction of travel or towards the identified steering mark.
   i. Determine a new steering mark or confirm direction of travel as needed.
Note: The direction of movement, when not using a steering mark, must be periodically confirmed.
3. Navigate using a combination of dead reckoning and terrain association.
   a. Follow the procedures outlined for both techniques.
   b. Use each technique to reinforce the accuracy of the other technique.

Evaluation Preparation:

Setup: Provide the Soldier with the equipment and or materials described in the conditions statement.

Brief Soldier: Tell the Soldier what is expected of him by reviewing the task standards. Stress to the Soldier the importance of observing all cautions, warnings, and dangers to avoid injury to personnel and, if applicable, damage to equipment.

Performance Measures	GO	NO GO
1 Navigated using terrain association.	_____	_____
2 Navigated using dead reckoning.	_____	_____
3 Navigated using a combination of dead reckoning and terrain association.	_____	_____

Evaluation Guidance: Refer to chapter 1, paragraph 1-9e, (1) and (2).

References
Required:
Related: FM 3-25.26

071-COM-1030

Navigate from One Point on the Another Point while Mounted

Conditions: You are a member of a squad or team in a field environment and have been directed to conduct mounted movement to a designated point. You have a 1:50,000-scale topographic map of the area, a coordinate scale, a protractor, a magnetic compass, and a vehicle with cross-country capability.

Standards: Navigate to the designated point using terrain association, dead reckoning, or combination of the two.

Special Condition: None

Special Equipment:

Cue: None

Note: None

Performance Steps

1. Navigate using terrain association.
    a. Identify the start point and destination point on the map.
    b. Analyze the terrain between these two points for both movement and tactical purposes.
    c. Identify terrain features that can be recognized during movement, such as hilltops, roads, rivers, etc..
    d. Plan the best route, including checkpoints, if needed.
    e. Determine the map distances between identified checkpoints and the total distance to be traveled.
    f. Determine the actual ground distance by adding 20 percent to the map distance.
Note: 20 percent is a general rule of thumb for cross country terrain; road movement and flat terrain do not require this 20 percent increase.
    g. Move to the designated end point (or intermediate point) using identified terrain features as aiming points or handrails.
Note: Handrails are linear features like roads or highways, railroads, power transmission lines, ridgelines, or streams that run roughly parallel to your direction of travel.
2. Navigate using dead reckoning.
Note: The use of steering marks is recommended when navigating by dead reckoning. A steering mark is a distant feature visible along one's route that is used as distant aiming point that one moves towards. Once reached another steering point is identified until a change of direction or the final destination is reached.
    a. Identify the start point and destination point on the map.
    b. Analyze the terrain between these two points for both movement and tactical purposes.
    c. Plan the best route, including checkpoints, if needed.
    d. Determine the grid azimuths between identified checkpoints (if any) and the final point.
    e. Convert the grid azimuth(s) taken from the map to a magnetic azimuth(s).
    f. Determine the map distances between identified checkpoints and the total distance to be traveled.
    g. Navigate using dead reckoning with steering marks.
        (1) Dismount a crew member and have them move 18 meters away from the front of the vehicle.
        (2) Set an azimuth using a compass.
        (3) Identify a steering mark.
          (a) Rock.
          (b) Tree.
          (c) Hilltop.
        (4) Notify the driver of the steering mark.
        (5) Move in the identified direction of travel or towards the identified steering mark.

Note: On arrival at the steering mark or on any changes in direction, the navigator repeats the first three steps for the next leg of travel.

      (6) Determine a new steering mark or confirm direction of travel as needed.

Note: The direction of movement, when not using a steering mark, must be periodically confirmed.

    h. Navigate using dead reckoning without steering marks.

Note: This procedure is used only on flat, featureless terrain.

      (1) Dismount a crew member to act as the navigator.

      (2) Direct the navigator to orient in the direction of travel.

      (3) Direct the navigator to move at least 18 meters to the front of the vehicle.

      (4) Direct the driver to drive in a straight line to the navigator.

      (5) Remount the navigator.

      (6) Holds the compass as it will be held while the vehicle is moving.

      (7) Read the azimuth in the direction of travel.

      (8) Use your vehicle odometer to be sure you travel the proper distance.

   3. Navigate using a combination of dead reckoning and terrain association.

    a. Follow the procedures outlined for both techniques.

    b. Use each technique to reinforce the accuracy of the other technique.

Evaluation Preparation:

Setup: Provide the Soldier with the equipment and or materials described in the conditions statement.

Brief Soldier: Tell the Soldier what is expected of him by reviewing the task standards. Stress to the Soldier the importance of observing all cautions, warnings, and dangers to avoid injury to personnel and, if applicable, damage to equipment.

	Performance Measures	GO	NO GO
1	Navigated using terrain association.	_____	_____
2	Navigated using dead reckoning.	_____	_____
3	Navigated using a combination of dead reckoning and terrain association.	_____	_____

Evaluation Guidance: Refer to chapter 1, paragraph 1-9e, (1) and (2).

References
Required:
Related: FM 3-25.26

113-610-2005

Navigate using the Defense Advanced Global Positioning System (GPS) Receiver (DAGR)

Conditions: Given a DAGR GPS in any environment where the Soldier has to maintain constent awareness at all times. The student will be aware of Contemporary Operational Environment factors such as extreme temperature differences, unstable political state and hostile locals are of the essence to maintain vital communications.

Standards: Met when the Soldier successfully navigates to two out of three assigned locations using the DAGR GPS in any environment while observing the Contemporary Operational Environment.

Special Condition: None

Special Standards: None

Special Equipment: None

Cue: None

Note: None

Performance Steps

    1. Enter Menu by pushing the menu button once.
      a. Select OP mode by pressing Enter. (Contineous, Standby, Fix, Average, Time only, Test, or Off.
    2. Enter Main menu by pushing the menu button twice.
      a. Select Display Setup.
        (1) Select Units and enter or verify all settings.
        (2) Select Internal Compass and enter settings and calibrate the DAGR.
        (3) Select Light/Contrast and enter settings.
      b. Select Receiver Setup.
        (1) Select Crypto Fill and verify settings.
        (2) Select GPS Setup and verify settings.
        (3) Select Power Saver and verify settings.
        (4) Select Battery and enter proper settings.
        (5) Select Auto-Run and verify settings.

3. Enter or verify the correct setup displays.
   a. Select setup mode.
4. Enter crypto keys.
5. Enter or verify initialization displays.
   a. Verify position and time by acquiring satellites.
6. Enter, edit, or review waypoint data.
   a. Mark present position waypoint.
   b. Create a new waypoint.
   c. Clear waypoints.
7. Navigate to five waypoints.

Evaluation Preparation:

Provide the Soldier with all material and equipment listed in the condition statement.

Performance Measures		GO	NO GO
1	Entered Menu and selected the Op mode.	_____	_____
2	Entered main menu and set the Display Setup.	_____	_____
3	Entered Main menu and set the Receiver Setup.	_____	_____
4	Entered or verified correct setup displays.	_____	_____
5	Entered crypto keys.	_____	_____
6	Entered and verified initialization displays.	_____	_____
7	Entered waypoint information.	_____	_____
8	Navigated to five waypoints.	_____	_____

Evaluation Guidance: Refer to chapter 1, paragraph 1-9e, (1) and (2).

References
Required: TB 11-5820-1172-10 and TM 11-5820-1172-13
Related:

071-COM-0502

Move Under Direct Fire

Conditions: You are a member of a team conducting movement to contact and are under fire from an enemy position that is 250 to 300 meters away from your position. You have an individual weapon, individual combat equipment, and a current firing position that provides cover from the enemy's direct fire.

Standards: Move within 100 meters of the enemy position using the appropriate movement techniques based on the situation and terrain.

Special Condition: None

Special Standards: None

Special Equipment:

Cue: None

Note: While this task may be performed by an individual Soldier, it is best performed as a member of a team or as part of a two-man buddy team.

Performance Steps

1. Select an individual movement route that adheres to the instructions provided by your team leader.
Note: When part of a team your movement route and general firing positions may be determined by your team leader. When moving as part of a team you must be prepared to follow your team leader's example.
   a. Search the terrain to your front for good firing positions.
Note: Large trees, rocks, stumps, fallen timber, rubble, vehicle hulls, man-made structures, and folds or creases on the ground may provide both cover and concealment and can be used as fighting positions.
   b. Select the best route to the positions.
Note: A gully, ravine, ditch, or wall at a slight angle to your direction of travel may provide cover and concealment when using the low or high crawl movement techniques. Hedge rows or a line of thick vegetation may provide concealment only when using the low or high crawl technique.
      (1) Pick a route that minimize your exposure to enemy fire.
      (2) Ensure route does not cross in front of other team members.

2. Communicate your movement intent to your buddy and team leader, as appropriate, using hand and arm signals.

3. Suppress the enemy as required.

Note: Do not expose yourself to fire unless the enemy is suppressed. Suppression of the enemy may be accomplished by another element, a buddy, or by yourself. With the enemy suppressed you can select an individual movement route or initiate movement.

4. Conduct movement using the appropriate technique(s) to reach each position.

a. Move using the high crawl technique (Figure 071-COM-1502-1).

Note: The high crawl lets you move faster than the low crawl and still gives you a low silhouette. Use this crawl when there is good cover and concealment but enemy fire prevents you from getting up.

Figure 071-COM-1502-1. High Crawl.

(1) Keep your body off of the ground.

(2) Rest your weight on your forearms and lower legs.

(3) Cradle your weapon in your arms.

(4) Keep the muzzle of the weapon off the ground.

(5) Keep your knees well behind your buttocks so it stays low.

(6) Move forward by alternately advancing your right elbow and left knee, and left elbow and right knee.

b. Move using the low crawl technique (Figure 071-COM-1502-2).

Note: The low crawl gives you the lowest silhouette. It is used to cross places where the cover and/or concealment are very low and enemy fire or observation prevents you from getting up.

Figure 071-COM-1502-2. Low Crawl.

(1) Keep your body as flat as possible to the ground.

(2) Grasp the sling of the weapon at the upper sling swivel with your right hand.

(3) Let the hand guard rest on your forearm.

(4) Keep the muzzle of the weapon off the ground.

(5) Move forward.

(a) Push both arms forward while pulling your right leg forward.

(b) Pull on the ground with both arms while pushing with your right leg.

(c) Repeat steps (a) and (b) until you reach your next position.

c. Moved using the rush technique (Figure 071-COM-1502-3).

Note: The rush is the fastest way to move from one position to another. Use when you must cross an open area and time is critical.

Figure 071-COM-1502-3. Rush.

(1) Raise your head.

(2) Select your next position.

(3) Lower your head.

(4) Draw your arms into your body.

(5) Pull your right leg forward.

(6) Raise your body.

(7) Get up quickly.

(8) Run for 3-5 seconds to your next position.

(9) Plant both feet just before hitting the ground.

(10) Fall forward.

    (a) Drop to your knees.

    (b) Slide your right hand down to the heel of the butt of your weapon.

    (c) Break your fall with the butt of your weapon.

    d. Continue using movement techniques until you reach your final firing position.

    5. Occupy your identified firing position within 100 meters of the enemy position.

        a. Assume a firing position.

        b. Engage enemy with your individual weapon.

Evaluation Preparation:

Setup: Provide the Soldier with the equipment and/or materials described in the conditions statement.

Brief Soldier: Tell the Soldier what is expected of him by reviewing the task standards. Stress to the Soldier the importance of observing all cautions, warnings, and dangers to avoid injury to personnel and, if applicable, damage to equipment.

Performance Measures		GO	NO GO
1	Selected an individual movement route that adhered to the instructions provided by your team leader.	_____	_____
2	Communicated movement intent to buddy and team leader, as appropriate, using hand and arm signals.	_____	_____
3	Suppressed the enemy as required.	_____	_____
4	Conducted movement using the appropriate technique(s) to reach each position.	_____	_____
5	Occupied your identified firing position within 100 meters of the enemy position.	_____	_____

Evaluation Guidance: Refer to chapter 1, paragraph 1-9e, (1) and (2).

References
Required:
Related: FM 3-21.75

071-326-0503

Move Over, Through, or Around Obstacles (Except Minefields)

Conditions: Given an individual weapon and individual protective equipment. You are moving and encounter a natural or manmade and obstacle. You must move over, through, or around the obstacle.

Standards: Identify chain of command of obstacle encountered, evaluate obstacle, identify nearest covered position on far side of obstacle, negotiate a wall obstacle, a wire obstacle, a ditch type obstacle and cover buddy during crossing of obstacle.

Special Condition: This task is being superseded by 071-COM-0503, refer to DTMS or CAR (https://atiam.train.army.mil/catalog/catalog/search.html) for the new task.

Special Standards: None

Special Equipment:

Cue: None

Note: An obstacle is any obstruction designed or employed to disrupt, fix, turn, or block the movement of an opposing force, and to impose additional losses in personnel, time, and equipment on the opposing force. Obstacles can be natural, manmade, or a combination of both.

Performance Steps

1. Notify your chain of command of the presence and type of obstacle encountered.
Note: Most obstacles, for maximum effectiveness, are covered by either fire or observation. Many obstacles, due to enemy fire or complexity of the obstacle, require a unit breaching operation and the appropriate collective task should also be followed.

2. Evaluate the obstacle, from a covered position, to determine whether to move around, through or over the obstacle
Note: Typically it is best to move around (or bypass) an obstacle, however this is not always possible.

3. Identify the nearest covered position on the far side of the obstacle.

4. Ensure a buddy, if present, covers your movement as you negotiate the obstacle.

5. Negotiate a wall obstacle.

a. Identify your immediate landing position on the far side of the wall.

Note: The far side must be relatively safe from enemy fire, as once across the wall, you are fully exposed. Additionally, the immediate opposite side of the wall must be safe for landing as long drops and debris can cause injury.

b. Assume a crouching position near the wall, while holding your weapon with one hand and grabbing the top of the wall with the other hand.

c. Pull with the hand on the wall while simultaneously swinging both legs over the wall, one right after the other.

d. Roll quickly over the top to other side, keeping a low silhouette.

e. Move to the identified covered position on the far side.

WARNING

An enemy may attach booby traps or tripwire-activated mines to wire obstacles.

---

6. Negotiate a wire obstacle.

a. Move to your designated crossing position.

b. Check for booby traps or early warning devices.

c. Cross over a wire obstacle.

(1) Place an object such as a piece of wood, metal, or mats, over the wire.

(2) Move over the wire by stepping on this object to avoid the wire entanglements.

d. Cross under a wire obstacle.

(1) Slide head first on your back under the bottom strands.

(2) Push yourself forward with your shoulders and heels, carrying your weapon lengthwise on your body and holding the barbed wire with one hand while moving.

(3) Let the barbed wire slide on the weapon to keep wire from catching on clothing and equipment.

e. Cut through a wire obstacle.

Note: If stealth is not needed then quickly cut all wires and proceed through the gap.

(1) Wrap cloth around the barbed wire between your hands.

(2) Cut partly through the barbed wire.

Note: Cutting the wire near a picket reduces the noise of a cut.

(3) Bend the barbed wire back and forth quietly until it separates.

(4) Cut only the lower strands.

(5) Cross under the remaining top wires.

7. Cross a ditch type obstacle.

a. Select a point that has cover and concealment on both sides, such as a bend in the ditch.

b. Move to your designated crossing site.

c. Crawl up to the edge of the open area.

d. Observe both the floor of the ditch and the far side for dangers.

e. Move rapidly but quietly across the exposed area.

f. Assume a covered position on the far side.

8. Cover your buddy, if present, as he or she crosses the obstacle.

Evaluation Preparation:

Setup: Provide the Soldier with the equipment and or materials described in the conditions statement.

Brief Soldier: Tell the Soldier what is expected of him by reviewing the task standards. Stress to the Soldier the importance of observing all cautions, warnings, and dangers to avoid injury to personnel and, if applicable, damage to equipment.

Performance Measures	GO	NO GO
1 Notified the chain of command of the presence and type of obstacle encountered.	___	___
2 Evaluated the obstacle, from a covered position, to determine whether to move around, through or over the obstacle.	___	___
3 Identified the nearest covered position on the far side of the obstacle.	___	___
4 Ensured a buddy, if present, was covering his movements.	___	___
5 Negotiated a wall obstacle.	___	___
6 Negotiated a wire obstacle.	___	___
7 Negotiated a ditch type obstacle.	___	___
8 Covered his buddy, if present, as the buddy crossed the obstacle.	___	___

Evaluation Guidance: Refer to chapter 1, paragraph 1-9e, (1) and (2).

References
Required: FM 3-21.75
Related:

071-COM-0510

React to Indirect Fire while Dismounted

Conditions: You are a member of a dismounted element, you are not the leader, and the element is moving or stationary. You hear indirect fire rounds exploding or passing overhead, or someone shouting "incoming."

Standards: Obtain the best available cover while following the leader's directions. Assess and report the situation to higher. Continue the mission.

Performance Steps

1. Shout "Incoming!" in a loud, recognizable voice.
2. React to the instructions of your leader by listening and looking for guidance.
Note: In general, if moving, the leader will give a direction and distance to move to. If possible, follow your leader; if you cannot see or hear your leader, follow other team members.
3. Seek the nearest appropriate cover.
    a. Remain in your defensive position if it has appropriate cover.

  Note: Prepared defensive positions include overhead cover to protect against indirect fires. As necessary adjust your position to maximize the protection of your available cover.
    b. Avoid the impact area if not already in it.
    c. Run out of the impact area in a direction away from the incoming fire.
4. Assess your situation.
5. Report your situation to your leader.
6. Continue the mission.

Evaluation Preparation: *Setup*: Provide the Soldier with the equipment and/or materials described in the conditions statement.
Brief Soldier: Explain what is expected from the Soldier by reviewing the task standards. Stress the importance of observing all cautions, warnings, and dangers to avoid injury to personnel and, if applicable, damage to equipment.

Performance Measures	GO	NO GO
1 Shouted "Incoming!" in a loud, recognizable voice.	_____	_____
2 Reacted to the instructions of your leader by listening and looking for instructions.	_____	_____
3 Sought the nearest appropriate cover.	_____	_____
5 Reported the situation to the leader.	_____	_____
6 Continued the mission.	_____	_____

Evaluation Guidance:. Refer to chapter 1, paragraph 1-9e, (1) and (2).

References
Required: FM 3-21.8
Related:

071-326-3002

React to Indirect Fire while Mounted

Conditions: You are mounted in a moving or stationary vehicle and you hear indirect fire rounds exploding or passing overhead, or someone shouting "incoming."

Standards: Seek cover, as appropriate, while following the chain of command's orders, assess and report the situation to the chain of command, and continue the mission as directed by the chain of command.

Performance Steps

Note: If a member of an established vehicle crew, such as a Bradley, M1 tank, or Stryker, then execute the appropriate crew drill, battle drill, or collective task.

    1. Return fire, as appropriate, to destroy or suppress enemy .NOTE:

    2. (LEADER) Issue orders after fast assessing the initial situation.

Note: Typical orders include—
- Directing the driver to a position that provides cover.
- Directing the driver to accelerate in a safe manner through the engagement area.
- Directing the gunner (if present) to engage the enemy.
- Directing an assault on the enemy position.

    3. React to the instructions of the leader by listening and looking for guidance.

    4. Seek the nearest appropriate cover (based on orders from the leader).

a. (DRIVER) Remain in a defensive position if there is appropriate cover.

b. (DRIVER) Drive in the direction designated by the leader or towards the nearest appropriate cover.

c. Occupy a covered position within the vehicle.

d. Close personnel hatches, if present.

e. Remain in the vehicle unless directed to dismount by the vehicle commander.

5. Analyze your situation.

Note: The leader checks the status of the vehicle and all occupants by sight or by calling out.

6. Develop the situation based on orders from the chain of command.

Note: If the vehicle is disabled, the leader must consider the option of dismounting some or all of the vehicle occupants to engage the enemy from outside the vehicle.

7. Report your situation to your chain of command.

8. Continue the mission as directed by the chain of command.

Evaluation Preparation: *Setup:* Provide the Soldier with the equipment and/or materials described in the conditions statement.

Brief Soldier: Tell the Soldier what is expected of him by reviewing the task standards. Stress the importance of observing all cautions, warnings, and dangers to avoid injury to personnel and, if applicable, damage to equipment.

Performance Measures	GO	NO GO
1 Returned fire, as appropriate, to destroy or suppress enemy.	_____	_____
2 (LEADER) Issued orders after fast assessing the initial situation.	_____	_____
3 Reacted to the instructions of the leader by listening and looking for guidance.	_____	_____
4 Sought the nearest appropriate cover (based on orders from the leader).	_____	_____
5 Analyzed the situation.	_____	_____

Performance Measures	GO	NO GO
6 Developed the situation based on orders from the chain of command.	____	____
7 Reported the situation to the chain of command.	____	____
8 Continued the mission as directed by the chain of command.	____	____

Evaluation Guidance:. Refer to chapter 1, paragraph 1-9e, (1) and (2).

References
Required: FM 3-21.9
Related:

071-COM-0513

Select Temporary Fighting Positions

Conditions: Given a requirement to occupy an area; an individual or crew-served weapon; combat equipment; and a requirement to select a temporary fighting position.

Standards: Select a fighting position that protects you from enemy observation and fire, and allows effective fires to be placed on enemy positions without exposing yourself or your equipment.

Special Condition: Refer to DTMS or CAR (https://atiam.train.army.mil/catalog/catalog/search.html) for the new task.

Special Standards: None

Special Equipment:

Cue: None

Note: None

1. Select a position that maximizes available cover.

Note: Cover, made of natural or man-made materials, gives protection from bullets, fragments of exploding rounds, flame, nuclear effects, biological and chemical agents, and enemy observation.

2. Select a position that maximizes available concealment.

Note: Concealment is anything that hides personal, equipment and/or vehicles from enemy observation. Concealment does not protect you from enemy fire.

    a. Use natural, undisturbed concealment, if available.

    b. Ensure man-made concealment blends with surroundings.

3. Maintain camouflage.

Note: Camouflage is anything you use to keep yourself, your equipment, and your position from being identified.

    a. Prevent attention by controlling movement and activities.

    b. Avoid putting anything where the enemy expects to find it.

    c. Break up outlines and shadows.

    d. Conceal shining objects.

    e. Break up familiar shapes to make them blend in with their surroundings.

    f. Camouflage yourself and your equipment to blend with the surroundings.

    g. Ensure proper dispersion.

    h. Study the terrain and vegetation of the area in which you are operating.

    i. Use camouflage material that best blends with the area.

4. Select a position that allows effective weapon emplacement.

    a. Ensure proper sector of fires for appropriate weapon system.

    b. Ensure proper field of fires.

        (1) Avoid disclosing your position by careless or excessive clearing.

        (2) Leave a thin, natural screen of vegetation to hide your position.

        (3) Cut off lower branches of large, scattered trees, in sparsely wooded areas.

        (4) Clear underbrush only where it blocks your view.

        (5) Remove cut brush, limbs, and weeds so the enemy will not spot them.

        (6) Cover cuts on trees and bushes forward of your position with mud, dirt, or snow.

        (7) Leave no trails as clues for the enemy.

5. Continue to follow the leader's directions after selection of a fighting position.

Evaluation Preparation:

Setup: Provide the Soldier with the equipment and or materials described in the conditions statement.

Brief Soldier: Tell the Soldier what is expected of him by reviewing the task standards. Stress to the Soldier the importance of observing all cautions, warnings, and dangers to avoid injury to personnel and, if applicable, damage to equipment.

Performance Measures	GO	NO GO
1 Selected a position that maximized available cover.	___	___
2 Selected a position that maximized available concealment.	___	___
3 Maintained camouflage.	___	___
4 Selected a position that allowed effective weapons emplacement.	___	___
5 Continued to follow the leader's directions after selecting a fighting position.	___	___

Evaluation Guidance:. Refer to chapter 1, paragraph 1-9e, (1) and (2).

References
Required: FM 3-21.75 and FM 3-21.8
Related:

Subject Area 3: Communicate

113-587-2070

Operate SINCGARS Single-Channel (SC)

Conditions: Given an operational SINCGARS, KYK-13/TSEC with keys or AN/CYZ-10, distant station, TM 11-5820-890-10-8, TM 11-5820-890-10-3, ACP 125 US Suppl-1, DA Pam 738-750, FM 24-19, FM 24-18, and unit SOI or ANCD w/SOI data loaded.

Standards: The standards are met when a secure communications check is conducted in SC mode with a distant station.

Special Condition: None

Special Standards: None

Performance Steps

1. Perform starting procedures.
2. Load the traffic encryption key (TEK).
3. Enter the net.
   a. Use the correct procedures.
   b. Conduct a secure communications check
4. Prepare the control monitor for operation.
5. Change the radio functions using the control monitor.
6. Perform stopping procedures.
7. Perform stopping procedures.

Evaluation Preparation:

Performance Measures	GO	NO GO
1 Performed starting procedures.	_____	_____
2 Load traffic encryption key (TEK).	_____	_____
3 Entered net.	_____	_____
4 Exited net.	_____	_____
5 Performed stopping procedures.	_____	_____

Evaluation Guidance:. Refer to chapter 1, paragraph 1-9e, (1) and (2).

References
Required: ACP 125 US SUPP-1, TM 11-5820-890-10-1,
TM 11-5820-890-10-3, and TM 11-5820-890-10-8
Related:

112-571-1022

Perform Voice Communications

Conditions: Given: 1. One operational radio set for each net member, warmed up and set to the net frequency. 2. A call sign information card (5 x 8) consisting of net member duty position (S-1, S-2), net call sign (letter-number-letter), suffix list (Net Control Station [NCS] - 46, S-1 - 39, S-2 - 13), and a message to be transmitted. 3. Situation: The net is considered to be secure and authentication is not required. 4. FM 24-18. Note: This task may have as many net members as there is equipment available. Each net member must have a different suffix and message to transmit.

Standards: Enter a radio net, send a message, and leave a radio net using the proper call signs, call sign sequence, prowords, and phonetic alphabet and numerals with 100 percent accuracy.

Special Condition: None

Special Standards: None

Special Equipment: None

Cue: None

Note: None

Performance Steps

   1. Enter the net.
     a. Determine the abbreviated call sign and answering sequence for your duty position.
     b. Respond to the NCS issuing a net call.
     c. Answer in alphanumeric sequence.
Note: At this time, the NCS acknowledges and the net is open.
   2. Send a message.
     a. Listen to make sure the net is clear. Do not interrupt any ongoing communications.
     b. Call the NCS and tell the operator the priority of the message you have for his or her station.
     c. Receive a response from the NCS that he or she is ready to receive.
     d. Send your message using the correct prowords and pronunciation of letters and numbers.
     e. Get a receipt for the message.

3. Leave the net in alphanumeric sequence.

Note: The NCS acknowledges and the net is closed. Note: The following call signs are used in this task as an example: Net call sign - E3E, NCS - E46, S-1 - E39, S-2 - E13.

    a. Answer in alphanumeric sequence.

    b. You receive a call from the NCS who issues a close down order.

Evaluation Preparation: *Setup*: Position operational radio sets in different rooms or tents or at least 70 feet apart outside. Obtain call signs, suffixes, and a radio frequency through the normal command chain. Select a message 15-25 words in length, containing some number groups such as map coordinates and times. Print the call signs for the sender and the receiver, along with the message to be sent, on 5 x 8 cards. Perform a communications check to ensure operation of the radios. Have an assistant who is proficient in radio operation man the NCS. Provide the assistant with the call signs. If the soldier has not demonstrated sufficient progress to complete the task within 5 minutes, give him or her a NO-GO. This time limit is an administrative requirement, not a doctrinal one; so if the soldier has almost completed the task correctly, you may decide to allow him or her to finish.

Brief Soldier: Give the soldier to be tested the card containing the message and call signs. Tell him or her the radio is ready for operation, the net is considered to be secure and authentication is not required, and to send the message to the NCS and get a receipt. Tell the soldier, if sufficient progress in completing the task within 5 minutes has not been demonstrated, he or she will receive a NO-GO for the task.

Performance Measures	GO	NO GO
1 Entered the net in alphanumeric sequence.	_____	_____
2 Sent a message of 15 to 25 words using the correct prowords and phonetic alphabet and numerals.	_____	_____
3 Left the net in alphanumeric sequence.	_____	_____

Evaluation Guidance:. Refer to chapter 1, paragraph 1-9e, (1) and (2).

References
Required:
Related:

081-COM-0101

Request Medical Evacuation

Conditions: You have a casualty requiring medical evacuation (MEDEVAC) and you will need a patient pickup site. You will need operational communications equipment, MEDEVAC request format, and unit signal operation instructions (SOI).

Standards: Transmit a MEDEVAC request, providing all necessary information as quickly as possible. Transmit, as a minimum, line numbers 1 through 5 during the initial contact with the evacuation unit. Transmit lines 6 through 9 while the aircraft or vehicle is en route, if not included during the initial contact. IAW FM 4-02.2

Special Condition: None

Special Standards: None

Special Equipment:

Cue: None

*Note:*None

Performance Steps

1. Collect all applicable information needed for the MEDEVAC request.
   a. Determine the grid coordinates for the pickup site. (See STP 21-1-SMCT.)
   b. Obtain radio frequency, call sign, and suffix.
   c. Obtain the number of patients and precedence.
   d. Determine the type of special equipment required.
   e. Determine the number and type (litter or ambulatory) of patients.
   f. Determine the security of the pickup site.
   g. Determine how the pickup site will be marked.
   h. Determine patient nationality and status.
   i. Obtain pickup site chemical, biological, radiological, and nuclear (CBRN) contamination information normally obtained from the senior person or medic.
Note: CBRN line 9 information is only included when contamination exists.
2. Record the gathered MEDEVAC information using the authorized brevity codes. (See tables 081-COM-0101-1 and 081-COM-0101-2.)
Note: Unless the MEDEVAC information is transmitted over secure communication systems.

Table 081-831-0101-1. Line numbers 1–6

LINE	ITEM	EXPLANATION	WHERE/HOW OBTAINED	WHO NORMALLY PROVIDES	REASON
1	Location of pickup site	Encrypt the grid coordinates of the pickup site. When using the DRYAD Numeral Cipher, the same "SET" line will be used to encrypt the grid zone letters and the coordinates. To preclude misunderstanding, a statement is made that grid zone letters are included in the message (unless unit SOP specifies its use at all times).	From map	Unit leader(s)	Required so that evacuation vehicle knows where to pick up patient. Also, so that the unit coordinating the evacuation mission can plan the route for the evacuation vehicle (if the evacuation vehicle must pick up from more than one location).
2	Radio frequency, call sign, and suffix	Encrypt the frequency of the radio at the pickup site, not a relay frequency. The call sign (and suffix if used) of person to be contacted at the pickup site may be transmitted in the clear.	From SOI	RTO	Required so that evacuation vehicle can contact requesting unit while en route (obtain additional information or change in situation or directions).
3	Number of patients by precedence	Report only applicable information and encrypt the brevity codes. A - URGENT B - URGENT-SURG C - PRIORITY D - ROUTINE E - CONVENIENCE If two or more categories must be reported in the same request, insert the word "BREAK" between each category.	From evaluation of patient(s)	Medic or senior person present	Required by unit controlling vehicles to assist in prioritizing missions.
4	Special equipment required	Encrypt the applicable brevity codes. A - None B - Hoist C - Extraction equipment D - Ventilator	From evaluation of patient/situation	Medic or senior person present	Required so that the equipment can be placed on board the evacuation vehicle prior to the start of the mission.
5	Number of patients by type	Report only applicable information and encrypt the brevity code. If requesting medical evacuation for both types, insert the word "BREAK" between the litter entry and ambulatory entry. L = # of patients - Litter A = # of patients - Ambulatory (sitting)	From evaluation of patient(s)	Medic or senior person present	Required so that the appropriate number of evacuation vehicles may be dispatched to the pickup site. They should be configured to carry the patients requiring evacuation.
6	Security of pickup site (wartime)	N - No enemy troops in area P - Possibly enemy troops in area (approach with caution) E - Enemy troops in area (approach with caution) X - Enemy troops in area (armed escort required)	From evaluation of situation	Unit leader	Required to assist the evacuation crew in assessing the situation and determining if assistance is required. More definitive guidance can be furnished while the evacuation vehicle while it is en route (specific location of enemy to assist an aircraft in planning its approach).

Table 081-831-0101-2. Line numbers 6–9

LINE	ITEM	EXPLANATION	WHERE/HOW OBTAINED	WHO NORMALLY PROVIDES	REASON
6	Number and type of wound, injury, or illness (peacetime)	Specific information regarding patient wounds by type (gunshot or shrapnel). Report serious bleeding, along with patient's blood type, if known.	From evaluation of patient(s)	Medic or senior person present	Required to assist evacuation personnel in determining treatment and special equipment needed.
7	Method of marking pickup site	Encrypt the brevity codes. A - Panels B - Pyrotechnic signal C - Smoke signal D - None E - Other	Based on situation and availability of materials	Medic or senior person present	Required to assist the evacuation crew in identifying the specific location of the pickup. Note that the color of the panels or smoke should not be transmitted until the evacuation vehicle contacts the unit (just prior to its arrival). For security, the crew should identify the color and the unit verifies it.
8	Patient nationality and status	The number of patients in each category need not be transmitted. Encrypt only the applicable brevity codes. A - US military B - US citizen C - Non-US military D - Non-US citizen E - Enemy prisoner of war (EPW)	From evaluation of patient(s)	Medic or senior person present	Required to assist in planning for destination facilities and need for guards. Unit requesting support should ensure that there is an English-speaking representative at the pickup site.
9	CBRN contamination (wartime)	Include this line only when applicable. Encrypt the applicable brevity codes. C - Chemical B - Biological R - Radiological N - Nuclear	From situation	Medic or senior person present	Required to assist in planning for the mission (determine which evacuation vehicle will accomplish the mission and when it will be accomplished).
9	Terrain description (peacetime)	Include details of terrain features in and around proposed landing site. If possible, describe relationship of site to prominent terrain feature (lake, mountain, tower).	From area survey	Personnel present	Required to allow evacuation personnel to assess route/avenue of approach into area. Of particular importance if hoist operation is required.

a. Location of the pickup site (line 1).

b. Radio frequency, call sign, and suffix (line 2).

c. Numbers of patients by precedence (line 3).

d. Special equipment required (line 4).

e. Number of patients by type (line 5).

f. Security of the pickup site (line 6).

h. Patient nationality and status (line 8).

i. CBRN contamination (line 9).

3. Transmit the MEDEVAC request. (See STP 21-1-SMCT, task 113-571-1022.)

Note: Transmission may vary depending on individual experience level and situation.

a. Contact the unit that controls the evacuation assets.

(1) Make proper contact with the intended receiver.

(2) Use effective call sign and frequency assignments from the SOI.

(3) Give the following in the clear "I HAVE A MEDEVAC REQUEST;" wait 1 to 3 seconds for a response. If no response, repeat the statement.

b. Transmit the MEDEVAC information in the proper sequence.

(1) State all line item numbers in clear text. The call sign and suffix (if needed) in line 2 may be transmitted in the clear.

Note: Line numbers 1 through 5 must always be transmitted during the initial contact with the evacuation unit. Lines 6 through 9 may be transmitted while the aircraft or vehicle is en route.

(2) Follow the procedure provided in the explanation column of the MEDEVAC request format to transmit other required information.

(3) Pronounce letters and numbers according to appropriate radiotelephone procedures.

(4) End the transmission by stating "OVER."

(5) Keep the radio on and listen for additional instructions or contact from the evacuation unit.

Evaluation Preparation: *Setup*: Evaluate this task during a training exercise involving a MEDEVAC aircraft or vehicle, or simulate it by creating a scenario and providing the information as the Soldier requests it. You or an assistant will act as the radio contact at the evacuation unit during "transmission" of the request. Give a copy of the MEDEVAC request format to the Soldier.

Brief Soldier: Tell the Soldier to prepare and transmit a MEDEVAC request. State that the communication net is secure.

Performance Measures	GO	NO GO
1 Collected all information needed for the MEDEVAC request line items 1 through 9.	___	___
2 Recorded the information using the authorized brevity codes.	___	___

Performance Measures	GO	NO GO
3 Transmitted the MEDEVAC request as quickly as possible, following appropriate radiotelephone procedures.	___	___

Evaluation Guidance:. Refer to chapter 1, paragraph 1-9e, (1) and (2).

References:
Required: FM 4-02.2, FM 8-10-6, and STP 21-1-SMCT
Related:

171-COM-4079

Send a Situation Report (SITREP)

Conditions: You are a member of a squad or team in a field environment and have been directed to send a situation report. You have a map, an overlay and/or sketch map with graphic control measures, and a operational communications system. Your unit may be digitally equipped.

Standards: Prepare a SITREP in standard format and send to the next higher element. Maintain situational awareness (SA).

Special Condition: None

Special Standards: None

Special Equipment:

Cue: None

Note: The operational environment must be considered at all times during this task. All Army elements must be prepared to enter any environment and perform their missions while simultaneously dealing with a wide range of unexpected threats and other influences. Units must be ready to counter these threats and influences and, at the same time, be prepared to deal with various third-party actors, such as international humanitarian relief agencies, news media, refugees, and civilians on the battlefield. These groups may or may not be hostile to us, but they can potentially affect the unit's ability to accomplish its mission.

Note: Units equipped with digital communication systems will use these systems to maximize information management, maintain SA, and minimize electronic signature.

1. Prepare a SITREP in standard format.

Note: The SITREP is used to report any change since the last report, to request resupply, and to report the current location of the element; only lines or parts of lines that contain new information will be sent. It may require additional follow-up reports.

Note: Timely and accurate reporting of friendly elements locations, obstacles and contacts are essential to maintaining SA and the reduction of potential fratricide incidents.

    a. Line 1: Date and Time Group (DTG)-Report date and time the report is being submitted.

Note: Date is the date that the report is being submitted. Time is the local time or zulu time that the report is being initiated.

    b. Line 2: Unit-Identify the unit making the report.

    c. Line 3: From-Report the time that the operational situation started or will start.

    d. Line 4: Until-Report the time that the operational situation ends or will end.

    e. Line 5: Map-Give a minimum six digit grid of the squad or team current location.

    f. Line 6: Enemy-Report enemy activity.

        (1) Nationality.

        (2) Location.

        (3) Mission.

        (4) Time of Sighting.

    g. Line 7: Nonhostile-Report nonhostile activity.

    h. Line 8: Own-Report activities of own forces.

        (1) Changes in location of units and/or formations.

        (2) Activities of forces not attached to originating unit.

2. Send the SITREP to the next higher element.

3. Maintain SA.

Evaluation Preparation:

Setup: Provide the Soldier with the equipment and or materials described in the conditions statement.

Brief Soldier: Tell the Soldier what is expected of him by reviewing the task standards. Stress to the Soldier the importance of observing all cautions, warnings, and dangers to avoid injury to personnel and, if applicable, damage to equipment.

Performance Measures	GO	NO GO
1 Prepared the SITREP in standard format.	_____	_____

Performance Measures	GO	NO GO
2 Sent the SITREP.	_____	_____
3 Maintained SA.	_____	_____

Evaluation Guidance:. Refer to chapter 1, paragraph 1-9e, (1) and (2).

References:
Required:
Related: FM 6-99.2

171-COM-4080

Send a Spot Report (SPOTREP))

Conditions: You are a member of a squad or team in an operational environment and have been directed to report current situation/status to higher headquarters. You have a tactical radio and/or other digital communication equipment.

Standards: Prepare a Spot Report (SPOTREP) in standard format and send to the next higher element.

Special Condition: None

Special Standards: None

Special Equipment:

Cue: None

Note: The SPOTREP is used to report timely intelligence or status regarding events that could have an immediate and significant effect on current and future operations. This is the initial means for reporting troops in contact and event information. Several lines of the SPOTREP provide sub-categories that structure reported data. Some lines may be omitted in an emergency. For example, the SPOTREP could provide only the reporting unit, event DTG, location, and activity. The format of a SPOTREP may also change based on unit's standing operating procedures (SOP).

If equipped with Force XXI Battle Command Brigade-and-Below (FBCB2), the FBCB2 operator must update observed enemy force locations, neutral organizations, civilians and other battlefield hazards.

Performance Steps

1. Prepare SPOTREP.
  a. LINE 1 – date time group (DTG) of report submission.
  b. LINE 2 – reporting unit (Unit Making Report).
Note: After the unit designation, the method of observation must be indicated: unaided, binoculars, infrared, thermal, night vision device (NVD), unmanned aircraft system (UAS), or other. Follow with narrative if needed.
  c. LINE 3 – size of detected element.
    (1) Persons: Military, Civilian.
    (2) Vehicles: Military, Civilian.
    (3) Equipment: Military, Civilian.
  d. LINE 4 - activity of detected element at DTG of report.
Note: The activity type or types must be indicated and an amplifying sub-type if Applicable. If necessary add a narrative to clarify, describe, or explain the type of activity.
    (1) Attacking (direction from).
      (a) Air defense artillery (ADA) (engaging).
      (b) Aircraft (engaging) (rotary wing [RW], fixed wing [FW]).
      (c) Ambush (IED [exploded], IED [unexploded], sniper, anti-armor, other).
      (d) Indirect fire (point of impact, point of origin).
      (e) Chemical, biological, radiological or nuclear (CBRN).
    (2) Defending (direction from).
    (3) Moving (direction from).
    (4) Stationary.
    (5) Cache.
    (6) Civilian (criminal acts, unrest, infrastructure damage).
    (7) Personnel recovery (isolating event, observed signal).
    (8) Other (give name and description).
  e. LINE 5 - location (universal transverse mercator (UTM) or grid coordinate with military grid reference system (MGRS) grid zone designator of detected element activity or event observed).
  f. LINE 6 - unit (detected element unit, organization, or facility).
Note: The type of unit, organization, or facility detected should be identified. If it cannot be clearly identified is should be described in as much detail as possible to include; the type uniform, vehicle markings, and other identifying information.
    (1) Conventional.
    (2) Irregular.
    (3) Coalition.
    (4) Host nation.
    (5) Nongovernmental organization (NGO).
    (6) Civilian.
    (7) Facility.
  g. LINE 7 – time (DTG of observation).
  h. LINE 8 – equipment (equipment of element observed).
Note: The equipment type or types, and amplifying sub-type should be identified, if

applicable. A narrative can be added if necessary to clarify, describe, or explain the type of equipment. The nomenclature, type, and quantity of all equipment observed should be provided, if known. If equipment cannot be clearly identified it should be describe in as much detail as possible.

(1) ADA (missile (man-portable air defense system [MANPADS]), missile (other), gun).

(2) Arty (gun (self-propelled [SP]), gun (towed), missile or rocket, mortar).

(3) Armored track vehicle (tank, armored personnel carrier [APC], command and control [C2], engineer, transport, other).

(4) Armored wheel vehicle (gun, APC, C2, engineer, transport, other).

(5) Wheel vehicle (gun, C2, engineer, transport, other).

(6) INF weapon (WPN) (anti-armor missile, anti-armor gun, rocket-propelled grenade [RPG], heavy [HVY] machine gun [MG], grenade launcher [GL], small arms, other).

(7) Aircraft (RW (attack helicopter [AH]), RW (utility helicopter [UH]), RW (observation helicopter), FW (atk), FW (trans), UAS, other).

(8) Mine or IED (buried, surface, vehicle-borne improvised explosive device [VBIED], person-borne improvised explosive device [PBIED], other).

(9) CBRN.

(10) Supplies (class III, class V, other).

(11) Civilian.

(12) Other.

i. LINE 9 – assessment (apparent reason for or purpose of the activity observed, and apparent threats to or opportunities for friendly forces).

j. LINE 10 –narrative (free text for clarifying report).

Note: The narrative should describe the actions related to the detected activity: attack, withdraw, continue to observe, or other. When feasible, the narrative should also state potential for subsequent reports such as air support request, battle damage assessment (BDA) report, call for fire, casualty report, explosive ordinance disposal (EOD) support, medical evacuation (MEDEVAC) or other reports.

k. LINE 11 – authentication (report authentication) per SOP.

2. Send SPOTREP to next higher element.

Note: The unit SOP may have additional guidance on who receives the SPOTREP.

Evaluation Preparation:*Setup*: Provide the Soldier with the equipment and or materials described in the conditions statement.

Brief Soldier: Tell the Soldier what is expected of him by reviewing the task standards. Stress to the Soldier the importance of observing all cautions, warnings, and dangers to avoid injury to personnel and, if applicable, damage to equipment.

Performance Measures	GO	NO GO
1 Prepared the SPOTREP.	_____	_____

Performance Measures	GO	NO GO
2 Sent the SPOTREP to higher headquarters.	_____	_____

Evaluation Guidance:. Refer to chapter 1, paragraph 1-9e, (1) and (2).

References:
Required:
Related: FM 6-99.2

071-326-0608

Use Visual Signaling Techniques

Conditions: Given a flashlight (night only); signaling flags (mounted signals only; and a requirement to perform visual signals or identify visual signals performed by another.

Standards: Demonstrate the proper actions for each required visual signal or identify each visual signal demonstrated by another.

Special Condition: None

Special Standards: None

Special Equipment: None

Cue: None

*Note:*Visual signals are any means of communication that require sight and can be used to transmit planned messages rapidly over short distances. This includes the devices and means used for the recognition and identification of friendly forces.

Performance Steps

1. Perform formation signals.
   a. Perform a coil formation signal (Figure 071-326-0608-1).

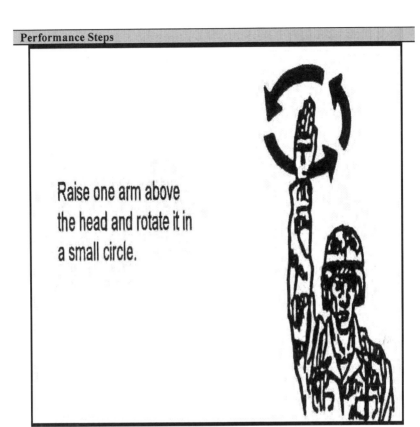

Raise one arm above the head and rotate it in a small circle.

Figure 071-326-0608-1. Coil

b. Perform a herringbone formation signal (Figure 071-326-0608-2).

Extend the arms parallel to ground. Bend the arms until the forearms are perpendicular.

Figure 071-326-0608-2. Herringbone.

2. Perform drill signals.
   a. Perform a contact left signal (Figure 071-326-0608-3).

Extend the left arm parallel to the ground. Bend the arm until the forearm is perpendicular. Repeat.

Figure 071-326-0608-3. Contact Left.
b. Perform a contact right signal (Figure 071-326-0608-4).

Extend the right arm parallel to the ground. Bend the arm until the forearm is perpendicular. Repeat.

Figure 071-326-0608-4. Contact Right.

c. Perform a action left signal (Figure 071-326-0608-5).

Extend both arms parallel to the ground. Raise the right arm until it is overhead. Repeat.

Figure 071-326-0608-5. Action Left.

d. Perform a action right signal (Figure 071-326-0608-6).

Figure 071-326-0608-6. Action Right.

e. Perform a action front (right, left, or rear) signal (Figure 071-326-0608-7).

Raise the fist to shoulder level and thrust it several times in the desired direction of action.

Figure 071-326-0608-7. Action Front (Right, Left, or Rear).
f. Perform a air attack signal (Figure 071-326-0608-8).

Bend the arms with fore-
arms at a 45-degree
angle. The forearms are
crossed. Repeat.

Figure 071-326-0608-8. Air Attack.

g. Perform a Chemical, Biological, Radiological, and Nuclear (CBRN) signal (Figure 071-326-0608-9).

Extend the arms and fists. Bend the arms to the shoulders. Repeat.

Figure071-326-0608- 9. Chemical, Biological, Radiological, and Nuclear (CBRN).

3. Perform proper movement techniques.
   a. Perform a traveling signal (Figure 071-326-0608-10).

Extend the arm over-
head and swing it in a
circle from the shoulder.

Figure 071-326-0608-10. Traveling.
b. Perform a traveling overwatch signal (Figures 11).

Extend both arms and raise them up and down.

Figure 11. Traveling Overwatch.

c. Perform a bounding overwatch, cover my move signal (Figure 071-326-0608-12).

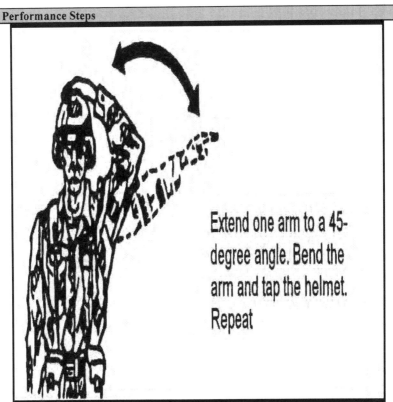

Extend one arm to a 45-degree angle. Bend the arm and tap the helmet. Repeat

Figure 071-326-0608-12. Bounding Overwatch, Cover My Move.
4. Perform proper signals to control the vehicle drivers and crews.
   a. Perform a move to the left signal (Figure 071-326-0608-13).

Figure 071-326-0608-13. Move to the Left.
b. Perform a move to the right signal (Figure 071-326-0608-14).

Figure 071-326-0608-14. Move to the Right.
c. Perform a move forward signal (Figure 071-326-0608-15).

Move the hands and forearms backward and forward, palms toward the chest.

Figure 071-326-0608-15. Move Forward.
d. Perform a attention signal (Figure 071-326-0608-16).

Extend the arm sideways, slightly above the horizontal, palm to the front. Wave the arm to and from the head several times.

Figure 071-326-0608-16. Attention.

e. Perform a I am ready, or ready to move, are you signal (Figure 071-326-0608-17).

Extend the arm toward the person being signaled; then raise the arm slightly above horizontal, palm outward.

Figure 071-326-0608-17. I am Ready, or Ready to Move, are you.
f. Perform a mount signal (Figure 071-326-0608-18).

Make two or three movements upward with the open hand, palm up.

Figure 071-326-0608-18. Mount.

g. Perform a disregard previous command signal (Figure 071-326-0608-19).

Raise both arms and cross wrists above the head, palms to the front.

Figure 071-326-0608-19. Disregard Previous Command.
h. Perform a I do not understand signal (Figure 071-326-0608-20).

Raise both arms sideways to the horizontal; bend both arms at the elbows and place both hands across the face, palms to the front.

Figure 071-326-0608-20. I Do Not Understand.

i. Perform a a start engine, or prepare to move signal (Figure 071-326-0608-21).

DAY

NIGHT

Simulate cranking of engines by making a fist and moving the army in a circular motion at waist level.

Move a light to describe a horizontal figure 8 in a vertical plane in front of the body.

Figure 071-326-0608-21. Start Engine, or Prepare to Move.

j. Perform a halt or stop signal (Figure 071-326-0608-22).

DAY

NIGHT

Raise the hand upward to the full extent of the arm, palm to the front. Hold that position until the signal is understood.

Move a light horizontally back and forth several times across the path of approaching traffic to stop vehicles. Use the same signal to stop engines.

NOTE: For alternate signal to stop vehicles, see Figure 34.

Figure 071-326-0608-22. Halt or Stop.

k. Perform a increase speed signal (Figure 071-326-0608-23).

DAY

Raise the fist to shoulder level; thrust the fist upward to the full extent of the arm and back to shoulder level rapidly several times.

NIGHT

Move a light vertically several times in front of the body.

Figure 071-326-0608-23. Increase Speed.

l. Perform a advance or move out signal (Figure 071-326-0608-24).

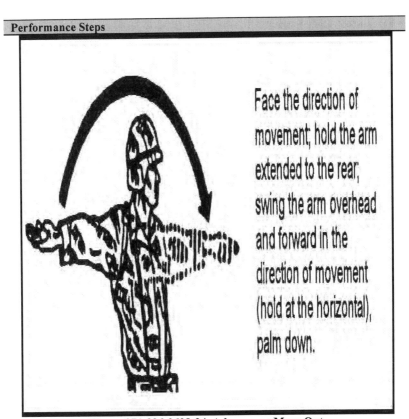

Face the direction of movement; hold the arm extended to the rear; swing the arm overhead and forward in the direction of movement (hold at the horizontal), palm down.

Figure 071-326-0608-24. Advance or Move Out.

m. Perform a open up signal (Figure 071-326-0608-25).

Extend the arms overhead, palms inward, then slowly lower arms to a horizontal position.

Figure 071-326-0608-25. Open Up.

n. Perform a close up signal (Figure 071-326-0608-26).

Extend both arms parallel to the ground, palms up, then move the arms up-ward and inward toward the head.

Figure 071-326-0608-26. Close Up.
o. Perform a right or left turn signal (Figure 071-326-0608-27).

Left

DAY

Extend the arm horizontally to side, palm outward.

left   right

NIGHT

Rotate a light to describe a circle 12 to 18 inches in diameter in the direction of the turn.

Figure 071-326-0608-27. Right or Left Turn.

p. Perform a slow down signal (Figure 071-326-0608-28).

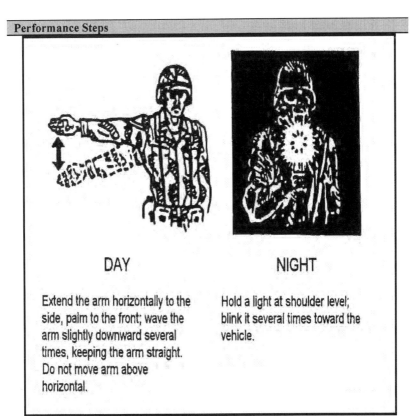

DAY

Extend the arm horizontally to the side, palm to the front; wave the arm slightly downward several times, keeping the arm straight. Do not move arm above horizontal.

NIGHT

Hold a light at shoulder level; blink it several times toward the vehicle.

Figure 071-326-0608-28. Slow Down.

q. Perform a move in reverse signal (Figure 071-326-0608-29).

DAY

Face the vehicle(s) (unit) being signaled, raise the hands to shoulder level, palms to the front. Move the hands forward and backward.

NIGHT

Hold a light at shoulder level; blink it several times toward vehicle(s).

Figure 071-326-0608-29. Move in Reverse.

r. Perform a close distance between vehicles signal (Figure 071-326-0608-30).

Face the vehicle(s) being signaled, extend the forearms to the front, palms inward and separated (width of the shoulders). Bring the palms together as the vehicle(s) approaches. The vehicle(s) must stop when the palms come together.

Figure 071-326-0608-30. Close Distance Between Vehicles.

s. Perform a stop engines signal (Figure 071-326-0608-31).

Extend the arm parallel to the ground, hand open, and move the arm across the body in a throat-cutting action.

Figure 071-326-0608-31. Stop Engines.

t. Perform a dismount signal (Figure 071-326-0608-32).

Extend the arms, make two or three movements up and down, hands open toward ground.

Figure 071-326-0608-32. Dismount.
u. Perform a neutral steer signal (Figure 071-326-0608-33).

Cross the wrists at the throat; point the index finger in direction of steer. Make a fist of the other hand.

Figure 071-326-0608-33. Neutral Steer.
v. Perform a stop signal (Figure 071-326-0608-34).

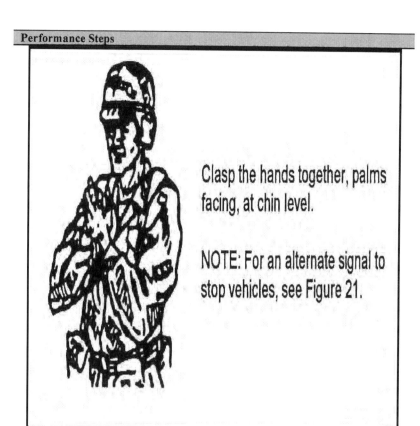

Clasp the hands together, palms facing, at chin level.

NOTE: For an alternate signal to stop vehicles, see Figure 21.

Figure 071-326-0608-34. Stop.
w. Perform a button up/unbutton signal (Figure 071-326-0608-35).

Figure 071-326-0608-35. Button Up/Unbutton.

x. Perform a message acknowleged signal (Figure 071-326-0608-36).

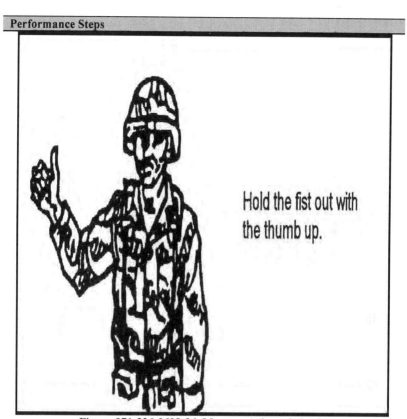

Hold the fist out with the thumb up.

Figure 071-326-0608-36. Message Acknowledged.

5. Perform flag signals.
   a. Perform a single signal flag signal (Figure 071-326-0608-37).

Figure 071-326-0608-37. Single Signal Flag.
b. Perform a mount signal (Figure 071-326-0608-38).

Figure 071-326-0608-38. Mount.
c. Perform a dismount signal (Figure 071-326-0608-39).

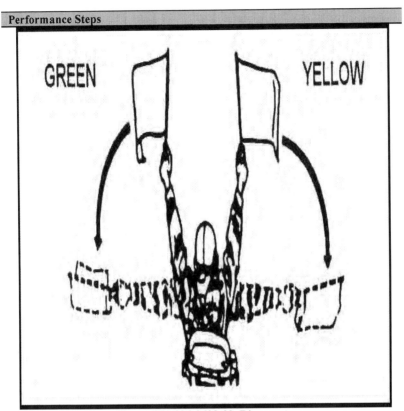

Figure 071-326-0608-39. Dismount.

d. Perform a dismount and assault signal (Figure 071-326-0608-40).

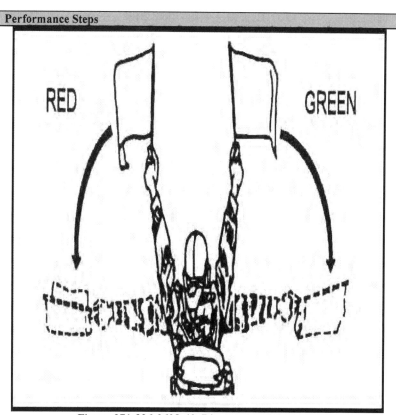

Figure 071-326-0608-40. Dismount and Assault.
e. Perform a assemble or close signal (Figure 071-326-0608-41).

Figure 071-326-0608-41. Assemble or Close.

f. Perform a move out signal (Figure 071-326-0608-42).

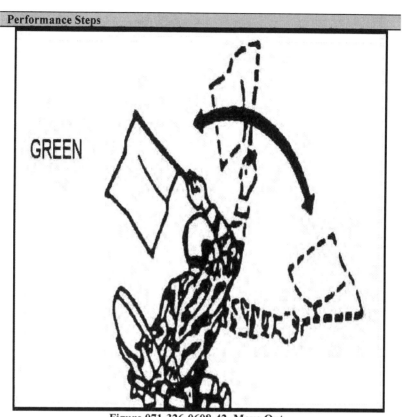

GREEN

Figure 071-326-0608-42. Move Out.
g. Perform a Chemical, Biological, Radiological, and Nuclear (CBRN) signal (Figure 071-326-0608-43).

Figure 071-326-0608-43. Chemical, Biological, Radiological, and Nuclear (CBRN).

Evaluation Preparation:

Setup: Provide the Soldier with the equipment and or materials described in the conditions statement.

Brief Soldier: Tell the Soldier what is expected of him by reviewing the task standards. Stress to the Soldier the importance of observing all cautions, warnings, and dangers to avoid injury to personnel and, if applicable, damage to equipment.

Performance Measures	GO	NO GO
1 Performed proper formation signals.	_____	_____
2 Performed proper drill signals.	_____	_____
3 Performed proper movement technique signals.	_____	_____
4 Performed proper signals to control vehicle drivers and crews.	_____	_____
5 Performed proper flag signals.	_____	_____

Evaluation Guidance:. Refer to chapter 1, paragraph 1-9e, (1) and (2).

References:
Required: FM 17-95 and FM 21-60
Related:

Subject Area 4: Survive

031-COM-1036

Maintain Your Assigned Protective Mask

WARNING

Read and adhere to all safety notes in your mask's operator's tm prior to beginning mask maintenance.

Conditions: You have used your assigned protective mask or must conduct a scheduled mask inspection. You have your assigned protective mask (with authorized accessories and components); cleaning materials in accordance with (IAW) the applicable operator technical manual (TM); a preventive maintenance checks and services (PMCS) Department of the Army (DA) Form 5988-E or DA Form 2404, Equipment Inspection and Maintenance Worksheet, IAW DA

Pamphlet (PAM) 750-8; mask replacement parts; and a new filter. This task cannot be performed in mission-oriented protective posture (MOPP) 4.

Standards: Maintain your assigned protective mask IAW the operator's TM by—
1) Performing operator's PMCS.
2) Cleaning your mask.

Special Condition: None

Special Standards: None

Special Equipment:

Cue: None

Note: None

Performance Steps

1. Inspect your protective mask, carrier, hood, and accessories according to the PMCS tables located in the mask operator TM.
   a. Identify deficiencies and shortcomings.
   b. Correct operator level deficiencies.
2. Clean and dry the mask, hood, and authorized accessories and components IAW the mask operator TM.
3. Record uncorrected deficiencies on DA Form 2404, Equipment Inspection and Maintenance Work Sheet, IAW DA Pam 750-8.
4. Provide the completed DA Form 2404 to your supervisor for his/her review and guidance.
5. Perform all maintenance without damaging your protective mask.

Evaluation Preparation:*Setup*: A good time to evaluate this task is during normal care and cleaning of the mask. Place the required equipment on a field table or another suitable surface. Simulate defects in the mask by removing components from the mask or using a defective mask not issued to the Soldier. During training and evaluation sessions, use an old set of filters or canister several times to avoid expending new ones each time. If the Soldier has not made adequate progress towards completing the task within 30 minutes, stop him and give him a NO GO. This time standard is administrative.

Brief Soldier: Tell the Soldier there is no time standard for this task on the job, but for testing purposes he must perform the task within 30 minutes. Tell him to perform operator level PMCS on the mask, clean his assigned protective mask, and replace the mask filter. Tell the Soldier that completing a DA Form 2404,

Equipment Inspection and Maintenance Work Sheet, IAW DA PAM 750-8 is not part of the task.

Performance Measures	GO	NO GO
1 Inspected protective mask, carrier, hood, and accessories according to the PMCS tables located in mask operator TM.	_____	_____
2 Cleaned and dried the mask, hood, and authorized accessories and components IAW mask operator TM.	_____	_____
3 Recorded uncorrected deficiencies on a DA Form 2404 Equipment Inspection and Maintenance Work Sheet IAW DA Pam 750-8.	_____	_____
4 Provided the completed DA Form 2404, Equipment Inspection and Maintenance Work Sheet, to his/her supervisor for review and guidance.	_____	_____
5 Performed all maintenance without damaging the protective mask.	_____	_____

Evaluation Guidance:. Refer to chapter 1, paragraph 1-9e, (1) and (2).

References:
Required: PAM 750-8, TM 3-4240-312-12&P, TM 3-4240-342-10, TM 3-4240-346-10, TM 3-4240-348-10, TM 3-4240-542-13&P
Related:

031-COM-1035

Protect Yourself from Chemical and Biological (CB) Contamination Using Your Assigned Protective Mask

Conditions: You are given your assigned protective mask, hood, carrier, a canteen with an M1 canteen cap or water canteen cap, and M8 detector paper. You find yourself in one of the following situations: (1) you hear or see a CB agent and/or unknown toxic industrial chemical attack/spill, (2) you realize, through other means, that you are under a CB agent and/or toxic industrial chemical attack, (3) you are ordered to mask, (4) you must enter a contaminated area, and (5) after having donned your protective mask, you need to drink from your canteen.

Standards: Protect yourself from CB agent and/or unknown toxic industrial chemical contamination by donning, clearing, and checking your assigned protective mask within 9 seconds without becoming contaminated. Drink water through your protective mask from your canteen without becoming a casualty.

Special Condition: Do not wear contact lenses when performing this task. Do not use masks with damaged filters because certain models contain hazardous materials. Do not change filter elements in a contaminated environment.

Special Standards: *Note*: The mask gives you immediate protection against traditional warfare agents. The mask may not be adequate to protect you from certain toxic industrial chemicals, but it provides the best available protection to enable you to evacuate the hazard area. You may be required to evacuate to a minimum safe distance of at least 300 meters upwind from the contamination (if possible) or as directed by the commander.

Special Equipment:

Cue: If you hear or see a chemical or biological attack.

Note: Soldier must complete steps 1 through 4 within 9 seconds.

Performance Steps
WARNING Before donning and adjusting the mask, female warfighters will remove earrings, hair fasteners (hair clips, hair pins, combs, and rubber bands), hair knots, buns, or braids that will interfere with the mask seal and will let hair hang freely. When wearing the Ground Crew Ensemble, hair will be neatly

tucked inside jacket. Facial hair could result in an improper mask fit resulting in illness or death.

Do not wear contact lenses (soft or hard) while wearing the masks. Inadequate oxygen supply to the corneal surface, and exposure to dust, dirt, and smoke or gas may cause serious vision loss or eye damage. Personnel requiring vision correction will use the optical inserts that have been provided to them with their protective masks.

1. Don the mask.
    a. Stop breathing, and close eyes.
    b. Remove helmet, put helmet between legs above knees or hold rifle between legs and place helmet on the muzzle. If helmet falls continue to mask.
    c. Take off glasses, if applicable.
    d. Open the mask carrier with left hand.
    e. Grasp the mask assembly with right hand, and remove it from the carrier.
    f. Place chin in the chin pocket, and press the facepiece tight against face.
Note: The temple and forehead straps have already been adjusted during fitting.
    g. Grasp the tab and pull the head harness over the head. Ensure that the ears are between the temple straps and the cheek straps. Ensure that the head harness is pulled far enough over the head that the forehead straps are tight.
    h. Use one hand to tighten the cheek straps, one at a time, while holding the head pad centered on the back of head with the other hand. Ensure that the straps lay flat against the head.
2. Clear the mask.
    a. Seal the outlet disk valve by placing one hand over the outlet valve cover assembly.
    b. Blow out hard to ensure that any contaminated air is forced out around the edges of the facepiece.
3. Check the mask.
    a. Cover the inlet port of the filter canister or the inlet port of the armor quick disconnect with the palm of the hand, and inhale.
    b. Ensure that the facepiece collapses against face and remains so while holding your breath, which indicates that the mask is airtight.
    c. Remove any hair, clothing, or other matter between the face and the mask if the facepiece does not collapse to face.
    d. Notify the chemical, biological, radiological, and nuclear (CBRN) noncommissioned officer (NCO) if the mask still does not collapse.
4. Resume breathing.
Note: There is no time standards for donning the hood.
5. Completes steps 1 through 4 within 9 seconds.

CAUTION
Be careful when pulling on the hood because it could snag and tear on the buckles of the head harness.

6. Secure the mask hood.

WARNING

Be careful not to break facepiece seal when pulling protective hood over your head.

    a. For the M50/M51-series protective mask.

      (1) Place hands up under the protective hood, stretch elasticized portion and raise protective hood up
and over filters.

      (2) Carefully pull excess protective hood material over head, neck and shoulders.

      (3) Grasp underarm straps.

      (4) Bring the male end of each underarm strap and fasten to female end.

      (5) Tighten underarm straps.

    b. For the M48 series protective mask.

      (1) Carefully pull the back of the hood assembly over the head so hood covers the head, neck and shoulders.

      (2) Tuck inner skirt inside the collar of the CBRN protective suit. This can be done using the buddy system.

    c. For the M42- or M43-series protective mask, pull the hood over the head and zip the front closed to cover the bare skin.

    d. For the M45-series protective mask, pull the M7 hood over the helmet and head so that the hood covers shoulders.

    e. For the M40-series protective mask, don the hood so that it lies smoothly on the head.

      (1) For masks equipped with the regular hood—

        (a) Grasp the back edge of the hood skirt.

        (b) Pull the hood completely over the head so that it covers the back of the head, neck, and shoulders.

        (c) Zip the front of the hood closed by pulling the zipper slider downward.

        (d) Tighten the draw cord.

        (e) Secure the underarm straps by fastening and adjusting them.

        (f) Close your mask carrier.

        (g) Continue your mission.

      (2) For masks equipped with the quick-doff hood—

        (a) Place hands inside the hood and expand the elastic gathering around the neck of the hood.

        (b) Stretch and carefully pull the hood over head so that the hood covers your head, neck and shoulders.

        (c) Fasten the underarm straps.

        (d) Put on the helmet.

Note: For combat vehicle crewman (CVC) helmet, perform the following steps: (1) disconnect the boom microphone from the helmet, (2) connect the mask microphone to the receptacle in the helmet, (3) grasp the helmet next to the ear cups with the hand, and spread the helmet as far as possible, (4) place the helmet over head, tilting the helmet forward slightly so that the first contact when putting it on is with the forehead surface of the mask and (5) rotate the helmet back and down over the head until it is seated in position.

(e) Close mask carrier.

(f) Continue the mission.

Note: If the Soldier is using the mask in conjunction with the joint-service, lightweight integrated suit technology (JSLIST), he/she skips this step (the mask lacks a hood because it is built in on the JSLIST).

WARNING

Use M8 detector paper to check for contamination before using the drinking system. If contamination is detected, decontaminate using the M295 decontamination kit. Do not connect the quick-disconnect coupling to your canteen until all surfaces are free of contamination. Chemical contamination could enter your mouth, and you could become a casualty.

Do not break the mask seal while drinking from the canteen.

---

7. Drink water while wearing the mask.

a. Press in on the top of the outlet valve cover until the internal drink tube can be grasped between your teeth.

b. Steady the mask assembly with one hand and pull the quick-disconnect coupling out of the outlet valve cover. For the M50/M51 protective mask pull drink coupler out of coupler receptacle, below the front module.

c. Flip open the cover on the M1 canteen cap or open retaining strap on water canteen cap for the M50/M51 protective mask.

d. Push the quick-disconnect coupling into the canteen cap so that the pin enters the quick-disconnect coupling. For the M50/M51 protective mask push drink coupler into canteen cap so that seal snaps into the groove in the cap.

e. Turn drink tube lever on front module assembly upward, until it stops and is fully opened, to positioninternal drink tube in front of mouth, and grasp internal drink tube between your lips (for the M50/M51 and M48 protective mask only.)

WARNING

Do not tilt your head back while drinking.

---

f. Blow to create positive pressure. You should feel some resistance.

g. Raise the canteen upside down and drink (if the system does not leak.)

h. Stop drinking after several swallows and lower the canteen. Blow into the internal drink tube to prevent the canteen from collapsing. Repeat the drinking procedure as required.

8. Doff the mask for storage.

a. M50/M51 protective mask

(1) Remove headgear.

(2) Loosen cheek straps completely by placing your thumbs behind the buckles and pulling forward so straps become loose. Grasp the front of the mask and lift it off your head.

(3) Replace headgear.

(4) Stow the audio frequency amplifier in the retaining loop located in the bottom of the mask carrier main stowage area before stowing the mask.

(5) Grasp the cheek straps and carefully pull the head harness over the front of the mask.

(6) Grasp the mask carrier flap tab and pull to open mask carrier flap.

(7) Grasp the mask by the front module assembly, place in mask carrier eyelens first, covered by head harness skullcap and face it away from the body.

b. M40A1 protective mask

(1) Remove helmet.

(2) Loosen cheek straps.

(3) Place one hand on the front voicemitter to hold mask assembly on face, with other hand grasp head harness tab, pull the head harness over the front of the mask assembly and remove mask assembly.

(4) Replace helmet.

(5) Pull head harness over front of mask assembly.

(6) Smooth the second skin/universal second skin over the front of the mask assembly.

(7) Pull the forehead straps tight over the second skin/universal second skin, by pulling the head harness down as far as possible, by pulling on the harness tab.

(8) Hold the facepiece assembly up and put it in the mask carrier with the lenses facing away from your body.

CAUTION

It is important to completely close the hook and pile fastener on the mask carrier cover. Failure to do this will result in collection of debris and damage to the mask assembly.

---

(9) Close the mask carrier. Seal the entire hook and pile fastener surface.

(10) Stowing M40A1/M42-Series Mask With Quick Doff Hood (QDH).

(a) Hold front of mask assembly in a horizontal position and smooth the QDH over it.

(b) Store the ends of the underarm straps in a "V".

(c) Fold the two edges of the QDH over the underarm straps to create a "V".

(d) Fold the "V" up to cover the eyelenses. Do not let the QDH cover the chin opening.

_1_ If stowing M42-series, wrap the two edges of the hood over the underarm straps and around the hose.

_2_ Grasp the hose through the hood and aligned hose to point down toward the chin.

CAUTION

To avoid damage to the mask assembly, DO NOT fold mask assembly when placing it in the mask carrier.

(e) Hold the facepiece assembly up and put it in the mask carrier with the lenses facing away from your body.

(f) Close the mask carrier. Seal the entire hook and pile fastener surface.

---

c. M43 protective mask

(1) Remove helmet.

(2) Detach canister disconnect along with canisters from top of blower. Let hose and canisters hang from facepiece.

(3) Turn blower off.

(4) Using both hands, gently lift hood up over head; let hood hang from front of facepiece.

(5) Loosen three head harness straps by rolling buckles forward.

(6) Grip head harness and pull facepiece up and off head.

(7) Check that the facepiece is dry and free of oil or solvents before stowing. If facepiece is not dry and free of oil or solvents, clean as directed.

(8) With hood hanging in front of facepiece, hold front of facepiece in a horizontal position (face down) and smooth the hood beneath it.

(9) Fold hood and microphone cable up around the back of facepiece.

(10) Open top flap on carrier.

(11) To stow the items in the proper locations proceed as follows:

(a) Place hose, canister disconnect and canisters into carrier section on the nametag side of the carrier.

(b) Place facepiece on top of canisters.

(c) Unsnap blower from harness.

(d) Insert blower with controls up, into carrier section on the back side of the carrier.

(e) Unclip shoulder, waist, leg straps and remove blower harness.

(f) Stow blower harness in carrier section with blower.

(g) Make sure technical manual is stowed in carrier section with blower.

(h) Close and seal top flap on carrier.

(i) Store carrier with contents in dark, dry location. Hang carrier by one of the straps for storage.

d. M45 protective mask.

(1) Remove helmet.

(2) Disconnect microphone (if issued) from helmet receptacle, then remove helmet.

(3) Loosen cheek straps ONLY.

(4) Place thumbs under both cheek tabs. Lift bottom of mask out and up over your head.

(5) Pull head harness over front of mask.

(6) With canister toward the bottom of the carrier, place mask in carrier with eyelenses facing up and away from body.

(7) Close carrier.

e. M48 protective mask

(1) Remove helmet.

(2) Using both hands, gently lift hood of facepiece assembly up over head; let hood hang from front of facepiece assembly.

(3) Loosen the three suspension harness straps by rolling buckles forward.

(4) Grip suspension harness and pull facepiece assembly up and off head.

(5) Turn blower assembly off.

WARNING

Any occurrences of redness, puffiness, or itchiness that persist for an extended period of time after removing the facepiece assembly should be referred to the flight surgeon for evaluation.

---

(6) Perform all After PMCS

(7) With hood assembly hanging in front of facepiece assembly, install facepiece assembly in facepiece carrier with open side of facepiece assembly toward the leg (back of facepiece carrier.)

(8) Tuck remainder of hood into facepiece carrier. Leave hose exposed from facepiece carrier.

(9) Close flap on facepiece carrier.

9. Perform all steps in sequence without becoming a casualty.

Evaluation Preparation:

Setup: Evaluate this task during a field exercise or a tactical training session. Use a mask earlier fitted to the Soldier's face. The Soldier will bring his/her flight or CVC helmet. The Soldier should be in mission-oriented protective posture 4 (MOPP4). Do not use a new decontamination kit for every Soldier; use the kit as long as possible. Ensure that the Soldier has M8 detector paper in the mask carrier before testing.

Brief Soldier: Tell the Soldier to stand, while wearing his/her mask carrier containing his/her assigned protective mask with the hood attached. Provide the Soldier with one of the scenarios described in the conditions statement (cue to begin masking). Tell the Soldier to keep the mask on until you issue the all clear order. Tell the Soldier to drink water while wearing his/her assigned mask.

Performance Measures	GO	NO GO
1 Donned the mask.	⎯⎯	⎯⎯
2 Cleared the mask.	⎯⎯	⎯⎯
3 Checked the mask.	⎯⎯	⎯⎯
4 Resumed breathing.	⎯⎯	⎯⎯

Performance Measures	GO	NO GO
5 Completed steps 1 through 4 in sequence within 9 seconds.	_____	_____
6 Secured the mask hood.	_____	_____
7 Consumed water while wearing the mask.	_____	_____
8 Doffed the mask for storage.	_____	_____
9 Performed all steps in sequence without becoming casualty.	_____	_____

Evaluation Guidance:. Refer to chapter 1, paragraph 1-9e, (1) and (2).

References:
Required: FM 3-11.3, FM 3-11.4, TM 3-4240-300-10-2, TM 3-4240-312-12&P, TM 3-4240-346-10, and TM 3-4240-542-13&P
Related:

031-COM-1019

React to Chemical or Biological (CB) Hazard/Attack

Conditions: You are in a tactical environment where the threat of an attack or exposure to chemical or biological agents (toxic industrial or conventional warfare) is high. You are given mission oriented protective posture (MOPP) gear, protective mask, an individual decontamination kit, reactive skin decontamination lotion (RSDL) and M8 and M9 detector paper. You may also be given eye protection, an Army combat helmet (ACH), an improved outer tactical vest (IOTV), and deltoid auxiliary protectors (DAPs). You are now in MOPP 0 and one of the following automatic-masking situations occurs: 1) a chemical alarm sounds, 2) a positive reading is obtained on detector paper, 3) individuals exhibit symptoms of chemical biological (CB) agents or toxic industrial chemical (TIC) poisoning, such as difficulty breathing, coughing, wheezing, vomiting, or eye irritation, 4) you observe a spill or cloud of unknown material(s), 5) you react to an improvised explosive device (IED) explosion where you suspect the release of a CB or toxic chemical, 6) you observe a contamination marker, 7) your supervisor orders you to mask, 8) you observe personnel wearing protective masks, and 9) you observe other signs of a possible CB agent or toxic industrial chemical attack/spill.

Standards: React to a CB agent or toxic industrial chemical hazard/attack without becoming a casualty by: donning your protective mask within 9 seconds, notifying your supervisor of identified or possible contamination, starting the steps to decontaminate yourself within 1 minute of finding contamination, (after decontaminating yourself all over) assuming MOPP 4 unless directed to a lower MOPP level, decontaminating your individual equipment using the decontaminating kit as necessary, and continuing the mission.

Special Condition: None

Special Standards: None

Special Equipment:

Cue: None

*Note:*None

Performance Steps

    1. Identify the CB hazard automatic-masking criteria.
      a. Don your protective mask automatically when any of the following situations occur:
        (1) A chemical alarm sounds.
        (2) A positive reading is obtained on detector paper.
        (3) Individuals exhibit symptoms of CB agent poisoning, such as difficulty breathing, coughing, wheezing, vomiting, or eye irritation.
        (4) You observe a spill or cloud of unknown material(s).
        (5) You react to an IED explosion where you suspect the release of a CB agent.
        (6) You observe a contamination marker.
        (7) Your supervisor orders you to mask.
        (8) You observe personnel wearing protective masks.
        (9) You observe other signs of a possible CB agent hazard/attack.
      b. Respond to the commander's policy of automatic masking.
Note: Commanders at all levels may establish a modified policy by designating additional criteria for automatic masking.
    2. Protect yourself from CB contamination by using your assigned protective mask without fastening the hood within 9 seconds.
Note: The mask provides protection against conventional warfare agents. The mask provides little if any protection from toxic industrial materials (TIMs), but it provides the best

available protection to enable you to evacuate the hazard area. You may be required to evacuate to a minimum safe distance of at least 300 meters upwind from the contamination (if possible) or as directed by the commander.

    a. Stop breathing and close your eyes.

    b. Don the protective mask with hood.

    c. Clear the mask.

    d. Check the mask.

    e. Do not fasten the hood.

    f. Go immediatley to the next step.

  3. Give the alarm.

    a. Shout, "Gas, Gas, Gas."

    b. Give the appropriate hand-and-arm signal.

    c. Hit two metal objects together.

  4. Take cover and/or assemble as directed, moving at least 300 meters upwind from the suspected contamination area to reduce exposure.

  5. Decontaminate exposed skin within 1 minute of becoming contaminated using the individual decontaminating kit as necessary.

  6. Cover all exposed skin and assume MOPP 4 as directed.

Note: This step is graded only if MOPP is available.

Note: If you are wearing an ACH, IOTV, or DAPs, proceed to performance step 6e through 6k.

    a. Don the overgarment trousers.

    b. Don the overgarment coat.

    c. Don the overboots.

Note: Combat boots provide limited protection. Cover them as soon as possible because they absorb chemicals. (It takes a long time to put on the overboots; in an emergency, put them on last.)

    d. Don the protective gloves.

    e. Remove the ACH and protective eyewear.

    f. Loosen the DAPs.

WARNING

When dofffing the iotv from the shoulder. Take care not to snag the filter canister and break the seal of your protective mask.

---

    g. Doff the IOTV by lifting the front flap and detach side plate carriers by separating hook and loop fastener tape. Lift front carrier and detach internal elastic bands at hook and loop interface. Open the medical access hook and pile closure, loosen the left shoulder adjustment strap and slide vest off the right shoulder.

    h. Perform performance steps 6a through 6d, and then proceed to performance step 6i.

    i. Don the IOTV over the right shoulder by tightening the left shoulder adjustment strap and fastening the medical access hook and pile closure. Attach internal elastic bands at hook and loop interface and close the front carrier. Attach side plate carriers and close the front flap.

j. Secure the DAP.

k. Don the ACH.

7. Decontaminate your individual equipment using your individual equipment decontamination kit, as necessary.

8. Notify your supervisor of any suspected CB hazard/attack.

9. Continue the mission and perform any additional requirements as outlined in your unit's standing operating procedure (SOP).

Note:

1. Use all means of CB detection to check your surrounding area for the presence of contamination.

2. Contact your higher headquarters if you find contamination or if you determine that the attack was non-CB related.

3. Await further guidance. The higher headquarters contacts all adjacent/attached units to check the status of CB contamination in their areas. All units will report the absence or presence of contamination to the chain of command.

4. Annotate the above actions on your duty log Department of the Army (DA) Form 1594, Daily Staff Journal or Duty Officer's Log, and as a siginificant activity (SIGAct) on units Combat Management System (CMS).

Evaluation Preparation:

Setup: A good time to evaluate this task is during a field exercise when a variety of CB hazards can be simulated. Select a site with adequate cover, and ensure that Soldiers have their assigned protective mask.

Brief Soldier: Tell the Soldier that there will be an encounter with simulated CB agents and/or a CB alarm will be given

Performance Measures	GO	NO GO
1 Identified automatic-masking criteria.	_____	_____
2 Donned protective mask without fastening the hood within 9 seconds.	_____	_____
3 Gave the alarm.	_____	_____
4 Took cover and/or assembled as directed. Moved at least 300 meters upwind from the suspected contamination area to reduce exposure.	_____	_____

Performance Measures	GO	NO GO
5 Decontaminated exposed skin as necessary within 1 minute of finding the contamination.	_____	_____
6   Covered all exposed skin and assumed MOPP 4 as directed.

(Graded only if MOPP is available. If Soldier is wearing an ACH, IOTV, or DAPs, proceed to performance step 6e and 6K.) | _____ | _____ |
7 Decontaminated individual equipment as necessary.	_____	_____
8 Notified the supervisor of any CB hazard/attacks.	_____	_____
9 Continued the mission and performed requirements outlined in unit's SOP.	_____	_____

Evaluation Guidance:. Refer to chapter 1, paragraph 1-9e, (1) and (2).

References:
Required: DA Form 1594, FM 3-11.4, FM 3-11.5, TM 3-4230-229-10, and TM 3-4230-235-10
Related:

031-COM-1040

Protect Yourself from CBRN Injury/Contamination with the JSLIST Chemical-Protective Ensemble

Conditions: You are given the Joint-Service, Lightweight, Integrated Suit Technology (JSLIST) chemical-protective ensemble consisting of JSLIST overgarments (coat and trousers), JSLIST compatible protective mask, JSLIST compatible footwear covers, and JSLIST compatible protective gloves, Field Manual (FM) 3-11.4, Technical Manual (TM) 10-8415-220-10, and Skin Exposure Reduction Paste Against Chemical Warfare Agents (SERPACWA). You are directed to assume mission-oriented protective posture (MOPP) level 4, or you are in a situation where you must automatically react to a chemical, biological, radiological, and nuclear (CBRN) hazard.

Standards: Protect yourself from CBRN injury/contamination with the JSLIST chemical protective ensemble by: 1) performing Before preventive maintenance checks and services (PMCS) according to TM 10-8415-220-10, 2) applying SERPACWA if command directed, 3) assuming MOPP Levels 1 through 4 in order within 8 minutes, 4) doffing the JSLIST ensemble, 5) performing After PMCS inspections, and 6) repackaging the JSLIST ensemble.

Special Condition: None

Special Standards: None

Special Equipment:

Cue: You are ordered to do so, learn a chemical attack is about to happen, must enter an area where chemical agents have been used, recognize a chemical hazard, or attacked with chemical agents without warning.

Note: None

Performance Steps

1. Perform Before PMCS on the JSLIST ensemble in accordance with (IAW) TM 10-8415-220-10.
    a. Using a new garment, first use.
        (1) Remove the coat or trousers from the factory vacuum-sealed bags and store in trouser pocket.
Note: Coat and trousers packaging includes resealable bags. Store bags in trousers pockets and retain for reuse in repackaging the JSLIST ensemble.
        (2) Perform Before PMCS according to table 2-1 located in TM 10-8415-220-10.
        (3) Mark the label with the date that the garment was removed from the package in permanent ink.
    b. Using a used garment.
        (1) Remove the coat or trousers from the clear plastic, resealable bag.

WARNING

SERPACWA is for military and external use only. Do not apply to the eyes or to mucous membranes. This product, its packaging, and clothing or other materials exposed to SERPACWA should not be destroyed by burning due to the release of toxic fumes. Smoking should be avoided, be sure to avoid getting SERPACWA on smoking products. Be sure to clean hands before handling smoking products.

---

2. Apply SERPACWA (if command-directed).
Note: SERPACWA is intended for use prior to exposure to chemical warfare agent (CWA) and only in conjunction with the JSLIST chemical protective ensemble.

a. Before you assume MOPP Level 1, use a dry towel to wipe off sweat, insect repellent, camouflage paint, sand, or dirt from your skin at the areas shown on the packet label.

b. Tear open the packet and squeeze about one-third of the pouch into the palm of your hand and rub it evenly around the wrists (site 1), neck (site 2), and boot tops of lower legs (site 3) until it forms a difficult to notice white film.

c. Remove the remaining two-thirds of the SERPACWA from the pouch and rub it evenly onto your armpits (site 4), groin area (site 5), and waistline (site 6).

d. After SERPACWA is applied, if exposure to CWA is either confirmed or suspected, follow the appropriate protocol for decontamination.

e. For removal of SERPACWA in the absence of exposure to CWA, scrub the sites with a dry towel, or if possible, with a cloth using both soap and water.

3. Don the JSLISTS chemical protective ensemble, in MOPP Level 1 through 4 sequence within eight minutes.

a. Assume MOPP Level 1.

(1) Don the JSLIST overgarment trousers.

(a) Extend your toes downward, put one leg into the trousers, and pull them up. Repeat the procedure for your other leg.

(b) Close the slide fastener, and fasten the two fly opening snaps.

(c) Pull the suspenders over your shoulders, and fasten the snap couplers. Adjust the suspenders to ensure that the trousers fit comfortably.
Note: The trouser length can be adjusted by raising or lowering the suspenders.

(d) Adjust the waistband hook-and-pile fasteners for a snug fit.

(2) Don the JSLIST overgarment coat.

(a) Don the coat, and close the slide fastener up as far as your chest.

(b) Secure the front closure hook-and-pile fasteners up as far as your chest.

(c) Pull the bottom of the coat down over the trousers. Pull the loop out and away from the overgarment coat, and bring it forward between the legs. Pull on the loop until the bottom of the coat fits snugly over the trousers.

b. Assume MOPP Level 2. Don the overboots.

(1) Don the overboots (multipurpose overboots/black vinyl overboots/green vinyl overboots (MULO/BVO/GVO) over the combat boots. Adjust and secure the strap-and-buckle fasteners.

(2) Pull the trouser legs over the overboots (MULO/BVO/GVO). Secure the hook-and-pile fasteners on each ankle to fit snugly around the boot.

c. Assume MOPP Level 3 by donning chemical-protective mask IAW task 031-503-1035.

d. Assume MOPP Level 4. Don the gloves.

(1) Push the sleeve cuffs up your arm.

(2) Put on the gloves and glove liners (inserts).

(3) Pull the sleeve cuffs over the top of the gloves, and secure the hook-and-pile fastener tape snugly on each wrist.

4. Doff the JSLIST chemical protective ensemble.

   a. Doff the gloves.

     (1) Unfasten the hook-and-pile fastener tape on each wrist, and remove the gloves (and liners if butyl rubber gloves are worn).

     (2) Put the gloves in the trouser pockets.

   b. Untie the bow in the coat retention cord, unfasten the webbing strip snap, and release the coat retention cord loop.

   c. Doff the helmet and cover, if worn.

   d. Doff the hood from the JSLIST coat.

     (1) Unfasten the barrel locks.

     (2) Loosen the hood.

     (3) Unfasten the hook-and-pile fastener tape at your neck.

     (4) Pull the hood off your head.

   e. Doff the protective mask, stow it in the carrier, remove the carrier, and place on an uncontaminated surface.

   f. Doff the overboots.

     (1) Unfasten the ankle hook-and-pile fastener tapes.

     (2) Unfasten the two strap-and-buckle fasteners on the MULOs.

     (3) Remove the MULOs.

   g. Doff the JSLIST coat.

     (1) Unfasten the front closure flap hook-and-pile fastener tape and the front slide fastener.

     (2) Remove the coat.

   h. Doff the JSLIST trousers.

     (1) Unfasten the suspender and waist hook-and-pile fastener tapes.

     (2) Unfasten the front closure snaps, and open the slide fastener.

     (3) Remove the JSLIST trousers.

5. Perform After PMCS inspections according to table 2-1 and paragraph 3-2 in TM 10-8415-220-10.

6. Repackage the JSLIST ensemble.

   a. Remove the clear plastic, resealable bags from the trousers pocket.

   b. Fold and repack the coat and trousers in individual clear plastic, resealable bags.

Evaluation Preparation:

Setup: Provide the Soldier with the items listed in the task conditions statement. Evaluate this task during a field exercise or during a normal training session. Ensure that adequate amounts of serviceable JSLIST ensembles are present or that the evaluated Soldier(s) bring their JSLIST ensemble to the evaluation site. The evaluator must be prepared to direct higher MOPP Levels at once as a Soldier reaches a preceding Level.

Brief Soldier: Read the action, conditions, and standards to the Soldier. Tell the Soldier to complete before PMCS and to inform you of any faults found with the suit (for example, the draw cord is unserviceable, and so forth). After the before PMCS has been completed, inform the Soldier that MOPP Levels 1 through 4 must be achieved in sequence and that the time limit for achieving MOPP Level 4 is 8 minutes. Ensure that the Soldier informs you as each MOPP Level is obtained (for example, "I am now at MOPP Level 1."). For performance measures or parts of performance measures requiring the Soldier to state an answer, lead the Soldier with an appropriate question (for example, "When would you put SERPACWA on?", or "What do you use the clear plastic, resealable bags for?").

Performance Measures	GO	NO GO
1 Performed Before PMCS inspection in accordance with (IAW) TM 10-8415-220-10.	___	___
2 SERPACWA was applied IAW the package instructions, if use was command directed.	___	___
3 Donned the JSLIST chemical protective ensemble, in MOPP Level 1 through 4 sequence, within 8 minutes.	___	___
4 Doffed the JSLIST chemical protective ensemble.	___	___
5 Performed After PMCS IAW TM 10-8415-220-10. (Labeled the coat and trouser in permanent ink with the days of wear, and the number of times they had been laundered IAW unit SOP.)	___	___
6 Repackaged JSLIST ensemble. Removed the clear-plastic resealable bags from the JSLIST trouser pocket, and placed the used JSLIST coat and trousers in them and resealed.	___	___

Evaluation Guidance: Evaluation Guidance:. Refer to chapter 1, paragraph 1-9e, (1) and (2).

References:
Required: FM 3-11.4 and TM 10-8415-220-10
Related:

031-COM-1013

Decontaminate Yourself and Individual Equipment Using Chemical Decontaminating Kits

Conditions: You are at mission-oriented protective posture (MOPP) Level 2. You are given Technical Manual (TM) 3-4230-229-10, TM 3-4230-235-10, TM 3-6505-001-10, a chemical protective mask, chemical protective gloves, chemical protective overboots, a full canteen of water, a poncho, load-bearing equipment (LBE) or load-bearing vest, Interceptor Body Armor (IBA), the Improved Outer Tactical Vest (IOTV), and M291 decontaminating kit(s) or the Reactive Skin Decontamination Lotion (RSDL). Your skin and eyes have been exposed to chemical agents, or you have passed through a chemically contaminated area and suspect that you have contamination on your skin.

Standards: Decontaminate yourself and your individual equipment using the chemical decontaminating kits. Start the steps to decontaminate your skin and eyes within 1 minute after contamination. Decontaminate your exposed skin and eyes, as necessary, before chemical-agent symptoms occur. Decontaminate all individual equipment after decontaminating your skin and eyes.

Special Condition: None

Special Standards: None

Special Equipment:

Cue: None

Note: None

Performance Steps

1. Assume MOPP Level 3 without securing the hook-and-pile fastener tape or drawcord on the integrated hood.

Note: For training purposes, use the Training RSDL. If the Reactive Skin Decontaminating Lotion (RSDL) is not available, use the M291 (skip to performance step 3).

2. Decontaminate your skin using the RSDL within 1 minute of contamination.

> **DANGER**
> Do not mix RSDL with solid, undiluted high-test hypochlorite (HTH) or super, tropical bleach (STB). Heat and/or fire may result.

WARNING

Under no circumstances should the training RSDL be used in place of the RSDL during actual combat operations. The training lotion does not contain active ingredients.

    a. Decontaminate your hands, face, and the inside of your mask.

      (1) Remove one RSDL packet from your carrying pouch.

      (2) Tear it open quickly at any notch.

      (3) Remove the applicator pad from the packet, and save the packet as the remaining lotion can be added to the applicator pad, if required.

      (4) Thoroughly scrub the exposed skin of your hand, palm, and fingers with the applicator pad.

Note: The applicator pad can be used from either side and may gripped in any manner allowing the applicator pad to be applied to the skin.

      (5) Switch the applicator pad to the other hand, and repeat the procedure.

DANGER

Death or injury may result if you breathe toxic agents while doing the following steps. If you need to breathe before you finish, reseal your mask, clear it, check it, get your breath, and then resume the decontaminating procedure.

      (6) Stop breathing, close eyes, grasp mask beneath chin and pull mask away from chin enough to allow one hand between the mask and your face. Hold the mask in this position during steps 2a(7) through 2a(13).

Note:

1. Do not discard the applicator pad at this time.

2. If you were masked with your hood secured when you became contaminated, stop. Put on your protective gloves, and proceed to step 2b.

3. If you were not masked with the hood secured when you became contaminated, continue decontaminating the exposed skin.

      (7) Thoroughly scrub the exposed skin of your face with lotion from the applicator pad.

      (8) Thoroughly scrub across your forehead.

      (9) Beginning at one side, scrub up and down across your cheeks, nose, chin, and closed mouth. Avoid ingesting.

      (10) Scrub under the chin from the ear along the jawbone to the other ear to coat your skin with lotion.

CAUTION

Do not apply lotion to the lens of the protective mask. The RSDL may cause loss of transparency.

      (11) Turn your hand over and scrub the inside surfaces of the mask that may touch your skin. Be sure to include the drinking tube.

      (12) Keep the applicator.

      (13) Seal your mask immediately, clear it, and check it.

(14) Use the applicator and any remaining lotion in the packet. Without breaking the mask seal, scrub the applicator pad across the forehead, exposed scalp, the skin of the neck, ears, and throat.

(15) Secure the hood.

(16) Thoroughly scrub your hands with lotion again as in steps 2a(4) through 2a(5).

(17) Assume MOPP Level 4 by putting on protective gloves.

> **WARNING**
>
> Do not discard the RSDL packaging or applicator pads into containers that contain HTH or STB. Heat and/or fire may result.

b. Use any remaining lotion to spot decontaminate weapons, personal equipment, and canteen cap that may have become contaminated.

c. Allow RSDL to remain on skin for at least 2 minutes to destroy the chemical agent.

d. Discard the used packet(s) and applicator pad(s) by leaving them in place.
Note: Do not put used packets in your pockets. Discard the carrying pouch after using the packets.

e. Remove the decontaminating lotion with soap and water when operational conditions permit, such as an "All Clear" directive or after detailed troop decontamination.
Note: Upon completion of training and evaluation, ensure that Soldiers have adequate mask cleaning supplies and water to clean training RSDL off of their protective mask.

3. Decontaminate your skin using the M291 decontaminating kit within 1 minute of contamination.

> **DANGER**
>
> Death or injury may result if you breathe toxic agents while decontaminating your face. If you need to breathe before you finish, reseal your mask, clear it, check it, get your breath, and then resume the decontaminating procedure.
>
> **CAUTION**
>
> The M291 decontaminating kit is for external use only. Keep decontaminating powder out of your eyes and out of any cuts or wounds. The decontaminating powder may irritate your skin or eyes.
>
> If your face has been contaminated, use water to wash the toxic agent out of your eyes, cuts, or wounds.
>
> After decontaminating with water, cover exposed cuts or wounds with appropriate first aid wrap or bandages before handling the decontaminating kit.
>
> Do not handle or hold leaking packets above your head. Do not touch or rub your eyes, lips, or the inside of your mouth with anything that has been in contact with the decontaminating powder.

Do not attempt to decontaminate a loaded weapon. Always unload and clear the weapon and place the weapon on safe before starting decontaminating procedures. Immediate decontaminating techniques remove only the liquid hazard. Certain items may still present a vapor hazard. See your supervisor for unmasking procedures.

    a. Decontaminate your hands and face and the inside of your mask.
       (1) Remove one skin decontamination packet from your carrying pouch.
       (2) Tear it open quickly at the notch.
       (3) Remove the applicator pad from the packet, and discard the empty packet.
       (4) Unfold the applicator pad, and slip your finger(s) into the handle.
       (5) Scrub the back of your hand, palm, and fingers until they are completely covered with black powder from the applicator pad.
       (6) Switch the applicator pad to the other hand, and repeat the procedure.

Note:
1. Do not discard the applicator pad at this time.
2. If you were masked with your hood zipped and the drawstring pulled tight when you were contaminated, stop. Discard the applicator pad, put on your protective gloves, and go to step 3b. However, if you were masked, but the zipper and drawstring were not secure, go to step 3a(16). The stars in the illustration on page 2-5 of TM 3-4230-229-10 show areas of the face that should be scrubbed with an extra stroke because they are hard to decontaminate.
3. The procedure is the same regardless of the type of protective mask. If you are using the Joint Service Lightweight Integrated Suit Technology (JSLIST) with a hood attached to the protective jacket, ignore the instructions for the hood.

DANGER
Death or injury may result if you breathe toxic agents while decontaminating your face. If you need to breathe before you finish, reseal your mask, clear it, check it, get your breath, and then resume the decontaminating procedure.

       (7) Scrub exposed skin of your face thoroughly until you are completely covered with black powder from the applicator pad.
       (8) Hold your breath, close your eyes, grasp the mask beneath your chin, and pull the hood and mask away from your chin enough to allow one hand between the mask and your face.
       (9) Scrub up and down across your face, beginning at the front of one ear, to your nose, and then to your other ear.
         (a) Scrub across your face to the corner of your nose.
         (b) Scrub an extra stroke at the corner of your nose.
         (c) Scrub across your nose, to the tip of your nose, and then to the other corner of your nose.
         (d) Scrub an extra stroke at the corner of your nose.
         (e) Scrub across your face to your other ear.
       (10) Scrub up and down across your face to your mouth and then to the other end of your jawbone.
         (a) Scrub across your cheek to the corner of your mouth.
         (b) Scrub an extra stroke at the corner of your mouth.

(c) Scrub across your closed mouth to the center of your upper lip.

(d) Scrub an extra stroke above your upper lip.

(e) Scrub across your closed mouth to the outer corner of your mouth

(f) Scrub an extra stroke at the corner of your mouth.

(g) Scrub across your cheek to the end of your jawbone.

(11) Scrub up and down across your face to your chin and then to the other end of your jawbone.

(a) Scrub across and under your jaw to your chin, cupping your chin.

(b) Scrub extra strokes at the center of your chin.

(c) Scrub across your upper jaw to the end of your jawbone.

(12) Turn your hand out, and quickly wipe the inside of your mask where it touches your face.

(13) Discard the applicator pad.

(14) Seal your mask immediately, clear it, and check it.

(15) Remove the second skin decontamination packet from the carrying pouch.

(16) Repeat steps 3a(2), (3), and (4) above.

(17) Scrub your neck and ears until they are thoroughly covered with black powder without breaking the seal between your face and your mask. Scrub your hands again until they are completely covered with black powder.

b. Assume MOPP Level 4.

(1) Discard the applicator pad.

(2) Put on your protective gloves.

(3) Fasten your hood.

c. Remove the decontaminating powder with soap and water when operational conditions permit.

4. Decontaminate your individual equipment using the M295 decontaminating kit.

a. Use the first mitt to decontaminate your gloves, the exposed areas of your mask and hood, your weapon, and your helmet.

(1) Remove one decontamination packet from your pouch.

(2) Tear the packet open at any notch.

(3) Remove the decontamination mitt.

(4) Discard the empty packet.

(5) Unfold the decontamination mitt.

(6) Grasp the green (nonpad) side of the decontamination mitt with your nondominant hand. Pat the other gloved hand with the decontamination mitt to start the flow of decontamination powder onto your glove. Rub your glove with the decontamination mitt until it is completely covered with decontaminating powder.

(7) Insert the decontaminated, gloved hand inside the decontamination mitt. Ensure that the pad side is in the palm of your hand and your thumb sticks through the appropriate thumbhole. Securely tighten the wristband on the gloved hand.

(8) Decontaminate individual equipment by rubbing with the pad side of the decontamination mitt until the equipment is thoroughly covered with decontamination powder. Pay special attention to areas that are hard to reach (such

as cracks, crevices, and absorbent materials).

       (a) Decontaminate your other glove.

       (b) Decontaminate exposed areas of your mask and hood.

       (c) Decontaminate your weapon.

       (d) Decontaminate your helmet by patting it with the decontamination mitt.

    (9) Discard the decontamination mitt.

  b. Use the second mitt to decontaminate your LBE, IBA or IOTV and accessories, mask carrier, overboots, and gloves again.

    (1) Get another packet, and repeat steps 4a(1) through 4a(7). Then, perform the following:

       (a) Decontaminate load-carrying equipment (LCE), IBA, IOTV and accessories (such as canteen, ammo pouch, and first aid pouch).

       (b) Decontaminate your mask-carrying case.

       (c) Decontaminate your protective boots.

       (d) Repeat the decontamination process on your protective gloves.

    (2) Discard the decontamination mitt.

    (3) Get another packet and repeat steps 4a(1) through 4a(7) if liquid contamination is still suspected or detected. Rub or blot areas where contamination is still suspected or detected.

WARNING

The M295 kit only removes the liquid hazard. Decontaminated items may still present a vapor hazard. Do not unmask until it has been determined safe to do so.

---

  c. Remove the decontaminating powder when operational conditions permit.

  5. Notify your supervisor on the location of the used decontaminating materials, and await guidance on disposal procedures.

Evaluation Preparation:

Setup: Provide the Soldier with the items listed in the task conditions statement. A good time to evaluate this task is while in a field environment. Gather materials for the disposal of hazardous waste according to federal, state, and local rules and regulations.

Brief Soldier: Tell the Soldier what body parts and equipment are contaminated.

Performance Measures	GO	NO GO
1 Assumed MOPP Level 3 without securing the hook-and-pile fastener tape or drawcord.	_____	_____
2 Decontaminated skin using the RSDL within 1 minute of contamination.	_____	_____
3 Decontaminated skin using the M291 decontaminating kit within 1 minute of contamination.	_____	_____
4 Decontaminated individual equipment using the M295 decontaminating kit.	_____	_____
5 Notified supervisor on the location of the used decontaminating materials, and awaited guidance on disposal procedures.	_____	_____

Evaluation Guidance:. Refer to chapter 1, paragraph 1-9e, (1) and (2).

References:
Required: FM 3-11.4, FM 3-11.5, TM 10-8415-209-10, TM 10-8415-220-10, TM 3-4230-229-10, TM 3-4230-235-10, and TM 3-6505-001-10
Related:

031-COM-1037

Detect Chemical Agents Using M8 or M9 Detector Paper

> **WARNING**
> Always wear protective gloves when touching M9 detector paper. Do not get M9 detector paper in or near your mouth or on your skin. The M9 detector paper dye may cause cancer, but the risk is small because very little dye is used.

Conditions: You are in mission-oriented protective posture (MOPP) 2 in a tactical environment or an area where there is a chemical threat. You are given a protective mask, a booklet of M8 detector paper, a dispenser of M9 detector paper, M256A1 or M256A2 chemical-agent detector kit, assigned M291 skin decontaminating kit or reactive skin decontamination lotion (RSDL), M295 individual equipment decontamination kit, DA Form 1594 Daily Staff Journal or

Duty Officer's Log, FM 3-11.4, FM 3-11.3, TM 3-6665-307-10, TM 3-6665-311-10, and a complete set of MOPP gear or a chemical-protective ensemble.

Standards: Detect chemical agents using M8 and M9 detector paper, ensuring that the M9 detector paper is attached to places likely to come into contact with liquid chemical agents. Detect and identify all liquid chemical agents in the area that are within the capabilities of the M8 or M9 detector paper without becoming a casualty.

Special Condition: 1) Do not wear contact lenses when performing this task, 2) do not use masks with damaged filters because certain models contain hazardous materials, and 3) do not change the filter element in a contaminated environment.

Special Standards: None

Special Equipment:

Cue: None

Note: None

Performance Steps

1. Detect chemical agents using M9 detector paper.
Note: M8 and M9 detector paper will not detect chemical-agent vapors.

a. Attach the M9 detector paper to your MOPP gear and equipment while wearing chemical-protective gloves.

(1) Place the M9 detector paper on the MOPP gear on opposite sides of your body.

(a) If you are right-handed, place a strip of M9 detector paper around your right upper arm, left wrist, and right ankle.
Note: These are the places where a moving Soldier will most likely brush against a surface (such as undergrowth) that is contaminated with a liquid chemical agent.

(b) If you are left-handed, place a strip of M9 detector paper around your left upper arm, right wrist, and left ankle.
Note: Do not attach M9 detector paper to hot, dirty, oily, or greasy surfaces because it may give a false positive reading.

(2) Place M9 detector paper on equipment where it will come in contact with contaminated objects and is visible to the operator.

CAUTION
Firing weapons lubricated with lubricating oil, semi-fluid; lubricant, small arms; or lubricant, semifluid, automatic weapons (LSA) may cause false positive responses on the olive drab (OD) detector paper.

b. Monitor the M9 detector paper constantly for any color change. If you observe a color change, immediately do the following:

(1) Mask.

(2) Give the alarm.

(3) Decontaminate as necessary.

(4) Assume MOPP 4.

2. Detect chemical agents using M8 detector paper if you see a liquid that might be a chemical agent or if you observe a color change on the M9 detector paper.

a. Assume MOPP 4 immediately.

b. Prepare the M8 detector paper. Tear out a sheet from the book (use one-half sheet if it is perforated).

Note: You may want to put the paper on the end of a stick or another object and then blot the paper on the suspected liquid agent.

c. Blot (do not rub) the M8 detector paper on the suspected liquid agent. Do not touch the liquid with your protective glove.

WARNING

Some decontaminants will give false positive results on the M8 detector paper. The M8 detector paper may indicate positive results if used in an area where decontaminants have been used.

---

d. Observe the M8 detector paper for a color change. Identify the contamination by comparing any color change on the M8 detector paper to the color chart on the inside front cover of the booklet.

(1) A yellow-gold color indicates the presence of a nerve (G) agent.

(2) A red-pink color indicates the presence of a blister (H) agent.

(3) A dark green color indicates the presence of a nerve (V) agent.

(4) Any other color or no color change indicates that the liquid cannot be identified using M8 detector paper.

e. Store the booklet of M8 detector paper.

f. Remain in MOPP4 even if the liquid cannot be identified. Use other types of chemical-agent detector kits to verify the test results.

g. Notify your supervisor of the test results.

Note: M8 detector paper reacts positively to petroleum products, ammonia, and decontaminating solution number 2 (DS2). M9 detector paper reacts positively to petroleum products, insecticides, and antifreeze. Because M9 detector paper only detects (but does not identify) chemical agents, verify all readings with M8 detector paper. If you observe a color change on M8 or M9 detector paper, assume it is a liquid chemical agent. When conducting agent tests at night, remove any colored lens because it may provide a false negative response. Confirm the presence of contamination by using all means of chemical-agent detection available in your area of operation, including a visual check of your surroundings. If you determine that your reading is a false positive, perform the following actions before giving the all clear signal:

1. Ensure that every attempt has been made to recheck the area.

2. Contact your higher headquarters (HQ) or the person in charge, and report the negative results.

3. Await further guidance. The higher HQ contacts all adjacent/attached units to check the status of contamination in their areas. If all units report the absence of contamination, the information is reported up the chain of command.

4. Annotate the above actions on DA Form 1594 Daily Staff Journal or Duty Officer's Log.

Evaluation Preparation:

> **CAUTION**
> Ensure that stimulants are placed on detector paper only and never on the protective clothing.

Setup: Provide the items listed in the task condition statement. Simulate an unknown liquid chemical agent by using expedient training aids (such as brake fluid, cleaning compound, gasoline, insect repellent, or antifreeze). Place drops of the simulated agent on M9 detector paper to obtain a reading. For M8 detector paper, place the simulated agent on nonporous material (such as an entrenching tool).

Brief Soldier: Tell the Soldier that he/she will be entering an area where chemical agents have been used. Tell him/her to attach M9 detector paper to his/her MOPP gear and equipment. Tell him/her that if you observe any acts that are unsafe or that could produce a false reading you will stop the test and he/she will be scored a NO GO.

Performance Measures	GO	NO GO
1 Detected chemical agents using M9 detector paper.	_____	_____
2 Detected chemical agents using M8 detector paper.	_____	_____

Evaluation Guidance:. Refer to chapter 1, paragraph 1-9e, (1) and (2).

References:
Required: DA Form 1594, FM 3-11.3, FM 3-11.4, TM 3-6665-311-10, and TM 3-6665-426-10
Related:

031-COM-1021

Mark CBRN-Contaminated Areas

Conditions: You are given a nuclear, biological, and chemical (NBC) marking set and Technical Manual (TM) 3-9905-001-10 or the M328 chemical, biological, radiological, and nuclear (CBRN) marking kit and TM 3-9905-002-12&P in a tactical environment where CBRN weapons have been used. The contamination has been located and identified in an area. You are in the appropriate personal protective equipment (PPE). This task may be performed in mission-oriented protective posture (MOPP) level 4.

Standards: Mark the CBRN-contaminated area. Ensure that the required information is printed on the marker(s), and emplace the marker(s) according to the type of contamination. There is no change to standards if task is performed in MOPP level 4.

Special Condition: None

Special Standards: None

Special Equipment:

Cue: None

Note: If the M328 CBRN Marking Kit is available, proceed to step 2.

Performance Steps

1. Employ contamination markers using the NBC marking set.
   a. Emplace the RADIOLOGICAL markers.
     (1) Place markers at the location where a dose rate of 1 centigray per hour (cGyph) or more is measured.
     (2) Place markers so that the word "ATOM" faces away from the contamination.
     (3) Print the following information clearly on the front of the markers:
       (a) Dose rate in cGyph.
       (b) Date-time group (DTG) (specify local or Zulu) of the detonation. If the DTG is not known, print "unknown."
       (c) The DTG (specify local or Zulu) of the reading.
       (d) Go to steps d.
   b. Emplace the BIOLOGICAL markers.
     (1) Place markers at the location where contamination is detected.
     (2) Place markers so that the word "BIO" faces away from the contamination area.
     (3) Print the following information clearly on the front of the marker.
       (a) Name of agent, if known. If unknown, print "unknown."
       (b) DTG (specify local or Zulu) of detection.
     (4) Go to steps d.
   c. Emplace the CHEMICAL makers.
     (1) Place markers at the location where contamination is detected.
     (2) Place markers so that the word "GAS" faces away from the contamination area.
     (3) Print the following information clearly on the front of the marker:
       (a) Name of agent, if known. If unknown, print "unknown."
       (b) DTG (specify local or Zulu) of detection.
     (4) Go to step d.

d. Position the markers so that the recorded information faces away from the area of contamination and place adjacent marking signs at intervals of 25 to 100 meters, depending on terrain.

e. If marking contamination in open terrain (e.g., desert, plains, rolling hills), raise markers to heights that permit approaching forces to view them at a distance up to 200 meters.

2. Employ contamination markers using the M328 CBRN Marking Kit.

a. Emplace the RADIOLOGICAL markers.

(1) Place markers at the location where a dose rate of 1 centigray per hour (cGyph) or more is measured.

(2) Place markers so that the word "ATOM" faces away from the contamination.

(3) Print the following information clearly on the front of the markers:

(a) Dose rate in cGyph.

(b) Date-time group (DTG) (specify local or Zulu) of reading.

(c) DTG of detonation, if known. If the DTG is not known, print "unknown."

(4) If beacons are required, proceed to step e; if not, proceed to step f.

b. Emplace the BIOLOGICAL markers.

(1) Place markers at the location where contamination is detected.

(2) Place markers so that the word "BIO" faces away from the contamination area.

(3) Print the following information clearly on the front of the markers:

(a) Name of agent, if known. If unknown, print "unknown."

(b) DTG (specify local or Zulu) of detection. If the DTG is not known, print "unknown."

(4) If beacons are required, proceed to step e; if not, proceed to step f.

c. Emplace the CHEMICAL markers.

(1) Place markers at the location where contamination is detected.

(2) Place markers so that the word "GAS" faces away from the contamination area.

(3) Print the following information clearly on the front of the marker.

(a) Name of agent, if known. If unknown, print "unknown."

(b) DTG (specify local or Zulu) of detection. If the DTG is not known, print "unknown."

(4) If beacons are required, proceed to step e; if not, proceed to steps f.

d. Emplace the toxic makers.

(1) Place markers at the location where contamination is detected.

(2) Place markers so that the word "TOXIC" faces away from the contamination area.

(3) Print the following information clearly on the front of the marker:

(a) Name of agent, if known. If unknown, print "unknown."

(b) DTG (specify local or Zulu) of detection. If the DTG is not known, print "unknown."

(4) If beacons are required, proceed to step e; if not, proceed to steps f.

e. Emplace beacons at approximately 300-meter intervals.

Note: Beacons are visible at night over ranges of up to 1,500+ meters. Beacons are supplied in visual and IR only types. Flexlight chemical lights are emplaced between beacons attached to the flag clips.

f. Ensure that the recorded information on the markers faces away from the area contamination and place adjacent marking signs at intervals of 10 to 50 meters depending on terrain, approximately waist high. If beacons are used, the markers can be placed 10 to 100 meters apart.

g. Ensure that when in open terrain all markers are at a height that permits approaching forces to view them at a distance up to 300 meters, approximately waist high.

Evaluation Preparation: *Setup*: Provide the Soldier with the items listed in the task condition statemSetup: Provide the Soldier with the items listed in the task condition statement. Use simulants to produce a contaminated environment for toxic and chemical or biological agents. For radiological contamination, tell the Soldier the type and amount of radiation present.

Brief Soldier: Tell the Soldier that the test will consist of ensuring that NBC markers are properly emplaced and that all required information is placed on the markers.

Performance Measures	GO	NO GO
1 Employed contamination markers using the NBC marking set.	_____	_____
2 Employed contamination markers using the M328 CBRN Marking Kit.	_____	_____

Evaluation Guidance:. Refer to chapter 1, paragraph 1-9e, (1) and (2).

References:
Required: FM 3-11.19, FM 3-11.3, TM 3-9905-001-10, and TM 3-9905-002-12&P
Related:

081-COM-1001

Evaluate a Casualty (Tactical Combat Casualty Care)

Conditions: While in a tactical area of operations, you encounter a combat casualty. Your unit may be under fire.

Some iterations of this task should be performed in MOPP.

Standards: Evaluate the casualty following the correct sequence. Identify and treat all life-threatening conditions and other serious wounds.

Special Condition: None

Special Standards: None

Special Equipment:

Cue: None

Note: Tactical combat casualty care (TCCC) can be divided into three phases. The first is care under fire; the second is tactical field care; the third is combat casualty evacuation care. In the first, you are under hostile fire and are very limited as to the care you can provide. In the second, you and the casualty are relatively safe and no longer under effective hostile fire, and you are free to provide casualty care to the best of your ability. In the third, the care is rendered during casualty evacuation (CASEVAC).

WARNING

If a broken neck or back is suspected, do not move the casualty unless to save his/her life.

Performance Steps

1. Perform care under fire.
   a. Return fire as directed or required before providing medical treatment.
   b. Determine if the casualty is alive or dead.

Note: In combat, the most likely threat to the casualty's life is from bleeding. Attempts to check for airway and breathing will expose the rescuer to enemy fire. Do not attempt to provide first aid if your own life is in imminent danger. In a combat situation, if you find a casualty with no signs of life--no pulse, no breathing--do NOT attempt to restore the airway. Do NOT continue first aid measures.

   c. Provide care to the live casualty.

Note: Reducing or eliminating enemy fire may be more important to the casualty's survival than the treatment you can provide.

   (1) Suppress enemy fire.
   (2) Use cover or concealment (smoke).
   (3) Direct the casualty to return fire, move to cover, and administer self-aid (stop bleeding), if possible. If the casualty is unable to move and you are unable to move the casualty to cover and the casualty is still under direct enemy fire, have the casualty "play dead."
   (4) If the casualty is unresponsive, move the casualty, his/her weapon, and mission-essential equipment to cover, as the tactical situation permits.
   (5) Keep the casualty from sustaining additional wounds.
   (6) Reassure the casualty.

d. Administer life-saving hemorrhage control.

(1) Determine the relative threat of the tactical situation versus the risk of the casualty's bleeding to death.

(2) If the casualty has severe bleeding from a limb or has suffered amputation of a limb, administer life-saving hemorrhage control by applying a tourniquet before moving the casualty. (See task 081-COM-1032.)

e. Transport the casualty, his/her weapon, and mission-essential equipment when the tactical situation permits.

f. Recheck bleeding control measures as the tactical situation permits.

WARNING

If there are any signs of nerve agent poisoning, stop the evaluation, take the necessary protective measures, and begin first aid. (See task 081-831-1044.)

---

2. Perform tactical field care when no longer under direct enemy fire.

Note: Tactical field care is rendered by the individual when no longer under hostile fire. Tactical field care also applies to situations in which an injury has occurred during the mission but there has been no hostile fire. Available medical equipment is limited to that carried into the field by the individual Soldier. In the following situations communicate the medical situation to the unit leader and ensure that the tactical situation allows for time to perform these steps before initiating any medical procedure. When evaluating and/or treating a casualty, seek medical aid as soon as possible. Do NOT stop treatment. If the situation allows, send another person to find medical aid.

a. Form a general impression of the casualty as you approach (extent of injuries, chance of survival).

Note: If a casualty is being burned, take steps to remove the casualty from the source of the burns before continuing evaluation and treatment. (See task 081-COM-1007.)

b. Check for responsiveness.

(1) Ask in a loud, but calm, voice: "Are you okay?" Gently shake or tap the casualty on the shoulder.

(2) Determine the level of consciousness by using AVPU: A = Alert; V = responds to Voice; P = responds to Pain; U = Unresponsive.

Note: To check a casualty's response to pain, rub the breastbone briskly with a knuckle or squeeze the first or second toe over the toenail.

(3) If the casualty is conscious, ask where his/her body feels different than usual, or where it hurts. Skip steps 2c and 2d. Go to step 2e.

Note: If the casualty is conscious but is choking and cannot talk, stop the evaluation and begin treatment. (See task 081-COM-1003.)

(4) If the casualty is unconscious, continue with step 2c.

c. Identify and control bleeding.

(1) Check for bleeding.

(a) Remove only the minimum amount of clothing to expose and treat injuries. Protect the casualty from the environment (heat and cold).

(b) Look for blood-soaked clothes.

(c) Look for entry and exit wounds.

(d) Place your hands behind the casualty's neck and pass them upward toward the top of the head. Note whether there is blood or brain tissue on your hands from the casualty's wounds.

(e) Place your hands behind the casualty's shoulders and pass them downward behind the back, the thighs, and the legs. Note whether there is blood on your hands from the casualty's wounds.

(2) If life-threatening bleeding is present, stop the evaluation and control the bleeding. (See task 081-COM-1032).

(3) Dress all wounds, including exit wounds.

d. Position the casualty and open the airway. (See task 081-COM-1023.)

e. Assess for breathing and chest injuries.

(1) Look, listen, and feel for respiration. (See task 081-COM-1023.)

Note: If the casualty is breathing, insert a nasopharyngeal airway (see task 081-COM-1023) and place the casualty in the recovery position. On the battlefield the cost of attempting cardiopulmonary resuscitation (CPR) on casualties with what are inevitably fatal injuries may result in additional lives lost as care is diverted from casualties with less severe injuries. Only in the case of nontraumatic disorders such as hypothermia, near drowning, or electrocution should CPR be considered prior to the CASEVAC phase.

(2) Expose the chest and check for equal rise and fall and for any wounds.

(a) If the casualty has a penetrating chest wound and is breathing or making an effort to breathe, stop the evaluation to apply a dressing.

(b) Position or transport with the affected side down, if possible.

(c) Check for an exit wound. If found, apply a dressing.

f. Check for fractures.

(1) Check for open fractures by looking for bleeding or a bone sticking through the skin.

(2) Check for closed fractures by looking for swelling, discoloration, deformity, or unusual body position.

g. Check for burns.

(1) Look carefully for reddened, blistered, or charred skin. Also check for singed clothes.

(2) If burns are found, stop the evaluation and begin treatment. (See task 081-COM-1007.)

h. Administer pain medications and antibiotics (the casualty's combat pill pack) to any Soldier wounded in combat.

Note: Each Soldier will be issued a combat pill pack before deploying on tactical missions.

i. Document the casualty's injuries and the treatment given on the field medical card (FMC), if applicable.

Note: The FMC is usually initiated by the combat medic. However, a certified combat lifesaver can initiate the FMC if a combat medic is not available or if the combat medic directs the combat lifesaver to initiate the card. A pad of FMCs is part of the combat lifesaver medical equipment set.

j. Transport the casualty to the site where evacuation is anticipated. (See task 081-COM-1046.)

3. Document care on Field Medical Card (FMC). Enter primary information (blocks 1, 3, 4, 9, and 11).

Note: The back of the original card is impregnated so that the information written on the front of the card will also appear on the front of the duplicate sheet.

a. Block 1, Name and other identifying information. Required information is self-explanatory.

Note: If the casualty is a member of a foreign military, including a prisoner of war, enter the casualty's military service number instead of social security number. If the casualty is not military, leave the block blank.

    b. Block 3, Injury.

        (1) Horizontal row at top. Mark the box to indicate the type of injury:

            (a) If the casualty is suffering trauma (battle casualty), mark the box in front of "BC/BC."

            (b) If the casualty is a nuclear, biological agent, or chemical agent casualty, mark the box in front of "NBC/NBC."

            (c) If the casualty is ill and is not classifiable as one of the three other categories, mark the box in front of "DISEASE/MALADE."

            (d) If the casualty is suffering from combat stress or other psychological injury, mark the box in front of "PSYCH/PSYCH."

        (2) Left portion. Mark the location(s) of the casualty's injury(ies). Be sure that the casualty has been checked for both entrance wounds and exit wounds

        (3) Vertical row on the right. Mark the appropriate box or boxes to describe the casualty's injury or injuries. If the box for "OTHER" is checked, enter the description in the area below the boxes/descriptions. If the casualty's condition has been covered in one of the boxes in the column, then the "OTHER" block should not be marked.

    c. Block 4, Level of consciousness. Check the appropriate box for level of consciousness, using the AVPU system.

    d. Block 9, Treatment/Observations/Current Medications/Allergies/NBC (Antidote). Enter a brief description of the treatment given. Use approved abbreviations, if possible. If needed, use block 14 on the back of the card for additional space.

Note: Listed below are some of the abbreviations authorized to be used on the FMC:
- Abraded wound--Abr W
- Contused wound--Cont W
- Fracture (compound) open--FC
- Fracture (compound) open comminuted--FCC
- Fracture simple (closed)--FS
- Lacerated wound--LW
- Multiple wounds--MW
- Penetrating wound--Pen W
- Perforating wound--Perf W
- Severe--SV
- Slight-SL

    e. Block 11, Provider/Unit. Enter your initials in the far right of the signature box.

Note: This will let the medical personnel know who initially treated the casualty and still leave room for the medical officer to sign the card. These instructions assume that there is no combat medic present. If the combat medic is present, he should enter his initials in the box. Do not enter anything in the date box. This box is completed by the medical officer.

    f. Enter information in blocks 6 and 8, if applicable.

        (1) Block 6, Tourniquet. If a tourniquet was applied, mark the YES box. If you check YES, also indicate the date in YY/MM/DD format (last two digits of the year/number of the month/number of the day of the month) and time that it was applied (use military 24-hour time) in the "Time" box.

(2) Block 8, IV. If an intravenous (IV) infusion has been initiated, write the type of IV fluid in the "IV" box and the date (YY/MM/DD) and time (military) that the intravenous solution was begun in the "Time" box.

g. The other blocks, with the exception of block 2, will normally be filled out only by medical personnel.

(1) If time permits, enter the casualty's unit and country of whose armed forces he/she is a member in block 2.

(2) Check the box corresponding to the armed service of which the casualty is a member.

(3) Mark the "A/T" box for Army, the "AF/A" box for Air Force, the "N/M" box for Navy, and the "MC/M" box for Marine Corps.

h. Attach the FMC to the casualty.

(1) Remove the card from the pad, being careful not to tear out the duplicate (white sheet).

(2) Attach the card to the casualty by threading the wire through the top buttonhole of uniform and then twisting the wire.

(3) Position the FMC so that it remains in plain view.

4. Document the casualty's injuries and the treatment given on the tactical combat casualty care (TCCC) card, if applicable.

Note: Since electronic forms are not compatible with the battlefield environment, a new casualty card will be made available to document the care for injured Soldiers at the point of wounding. The proposed 4.5-inch by 6-inch card is based on the principles of tactical combat casualty care (TCCC) and addresses the initial lifesaving care provided at the point of wounding. Its format is simple, often with a circle or X in the appropriate block. This casualty card will be found in each Soldiers Improved First Aid Kit (IFAK). Use an indelible marker to fill it out. Attach it to the casualty's belt loop, or place it in their upper left sleeve, or the left trouser cargo pocket. Include as much information as you can.

a. Casualty's name and identification: (name/ID). The Soldier should have entered his last name and first name as a minimum in the "Name/ID" portion of his/her card before he placed the card in their IFAK

b. Allergies. The Soldier should have listed any allergic reactions to medications on his/her card before placed the card in their IFAK. If the information is not entered, obtain the information from the casualty or from any medical alert identification, if possible.

c. Date-Time Group (DTG). Enter the date and military time that you begin treatment of the casualty. For example: 17 May 1530. The year need not be entered.

d. Date-Time Group (DTG). Enter the date and military time that you begin treatment of the casualty. For example: 17 May 1530. The year need not be entered.

e. Type of Injury. Circle the type of injury: gunshot wound (GSW), blast, motor vehicle accident (MVA), or other. If "other" is indicated, enter an explanation in the blank following "Other

f. Time Tourniquet Applied (TQ Time). If a tourniquet has been applied to the casualty, enter the military time that the tourniquet was applied, such as "1540." The date and year does

g. Location of Wound(s). The card contains two body pictures, one of the casualty's front and another for the casualty's back. Place an "X" on the illustration to indicate the place of injury or the wound site. If there is an entrance wound and an exit wound, place one "X" on the front figure and another "X" on the back figure. Place as many X's as needed.

Note: The figures contain burn percentages based upon the rule of nines. Use these figures in estimating the percentage of body surface burned.

h. Vital Signs. The chart is used to record the casualty's level of consciousness and vital signs.

(1) Enter the time.

(2) Enter the casualty's level of consciousness using the AVPU system in the "AVPU" box. Enter
for alert, V for verbal, P for pain, or U for unresponsive.

(3) Enter the casualty's pulse rate in the "Pulse" box.

(4) Enter the casualty's respiration rate (complete breaths per minute-even or odd number) in the "Resp" box.

(5) Enter the casualty's blood pressure (if applicable) in the "BP" box.

5. Complete the back (reverse) side of the TCCC card.

a. Record airway interventions (Line A).

b. Record breathing interventions (Line B).

c. Record bleeding control measures (Line C).

d. Indicate the method used to administer the fluids. Circle "IV" for intravenous infusion and "IO" for intraosseous (through the bone) infusion.

e. Record drugs given. Enter the type, dose and route.

Note: Enter any pertinent notes or observations in the lines below the OTHER line in the DRUGS section.

f. Sign the card.

Note: If you are assisting a combat medic, he/she will sign the card. If you are acting as a combat lifesaver and no combat medic is present, print your name and rank in the medic's name line at the bottom of the card. Documentation of care. Record each specific intervention in each category. If you are not sure what to do, the card will prompt you where to go next. Simply circle the intervention you performed. Explain any action you want clarified in the remarks area. Documentation of care. You may not be able to perform all the interventions on the card or that the casualty needs. However, when the medic is available he/she can add additional treatments to the card. This card can be filled out in less than two minutes. It is important to document the care given to the casualty. Review TCCC Card Abbreviations.

6. Transport the casualty to the site where evacuation is anticipated. (See task 081-COM-1046.)

a. Monitor the patient for shock.

b. Continually reassess casualty until a medical person arrives

---

Evaluation Preparation:

Setup: Prepare a "casualty" for the Soldier to evaluate in step 2 by simulating one or more wounds or conditions. Simulate the wounds using a war wounds moulage set, casualty simulation kit, or other available materials. You can coach a "conscious casualty" on how to respond to the Soldier's questions about location of pain or other symptoms of injury. However, you will have to cue the Soldier during evaluation of an "unconscious casualty" as to whether the casualty is breathing and describe the signs or conditions, as the Soldier is making the checks.

Brief Soldier: To test step 1, tell the Soldier that his/her unit is under fire and ask him/her what he/she should do to provide aid to casualties. For step 2, tell the Soldier that the tactical situation permits full evaluation of the casualty. Tell him/her to do, in order, all necessary steps to evaluate the casualty and identify all wounds and/or conditions. Tell the Soldier that he/she will not perform first aid but will tell you what first aid action (give mouth-to-mouth resuscitation, bandage the wound, and so forth) he/she would take. After he/she has completed the checks (step 2f), ask him/her what else he/she should do. To test step 3, ask him/her what he/she should do while evacuating an unconscious casualty.

Performance Measures	GO	NO GO
1 Performed care under fire.	____	____
2 Performed tactical field care.	____	____
3 Documented care on a FMC.	____	____
4 Documented care on a TC3 card.	____	____
5 Completed the back of the TC3 card.	____	____
6 Transported the casualty to evacuation site.	____	____

Evaluation Guidance:. Refer to chapter 1, paragraph 1-9e, (1) and (2).

References:
Required:
Related:

081-COM-1003

Perform First Aid to Clear an Object Stuck in the Throat of a Conscious Casualty

Conditions: You see a conscious casualty who is having a hard time breathing because something is stuck in his/her throat.

Standards: Clear the object from the casualty's throat. Give abdominal or chest thrusts until the casualty can talk and breathe normally, you are relieved by a qualified person, or the casualty becomes unconscious requiring mouth-to-mouth resuscitation.

Special Condition: None

Special Standards: None

Special Equipment: None

Cue: None

Note: Conditions, standards, performance steps, and performance measures match task as it appears in STP 21-1-SMCT, 2 May 2011.

Performance Steps

1. Determine if the casualty needs help.
   a. If the casualty has a mild airway obstruction (able to speak or cough forcefully, may be wheezing between coughs), do not interfere except to encourage the casualty.
   b. If the casualty has a severe airway obstruction (poor air exchange and increased breathing difficulty, a silent cough, cyanosis, or inability to speak or breathe), continue with step 2.

Note: You can ask the casualty one question, "Are you choking?" If the casualty nods yes, help is needed.

CAUTION

Do not slap a choking casualty on the back. This may cause the object to go down the airway instead of out.

---

2. Perform abdominal or chest thrusts.

Note: Abdominal thrusts should be used unless the victim is in the advanced stages of pregnancy, is very obese, or has a significant abdominal wound.

Note: Clearing a conscious casualty's airway obstruction can be performed with the casualty either standing or sitting.

   a. Abdominal thrusts.
      (1) Stand behind the casualty.
      (2) Wrap your arms around the casualty's waist.

(3) Make a fist with one hand.

(4) Place the thumb side of the fist against the abdomen slightly above the navel and well below the tip of the breastbone.

(5) Grasp the fist with the other hand.

(6) Give quick backward and upward thrusts.

Note: Each thrust should be a separate, distinct movement. Thrusts should be continued until the obstruction is expelled or the casualty becomes unconscious.

b. Chest thrusts.

(1) Stand behind the casualty.

(2) Wrap your arms under the casualty's armpits and around the chest.

(3) Make a fist with one hand.

(4) Place the thumb side of the fist on the middle of the breastbone.

(5) Grasp the fist with the other hand.

(6) Give backward thrusts.

Note: Each thrust should be performed slowly and distinctly with the intent of relieving the obstruction.

3. Continue to give abdominal or chest thrusts, as required. Give abdominal or chest thrusts until the obstruction is clear, you are relieved by a qualified person, or the casualty becomes unconscious.

Note: If the casualty becomes unconscious, lay him/her down and then start mouth-to-mouth resuscitation procedures.

4. If the obstruction is cleared, watch the casualty closely and check for other injuries, if necessary.

Evaluation Preparation:

Setup: For training and evaluation, use another Soldier to simulate a patient in shock.

Brief Soldier: Tell the Soldier the simulated patient requires first aid for shock to be given.

Performance Measures	GO	NO GO
1 Determined if the casualty needed help.	___	___
2 Performed abdominal or chest thrusts, as required.	___	___
3 Continued abdominal or chest thrusts, as required.	___	___

Performance Measures	GO	NO GO
4 If the obstruction was cleared, watched the casualty closely and checked for other injuries, if necessary.	_____	_____

Evaluation Guidance:. Refer to chapter 1, paragraph 1-9e, (1) and (2).

References:
Required: FM 4-25.11
Related:

081-COM-1005

Perform First Aid to Prevent or Control Shock

Conditions: You see a casualty who is breathing. There is no uncontrolled bleeding. The casualty has one or more of the symptoms of shock. You will need a field jacket and blanket or poncho.

Standards: Attempt to prevent a casualty from going into shock by correctly positioning the casualty, loosening binding clothes, calming and reassuring the casualty, and providing shade from direct sunlight during hot weather or covering to prevent body heat loss during cold weather. Do not cause further injury to the casualty.

Special Condition: None

Special Standards: None

Special Equipment: None

Cue: None

Note: Conditions, standards, performance steps, and performance measures match task as it appears in STP 21-1-SMCT, 2 May 2011.

Performance Steps

1. Check the casualty for signs and symptoms of shock.
   a. Sweaty but cool skin.
   b. Pale skin.
   c. Restlessness or nervousness.
   d. Thirst.
   e. Severe bleeding.
   f. Confusion.

g. Rapid breathing.

h. Blotchy blue skin.

i. Nausea and/or vomiting.

2. Position the casualty.

a. Move the casualty to cover, if cover is available and the situation permits.

b. Lay the casualty on his/her back or in the recovery position (on his/her side) unless a sitting position will allow the casualty to breathe easier.

c. Elevate the casualty's feet higher than the heart using a stable object so the feet will not fall.

```
                            WARNING
            Do not loosen clothing if in a chemical area.
```

3. Loosen clothing at the neck, waist, or anywhere it is binding.

4. Splint the limb, if appropriate. (See task 081-831-1034.)

a. Apply a splint to the injured limb if one or more bones in the limb have been fractured.

b. Splint the arm, forearm, thigh, or leg when a severe wound is present even if the limb is not fractured.

5. Prevent the casualty from getting chilled or overheated.

a. Cover the casualty to avoid loss of body heat and, in cold weather, place cover under as well as over the casualty. Use a blanket or clothing, or improvise a cover.

b. Place the casualty under a permanent or improvised shelter in hot weather to shade him/her from direct sunlight.

6. Calm and reassure the casualty.

a. Take charge and show self-confidence.

b. Assure the casualty that he/she is being taken care of.

7. Watch the casualty closely for life-threatening conditions and check for other injuries, if necessary. Seek medical aid.

Evaluation Preparation:

Setup: For training and evaluation, use another Soldier to simulate a patient in shock.

Brief Soldier: Tell the Soldier the simulated patient requires first aidfor shock to be given.

Performance Measures	GO	NO GO
1 Checked the casualty for signs and symptoms of shock.	_____	_____
2 Positioned casualty correctly.	_____	_____
3 Loosened clothing at the neck, waist, or anywhere it was binding.	_____	_____
4 Splinted the limb, if appropriate.	_____	_____
5 Prevented the casualty from chilling or overheating.	_____	_____
6 Calmed and reassured the casualty.	_____	_____
7 Watched the casualty closely for life-threatening conditions and checked for other injuries, if necessary. Sought medical aid.	_____	_____

Evaluation Guidance:. Refer to chapter 1, paragraph 1-9e, (1) and (2).

References:
Required: FM 4-25.11
Related:

081-COM-1023

Perform First Aid to Restore Breathing and/or Pulse

Conditions: You see an adult casualty who is unconscious and does not appear to be breathing. You are not in a combat situation or chemical environment. You will need a nasopharyngeal airway (NPA).

This task should not be trained in MOPP.

Standards: Take appropriate action, in the correct sequence, to restore breathing and, if necessary, restore the pulse. Continue until the casualty's breathing/pulse returns, a qualified person relieves you, a physician stops you, or you are too tired to continue.

Special Condition: None

Special Standards: None

Special Equipment:

Cue: None

Note: Conditions, standards, performance steps, and performance measures match task as it appears in STP 21-1-SMCT, 2 May 2011.

Performance Steps

> **WARNING**
> The casualty should be carefully rolled as a whole, so the body does not twist.

    1. Roll the casualty onto his/her back, if necessary, and place him/her on a hard, flat surface.
        a. Kneel beside the casualty.
        b. Raise the near arm and straighten it out above the head.
        c. Adjust the legs so they are together and straight or nearly straight.
        d. Place one hand on the back of the casualty's head and neck.
        e. Grasp the casualty under the arm with the free hand.
        f. Pull steadily and evenly toward yourself, keeping the head and neck in line with the torso.
        g. Roll the casualty as a single unit.
        h. Place the casualty's arms at his/her sides.
    2. Open the airway.
Note: If foreign material or vomit is in the mouth, remove it as quickly as possible.

> **CAUTION**
> Do NOT use this method if a spinal or neck injury is suspected.

        a. Head-tilt/chin-lift method.
        (1) Kneel at the level of the casualty's shoulders.
        (2) Place one hand on the casualty's forehead and apply firm, backward pressure with the palm to tilt the head back.
        (3) Place the fingertips of the other hand under the bony part of the lower jaw and lift, bringing the chin forward.
Note: Do NOT use the thumb to lift.
Note: Do NOT completely close the casualty's mouth.

> **CAUTION**
> Do NOT press deeply into the soft tissue under the chin with the fingers.

> **CAUTION**
>
> Use this method if a spinal or neck injury is suspected.

Note: If you are unable to maintain an airway after the second attempt, use the head-tilt/chin-lift method.

    b. Jaw-thrust method.

        (1) Kneel above the casualty's head (looking toward the casualty's feet).

        (2) Rest your elbows on the ground or floor.

        (3) Place one hand on each side of the casualty's lower jaw at the angle of the jaw, below the ears.

        (4) Stabilize the casualty's head with your forearms.

        (5) Use the index fingers to push the angles of the casualty's lower jaw forward.

Note: If the casualty's lips are still closed after the jaw has been moved forward, use your thumbs to retract the lower lip and allow air to enter the casualty's mouth.

> **CAUTION**
>
> Do not tilt or rotate the casualty's head.

   3. Check for breathing.

    a. While maintaining the open airway position, place an ear over the casualty's mouth and nose, looking toward the chest and stomach.

    b. Look for the chest to rise and fall.

    c. Listen for air escaping during exhalation.

    d. Feel for the flow of air on the side of your face.

    e. Count the number of respirations for 15 seconds.

    f. Take appropriate action.

> **CAUTION**
>
> Do NOT use the NPA if there is clear fluid (cerebrospinal fluid-CSF) coming from the ears or nose. This may indicate a skull fracture.

        (1) If the casualty is unconscious, if respiratory rate is less than 2 in 15 seconds, and/or if the casualty is making snoring or gurgling sounds, insert an NPA.

           (a) Keep the casualty in a face-up position.

           (b) Lubricate the tube of the NPA with water.

           (c) Push the tip of the casualty's nose upward gently.

           (d) Position the tube of the NPA so that the bevel (pointed end) of the NPA faces toward the septum (the partition inside the nose that separates the nostrils).

Note: Most NPAs are designed to be placed in the right nostril.

> **CAUTION**
>
> Never force the NPA into the casualty's nostril. If resistance is met, pull the tube out and attempt to insert it in the other nostril. If neither nostril will accommodate the NPA, place the casualty in the recovery position.

           (e) Insert the NPA into the nostril and advance it until the flange rests against the nostril.

(f) Place the casualty in the recovery position by rolling him/her as a single unit onto his/her side, placing the hand of his/her upper arm under his/her chin, and flexing his/her upper leg.

(g) Watch the casualty closely for life-threatening conditions and check for other injuries, if necessary. Seek medical aid.

(2) If the casualty is not breathing, continue with step 4 if the tactical situation permits.

Note: If the casualty resumes breathing at any time during this procedure, the airway should be kept open and the casualty should be monitored. If the casualty continues to breathe, he/she should be transported to medical aid. Otherwise, the procedure should be continued.

4. Give breaths to ensure an open airway.

Note: When mouth-to-mouth resuscitation breathing cannot be performed because the casualty has jaw injuries or spasms, the mouth-to-nose method may be more effective. Perform the mouth-to-nose method as follows:

* Blow into the nose while holding the lips closed.
* Let air escape by removing your mouth and, in some cases, separating the casualty's lips.

a. Insert a face shield, if available, into the casualty's mouth, with the short airway portion over the top of the tongue, and flatten the plastic sheet around the mouth.

b. Maintain the airway and gently pinch the nose closed, using the hand on the casualty's forehead.

c. Take a normal breath and place your mouth, in an airtight seal, around the casualty's mouth.

d. Give two breaths (1 second each), taking a breath between them, while watching for the chest to rise and fall and listening and/or feeling for air to escape during exhalation.

Note: If the chest rises, go to step 7.

Note: If the chest does not rise after the first breath, continue with step 5.

5. Reposition the casualty's head slightly farther backward and repeat the breaths.

Note: If the chest rises, go to step 7.

Note: If the chest does not rise, continue with step 6.

6. Perform chest compressions to clear the airway.

a. Perform chest compressions.

(1) Kneel close to the side of the casualty's body.

(2) Locate the nipple line placing the heel of one hand on the lower half of the sternum (breastbone).

(3) Place the heel of the other hand on top of the first hand on the lower half of the breastbone, extending or interlacing the fingers.

(4) Straighten and lock the elbows with the shoulders directly above the hands.

(5) Without bending the elbows, rocking, or allowing the shoulders to sag, apply enough pressure to depress the breastbone 1½ to 2 inches.

Note: Give compressions at a rate of 100 per minute (hard and fast at a ratio of 30 compressions to 2 breaths) with the intent of relieving the obstruction.

> **WARNING**
>
> Only attempt to remove the object if you can see it. Do NOT force the object deeper into the airway.

b. Look in the mouth for the object between compressions and breaths and if you can see it, remove it.

c. Reopen the airway and repeat the breaths.

Note: If the chest rises, go to step 7. If the chest does not rise, repeat step 6 until the airway is clear.

7. Check for a pulse for 5 to 10 seconds.

Note: Use the first two fingers in the groove in the casualty's throat beside the Adam's apple on the side closest to you. Do NOT use the thumb.

a. If a pulse is found but the casualty is not breathing, continue mouth-to-mouth resuscitation.

(1) Give breaths at the rate of one every 5 to 6 seconds (10 to 12 breaths per minute).

(2) Recheck for pulse and breathing every 2 minutes. If the pulse stops, go to step 8.

(3) Continue until the casualty's breathing returns, a qualified person relieves you, a physician stops you, or you are too tired to continue. If the breathing returns, go to step 9.

b. If no pulse is found, you must perform cardiopulmonary resuscitation (CPR). Continue with step 8.

8. Perform CPR.

a. Position your hands and body for chest compressions as in step 6a.

b. Give 30 compressions.

(1) Press straight down to depress the breastbone 1 ½ to 2 inches.

(2) Come straight up and completely release the pressure on the breastbone to allow the chest to return to its normal position. The time allowed for release should equal the time required for compression.

(3) Give 30 compressions in about 23 seconds (at a rate of 100 per minute).

Note: Do NOT remove the heel of your hand from the casualty's chest or reposition your hand between compressions. However, all pressure must be released from the chest cavity to allow for full chest wall expansion.

c. Give two breaths.

(1) Open the casualty's airway.

(2) Give two breaths (1 second each).

d. Repeat steps 8b through 8c for five cycles or 2 minutes.

e. Reassess the casualty.

(1) Check for the return of the pulse for 3 to 5 seconds.

(a) If the pulse is present, continue with step 8e(2).

(b) If the pulse is absent, continue with step 8f.

(2) Check breathing for 3 to 5 seconds.

(a) If the casualty is breathing, continue with step 9.

(b) If the casualty is not breathing, continue mouth-to-mouth resuscitation (step 7a).

f. Resume CPR with compressions (step 8b).

g. Recheck for pulse every 2 minutes.

Performance Steps

h. Continue CPR until the casualty's pulse returns, you are relieved by a qualified person, stopped by a physician, or you are too tired to continue.

9. Once the casualty is breathing and has a pulse, place the casualty in the recovery position until help arrives. Watch the casualty closely for life-threatening conditions, maintain an open airway, and check for other injuries, if necessary.

Evaluation Preparation:

Setup: For training and testing, you must use a resuscitation training mannequin (DVC 08-15). Have a bottle of alcohol and swabs or cotton available. Place the mannequin on the floor and alcohol and cotton balls on the table. Clean the mannequin's nose and mouth before each Soldier is evaluated. If a mannequin that is capable of testing insertion of an NPA is available, use it to test step 3b. Brief Soldier: Tell the Soldier to do, in order, all necessary steps to restore breathing and pulse. For step 3b, tell the Soldier that the casualty's breathing rate is slow, and have him/her show you (on a mannequin) or tell you what he/she would do to insert an NPA. After step 3, tell the Soldier that the casualty is not breathing. When testing steps 4 and 5, you can vary the test by indicating whether the chest rises or not. If steps 6 and 7 are tested, tell the Soldier that the chest rises after he/she removes the foreign object. When testing step 8, tell the Soldier that a pulse is not found. You can stop the evaluation when the Soldier rechecks for the pulse in step 10. Do not evaluate step 12 in the simulated mode. Note: Reference made to the mouth-to-nose method within the task presents information on an alternate procedure that must be used under some circumstances. This method will not be evaluated.

Performance Measures	GO	NO GO
1 Rolled the casualty onto his/her back, if necessary, and placed him/her on a hard, flat surface.	_____	_____
2 Opened the airway using the head-tilt/chin-lift method.	_____	_____
3 Checked for breathing.	_____	_____
4 Gave breaths to ensure an open airway.	_____	_____

Performance Measures	GO	NO GO
5 Repositioned the casualty's head slightly farther backward and repeated teh breaths	_____	_____
6 Performed chest compressions to clear the airway, if necessary.	_____	_____
7 Checked for a pulse.	_____	_____
8 Performed CPR	_____	_____
9 Once the casualty was breathing and had a pulse, placed him/her in the recovery position. Watched the casualty closely for life-threatening conditions, maintained an open airway, and checked for other injuries, if necessary.	_____	_____

Evaluation Guidance:. Refer to chapter 1, paragraph 1-9e, (1) and (2).

References:
Required: FM 4-25.11
Related:

081-COM-1032

Perform First Aid for Bleeding of an Extremity

Conditions: You have a casualty who has a bleeding wound of the arm or leg. The casualty is breathing. You will need the casualty's emergency bandage, Kerlix field dressing, materials to improvise a pressure dressing (wadding and cravat or strip of cloth), and combat application tourniquet (C-A-T).

Some iterations of this task should be performed in MOPP.

Standards:

Control bleeding from the wound without causing further harm to the casualty.

Special Condition: None

Special Standards: None

Special Equipment:

Cue: None

Note: None

> **CAUTION**
> All body fluids should be considered potentially infectious. Always observe body substance isolation (BSI) precautions by wearing gloves and eye protection as a minimal standard of protection. In severe cases, you should wear gloves, eye protection, gown and shoe covers to protect yourself of splashes, projectile fluids, spurting fluids or splashes onto your clothing and foot wear.

1. Determine if the bleeding is life threatening. If bleeding is life threatening, immediately apply a CAT tourniquet. See step #4.
Note: If in a tactical environment, evaluate a casualty (See task 081-831-1001)
The tree methods of controlling external bleeding are direct pressure, pressure dressing, and tourniquet.

> **CAUTION**
> Once bleeding has been controlled, it is important to check a distal pulse to make sure that the dressing has not been applied too tightly. If a pulse is not palpable, adjust the dressing to re-establish circulation.

2. If bleeding is not life threatening, apply direct pressure.
    a. Expose the wound.
    b. Place a sterile gauze or dressing over the injury site and apply fingertips, palm or entire surface of one hand and apply direct pressure.
Note: If bleeding is profuse, apply direct pressure to the wound with your gloved hand initially while procuring a sterile dressing with your other hand. Larger wounds require a larger surface area of pressure and usually more pressure as well.
    c. Pack large, gaping wounds with sterile gauze and apply direct pressure.

> **WARNING**
> The emergency bandage must be loosened if the skin distal to the injury becomes cool, blue, numb, or pulseless.

2. If bleeding is not life threatening, apply direct pressure.
3. Apply the pressure dressing (casualty's emergency bandage).
    a. Open the plastic dressing package.
    b. Apply the dressing, white (sterile, non-adherent pad) side down, directly over the wound.

c. Wrap the elastic tail (bandage) around the extremity and run the tail through the plastic pressure bar.

d. Reverse the tail while applying pressure and continue to wrap the remainder of the tail around the extremity, continuing to apply pressure directly over the wound.

e. Secure the plastic closure bar to the last turn of the wrap.

f. Check the emergency bandage to make sure that it is applied firmly enough to prevent slipping without causing a tourniquet-like effect.

CAUTION

In combat, while under enemy fire, a tourniquet is the primary means to control bleeding. It allows the individual, his battle buddy, or the combat medic to quickly control life threatening hemorrhage until the casualty can be moved away from the firefight. Always treat life threatening hemorrhage while you and the casualty are behind cover.

---

4. Apply a Combat Application Tourniquet (CAT).

a. Pull the free end of the self-adhering band through the buckle and route through the friction adapter buckle.

b. Place combat application tourniquet (CAT), 2-3 inches above the wound on the injured extremity.

c. Pull the self-adhering band tight around the extremity and fasten it back on itself as tightly as possible.

d. Twist the windlass until the bleeding stops.

e. Lock the windlass in place within the windlass clip.

f. Secure the windlass with the windlass strap.

g. Assess for absence of a distal pulse.

h. Place a "T" and the time of the application on the casualty with a marker.

i. Secure the CAT in place with tape.

5. Initiate treatment for shock as needed. (See task 081-831-1005).

6. Record treatment given on the DD Form 1380, Field Medical Card (FMC), or DA Form 7656, Tactical Combat Casualty Care.

7. Evacuate the casualty.

Evaluation Preparation:

Setup: Have one Soldier play the part of the casualty. Use moulage or mark a place on the casualty's arm or leg to simulate a wound. For applying a tourniquet, use a mannequin or simulated arm or leg (padded length of 2-inch by 4-inch wood with a glove or boot on one end) with a dressing appropriately placed on the arm or leg. Under no circumstances will a live simulated casualty be used to evaluate the application of a tourniquet.

Brief Soldier: Tell the Soldier to do, in order, the first aid steps required to apply a dressing and, if necessary, a pressure dressing on the casualty's wound. After steps 2 and 3, tell the Soldier that the bleeding has not stopped. After step 4, tell the Soldier the bleeding is continuing and ask the Soldier to describe and perform the first aid steps needed on the simulated arm or leg provided.

Performance Measures	GO	NO GO
1 If the bleeding was life threatening. If bleeding was life threatening, went to step 4 immediately.	____	____
2 Applied direct pressure with sterile gauze.	____	____
3 Applied pressure dressing or emergency bandage if the wound continued to bleed.	____	____
4 Applied a tourniquet if the wound continued to bleed.	____	____
5 Initiated treatment for shock.	____	____
6 Recorded treatment given on DD Form 1380 Record of Individual Performance of Reserve Duty Training.	____	____
7 Evacuated the casualty.	____	____

Evaluation Guidance:. Refer to chapter 1, paragraph 1-9e, (1) and (2).

References:
Required:
Related:

081-831-1051

Transport a Casualty Using a Military Vehicle

Conditions: You have evaluated and provided first aid to a casualty. You have determined that the casualty must be evacuated to receive further medical treatment. A military vehicle (ground vehicle or rotary-wing aircraft) is available. You have a litter and straps to secure the patient and the litter.

Standards: Secure the casualty on a litter and load the litter onto a military vehicle (ground vehicle or rotary-wing aircraft) without causing undo pain or further harm to the casualty.

Special Condition: None

Special Standards: None

Special Equipment: None

Cue: None

Note: Shared - JFK

Performance Steps

1. Determine the order in which casualties are to be evacuated.
   a. First priority.
      (1) Serious respiratory problems.
      (2) Severe blood loss.
      (3) Second and third degree burns of the face, neck, or perineum.
      (4) Closed head injuries, with decreasing mental status.
      (5) Poor blood circulation in a limb or with no detectable circulation in a limb.
   b. Second priority.
      (1) Chest wounds.
      (2) Abdominal wounds.
      (3) Extensive, serious eye injuries.
      (4) Fractures.
      (5) Serious second and third degree burns not involving the face, neck, or perineum.
   c. Third priority.
      (1) Injuries which have been stabilized and do not threaten the casualty with loss of life or limb.
      (2) Injuries so severe that only extensive and complicated medical treatment can prolong life.
2. Move a casualty using a four-man litter squad.
   a. Prepare the litter.
      (1) Open a standard litter.
      (2) Lock the spreader bars at each end of the litter with your foot.
   b. Prepare the casualty.
      (1) Place the casualty onto the litter using the modified two-man arms carry or the modified two-man fore-and-aft carry.
      (2) Secure the casualty to the litter with litter straps.
   c. Lift the litter.
      (1) Position one squad member at each litter handle with the litter squad leader at the casualty's right shoulder.
Note: The leader should be at the right shoulder to monitor the casualty's condition.

(2) On the preparatory command, "Prepare to lift," the four bearers kneel beside and grasp the litter handles.

(3) On the command, "Lift," all bearers rise together.

(4) On the command, "Four man carry, move," all bearers walk forward in unison.

(a) If the casualty does not have a fractured leg, carry the casualty feet first on level ground and head first when going up hill.

(b) If the casualty has a fractured leg, carry the casualty head first, except when going up hill.

(5) To change direction of movement, such as from feet first to head first, begin in a litter post carry position. The front and back bearers release the litter and the middle bearers rotate the litter and themselves.

3. Load casualties onto a military vehicle.

a. Ground ambulance.

Note: Ground ambulances have medical specialists to take care of the casualties during evacuation. Follow any special instructions for loading, securing, or unloading casualties.

(1) Make sure each litter casualty is secured to his or her litter. Use the litter straps when available.

(2) Load the most serious casualty last.

(3) Load the casualty head first (head in the direction of travel) rather than feet first.

(4) Make sure each litter is secured to the vehicle.

Note: Unload casualties in reverse order, most seriously injured casualty first.

b. Air ambulance.

Note: Air ambulances have medical specialists to take care of the casualties during evacuation. Follow any special instructions for loading, securing, or unloading casualties.

(1) Remain 50 yards from the helicopter until the litter squad is signaled to approach the aircraft.

(2) Approach the aircraft in full view of the aircraft crew, maintaining visual confirmation that the crew is aware of the approach of the litter party. Ensure that the aircrew can continue to visually distinguish friendly from enemy personnel at all times. Maintain a low silhouette when approaching the aircraft

---

WARNING

Never go around the rear of UH-60 or UH-1 aircraft.

(a) Approach UH-60/UH-1 aircraft from the sides. Do not approach from the front or rear. If you must move to the opposite side of the aircraft, approach from the side to the skin of the aircraft. Then, hug the skin of the aircraft, and move around the front of the aircraft to the other side.

(b) Approach CH-47/CH-46 aircraft from the rear.

(c) Approach MH-53 aircraft from the sides to the rear ramp, avoiding the tail rotor.

(d) Approach nonstandard aircraft in full view of the crew, avoiding tail rotors, main rotors, and propellers.

(e) Approach high performance aircraft (M/C-130/-141B/-17/-5B) from the rear, under the guidance of the aircraft loadmaster or the ground control party.

(3) Load the most seriously injured casualty last.

(4) Load the casualty who will occupy the upper birth first, and then load the next litter casualty immediately under the first casualty.

Note: This is done to keep the casualty from accidentally falling on another casualty if his litter is dropped before it is secured.

(5) When casualties are placed lengthwise, position them with their heads toward the direction of travel.

(6) Make sure each litter casualty is secured to his or her litter.

(7) Make sure each litter is secured to the aircraft.

Note: Unload casualties in reverse order, most seriously injured casualty first.

c. Ground military vehicles.

Note: 1. Nonmedical military vehicles may be used to evacuate casualties when no medical evacuation vehicles are available.

2. If medical personnel are present, follow their instructions for loading, securing, and unloading casualties.

(1) When loading casualties into the vehicle, load the most seriously injured casualty last.

(2) When a casualty is placed lengthwise, load the casualty with his or her head pointing forward, toward the direction of travel.

(3) Ensure each litter casualty is secured to the litter. Use litter straps, if available.

(4) Secure each litter to the vehicle as it is loaded into place. Make sure each litter is secured.

Note: Unload casualties in reverse order, most seriously injured casualty first.

Evaluation Preparation:

Setup: Provide the soldier with litters, straps, a casualty, military vehicle(s), and assistants.

Brief Soldier: Tell the soldier that he has a stable casualty requiring evacuation and that a vehicle is available. He has assistants available, who must be directed in their efforts. Describe the casualty's injuries and tell the soldier to determine what priority to assign to the casualty, and then load the casualty for evacuation.

Performance Measures	GO	NO GO
1 Determine the order in which casualties are to be evacuated.	_____	_____
2 Move a casualty using a four-man litter squad.	_____	_____

Performance Measures	GO	NO GO
3 Load casualties onto a military vehicle.	_____	_____

Evaluation Guidance:. Refer to chapter 1, paragraph 1-9e, (1) and (2).

References:
Required:
Related:

081-COM-1046

Transport a Casualty

Conditions: You have evaluated and given first aid to a casualty. You need to move the casualty to get further medical aid and may have to remove him/her from a vehicle before transporting. Assistance from other Soldiers may be available. You will need material that will not cut or bind the casualty (cravat bandages or litter straps), poncho, shirts or jackets, and poles or tree limbs. A SKED or Talon litter may be available.

Standards: Transport the casualty using an appropriate carry or litter without dropping or causing further injury to the casualty.

Special Condition: None

Special Standards: None

Special Equipment: None

Cue: None

Note: Conditions, standards, performance steps, and performance measures match task as it appears in STP 21-1-SMCT, 2 May 2011.

Performance Steps

> **WARNING**
> If the casualty was involved in a vehicle crash you should always consider that he/she may have a spinal injury. Unless there is an immediate life-threatening situation (such as fire, explosion), do NOT move the casualty with a suspected back or neck injury. Seek medical personnel for guidance on how to transport the casualty.

1. Remove a casualty from a vehicle, if necessary.

a. Laterally.

(1) With the assistance of another Soldier grasp the casualty's arms and legs.

(2) While stabilizing the casualty's head and neck as much as possible, lift the casualty free of the vehicle and move him/her to a safe place on the ground.

Note: If medical personnel are available, they may stabilize the casualty's head, neck, and upper body with a special board or splint.

b. Upward.

Note: You may have to remove a casualty upward from a vehicle; for example, from the passenger compartment of a wheeled vehicle lying on its side or from the hatch of an armored vehicle sitting upright.

(1) You may place a pistol belt or similar material around the casualty's chest to help pull him/her from the vehicle.

(2) With the assistance of another Soldier inside the vehicle, draw the casualty upward using the pistol belt or similar material or by grasping his/her arms.

(3) While stabilizing the casualty's head and neck as much as possible, lift the casualty free of the vehicle and place him/her on the topmost side of the vehicle.

Note: If medical personnel are available, they may stabilize the casualty's head, neck, and upper body with a special board or splint.

(4) Depending on the situation, move the casualty from the topmost side of the vehicle to a safe place on the ground.

> **WARNING**
>
> Do NOT use manual carries to move a casualty with a neck or spine injury, unless a life-threatening hazard is in the immediate area. Seek medical personnel for guidance on how to move and transport the casualty.

2. Select an appropriate method to transport the casualty.

Note: The Hawes carry is more easily used to move a conscious casualty to cover. Grasp the injured Soldier's wrist with his/her arm over one shoulder and lean forward, raising him off the ground. When performed correctly, the rescuer can still employ his/her weapon.

a. Fireman's carry. Use for an unconscious or severely injured casualty.

> **CAUTION**
>
> Do NOT use the neck drag if the casualty has a broken arm or a suspected neck injury.

b. Neck drag. Use in combat, generally for short distances.

c. Cradle-drop drag. Use to move a casualty who cannot walk when being moved up or down stairs.

d. Use litters if materials are available, if the casualty must be moved a long distance, or if manual carries will cause further injury.

e. Roll the casualty toward you onto his/her abdomen.

3. Transport the casualty.

a. Fireman's carry.

(1) Kneel at the casualty's uninjured side.

(2) Place casualty's arms above his/her head.

(3) Cross the ankle on the injured side over the opposite ankle.

(4) Place one of your hands on the shoulder farther from you and your other hand on his/her hip or thigh.

(5) Roll the casualty toward you onto his/her abdomen.

(6) Straddle the casualty.

Note: This method is used if the rescuer believes that it is safer than the regular method due to the casualty's wounds. Care must be taken to keep the casualty's head from falling backward, resulting in a neck injury.

(7) Place your hands under the casualty's chest and lock them together.

(8) Lift the casualty to his/her knees as you move backward.

(9) Continue to move backward, thus straightening the casualty's legs and locking the knees.

(10) Walk forward, bringing the casualty to a standing position but tilted slightly backward to prevent the knees from buckling.

(11) Maintain constant support of the casualty with one arm. Free your other arm, quickly grasp his/her wrist, and raise the arm high.

(12) Instantly pass your head under the casualty's raised arm, releasing it as you pass under it.

(13) Move swiftly to face the casualty.

(14) Secure your arms around his/her waist.

(15) Immediately place your foot between his/her feet and spread them (approximately 6 to 8 inches apart).

(16) Again grasp the casualty's wrist and raise the arm high above your head.

(17) Bend down and pull the casualty's arm over and down your shoulder bringing his/her body across your shoulders. At the same time pass your arm between the legs.

(18) Grasp the casualty's wrist with one hand while placing your other hand on your knee for support.

(19) Rise with the casualty correctly positioned.

Note: Your other hand is free for use as needed.

WARNING

Do NOT use the neck drag if the casualty has a broken and/or fractured arm or a suspected neck injury. If the casualty is unconscious, protect his/her head from the ground.

---

b. Neck drag.

(1) Tie the casualty's hands together at the wrists. (If conscious, the casualty may clasp his/her hands together around your neck.)

(2) Straddle the casualty in a kneeling face-to-face position.

(3) Loop the casualty's tied hands over and/or around your neck.

(4) Crawl forward, looking ahead, dragging the casualty with you.

c. Cradle-drop drag.

(1) With the casualty lying on his/her back, kneel at the head.

(2) Slide your hands, palms up, under the casualty's shoulders.

(3) Get a firm hold under his/her armpits.

(4) Partially rise, supporting the casualty's head on one of your forearms.
Note: You may bring your elbows together and let the casualty's head rest on both of your forearms.

(5) With the casualty in a semisitting position, rise and drag the casualty backwards.

(6) Back down the steps (or up if appropriate), supporting the casualty's head and body and letting the hips and legs drop from step to step.

   d. SKED or Talon litter.

     (1) Prepare a SKED litter.

(a) Remove the SKED from the pack and place on the ground.

(b) Unfasten the retainer strap, step on the foot end of the SKED, and unroll it completely to the opposite end.

(c) Bend the SKED in half and back roll. Repeat with the opposite end of the litter. The SKED litter will now lay flat.

     (2) Prepare a Talon litter.

(a) Stand the litter upright and release buckles from the litter.

(b) Place the litter on the ground and completely extend it with the fabric side facing up.

(c) Keeping the litter as straight as possible, grab the handles and rotate them inward until all the hinges rotate and lock.
Note: This action is done best using two individuals on each end of the litter executing this step simultaneously.

(d) While maintaining the hinges in the locked position, apply firm, steady pressure on the spreader bar with your foot. Increase pressure with your foot until the spreader bar locks into place.

     (3) Place the casualty on the litter.

(a) Place the litter next to the casualty. Ensure that the head end of the litter is adjacent to the head of the casualty.

(b) Log roll the casualty and slide the litter as far under him/her as possible. Gently roll the casualty down onto the litter.

(c) Slide the casualty to the center of the litter. Be sure to keep the spinal column as straight as possible.

     (4) Secure the casualty to the litter using litter straps or other available materials.
Note: For a SKED litter, lift the sides of the SKED and fasten the four cross straps to the buckles directly opposite the straps. Lift the foot portion of the SKED and feed the foot straps through the unused grommets at the foot end of the SKED and fasten to the buckles.

   e. Improvised litter.

     (1) Use the poncho and two poles or limbs.

(a) Open the poncho and lay the two poles lengthwise across the center, forming three equal sections.

(b) Reach in, pull the hood up toward you, and lay it flat on the poncho.

(c) Fold one section of the poncho over the first pole.

(d) Fold the remaining section of the poncho over the second pole to the first pole.

(2) Use shirts or jackets and two poles or limbs.

(a) Button two or three shirts or jackets and turn them inside out, leaving the sleeves inside.

(b) Lay the shirts or jackets on the ground and pass the poles through the sleeves.

(3) Place the casualty on the litter.

(4) Lift the litter.

(a) Raise the litter together.

(b) Keep the litter as level as possible.

Note: Use caution when transporting on a slope, incline, and/or hill.

4. Lift the casualty onto your back.

a. Raise the casualty to a standing position and or face the casualty, grasp the casualty's wrist and raise his arm high above your head while continuing to support the casualty with your other arm. If you use your right hand to fire your weapon, grasp the casualty's right wrist with your left hand. This will leave your right hand free to use your weapon.

b. Rotate your body so that your back is to the casualty's chest. The casualty's arm will be across your shoulder.

c. Lean forward, lifting the casualty's off of his/her feet.

d. Adjust the casualty's body as needed and move forward, carrying the casualty. When the carry is performed correctly, the rescuer can still employ his weapon.

Note: Two-Man Supporting Carry. The two-man carry is similar to the Hawes carry. Two rescuers grasp the casualty's wrists over opposite shoulders, lean forward, and lift the casualty to move him. This carry is easier in that two rescuers are used instead of one. Other Carries. Other one-man and two-man carries may be appropriate for casualty movement but they must be based on the tactical situation and have been practiced for familiarity.

5. Evacuate a casualty using a SKED litter.

a. Prepare a SKED litter for use.

(1) Remove the SKED litter from its pack and place it on the ground.

(2) Unfasten the retainer strap.

(3) Step on the foot end of the SKED litter and unroll the SKED completely.

(4) Bend the SKED litter in half and back roll.

(5) Repeat with the opposite end of the litter so that the SKED litter should lay flat.

(6) Point out the handholds, straps for the casualty, and dragline at the head of the litter.

b. Place and secure a casualty to a SKED litter.

Note: Now that the SKED litter has been made ready, place the casualty onto the litter, secure the casualty to the litter so he will not fall off, and evacuate the casualty. Use an assistant student as the simulated casualty.

(1) Place the SKED litter next to the casualty so that the head end of the litter is next to the casualty's head.

(2) Place the cross straps under the SKED litter.

(3) Log roll the casualty onto his side in a steady and even manner.

Note: Suggest showing one-man rescuer method, then four-man rescuer method. Emphasize supporting the casualty's head and neck.

(4) Slide the SKED litter as far under the casualty as possible.

(5) Gently roll the casualty until he is again lying on his back with the litter beneath him.

(6) Slide the casualty to the middle of the SKED litter, keeping his spinal column as straight as possible.

(7) Pull out the straps from under the SKED litter.

(8) Bring the straps across the casualty.

(9) Lift the sides of the SKED litter and fasten the four cross straps to the buckles directly opposite the straps.

(10) Lift the foot portion of the SKED litter.

(11) Feed the foot straps over the casualty's lower extremities and through the unused grommets at the foot end of the SKED litter.

(12) Fasten the straps to the buckles.

(13) Check to make sure the casualty is secured to the SKED litter.

Note: Move the casualty by yourself (dragline), two person (one on each side grasping two handholds each), and four man (litter squad)bearer kneels at one of the handles on the knee closest to the litter and facing the direction of travel. The leader of the litter team is usually at the casualty's right shoulder. Usually, the casualty is evacuated with his feet pointing toward the direction of travel. Upon command from the leader, the bearers stand up in unison, lifting the casualty, carry the casualty and, adjusting as needed to keep the casualty as level as possible.

6. Evacuate a casualty using a Talon litter.

a. Stand upright and release buckles from litter.

b. Place litter on the ground and completely extend with fabric side facing up.

c. Keeping the litter straight as possible, grab handles and rotate inward until all hinges rotate and lock.

d. While maintaining hinges in the locked position, apply firm, steady pressure on the spreader bar with foot. Increase pressure with foot until spreader bar locks into place.

Note: To close and store the litter, repeat the directions in reverse.

7. Making Improvised litters.

a. Use the poncho and two poles or limbs.

(1) Open the poncho and lay the two poles (limbs) lengthwise across the center so that the poncho is divided into thirds.

(2) Reach in, pull the hood up (toward you) and lay it flat on the poncho.

(3) Fold one section of the poncho over the first pole.

(4) Fold the remaining section of the poncho over the second pole to the first pole.

b. Use shirts or jackets and two poles or limbs.

(1) Button two or three shirts or jackets and turn them inside out, leaving the sleeves inside.

(2) Lay the shirts or jackets on the ground and pass the poles through the sleeves.

c. Using a blanket.

Note: An improvised litter can be made using only a blanket or other material.

(1) Lay the blanket on the ground.

(2) Roll two opposite edges of the blanket toward the middle.

Note: When the casualty is placed on the blanket, the rolled edges of the blanket are used as grips. Four or more litter bearers should be used when transporting a casualty using the blanket litter.

8. Place the casualty on the improvised litter.

a. Place the litter next to casualty. Ensure the head end of the litter is adjacent to the head of the casualty.

Note: Tell the students: In order to prevent hypothermia in transport, cover the casualty with a blanket, poncho, or other available materials to keep him warm and dry. Place covering under the casualty to prevent chilling due to contact with cold or wet ground.

b. Log roll the casualty and slide the litter as far under him as possible. Gently roll the casualty down on to the litter.

c. Slide the casualty to the center of the litter. Be sure to keep the spinal column as straight as possible.

d. Secure the casualty to the litter using litter straps or other available materials.

9. Transport the casualty.

a. Four Soldiers will need to be available to evacuate the casualty. A four-man carry can be used to quickly and safely transport a casualty on a litter to a nearby collection point where he can be transferred to a ground or air ambulance.

b. If only one other Soldier is available, position yourselves on opposite sides of the litter and face toward the casualty, kneel on one knee, and grab the two poles. Upon the command from the leader, both rise in unison, lifting the casualty.

c. Lift the litter.

(1) Raise the litter at the same time as the other carrier/bearer.

(2) Keep the litter as level as possible.

(3) Place and transport the casualty on the improvised litter.

Note: Use caution when transporting on a slope, incline, and/or hill.

Evaluation Preparation: *Setup*: For training and evaluation, use other Soldiers to be simulated casualties to be transported. Place Soldiers in both vehicles and on theground for transport.

Brief Soldier: Tell the Soldier the simulated casualties require movementto another location.

Performance Measures	GO	NO GO
1 Removed the casualty from a vehicle, if necessary.	_____	_____
2 Selected an appropriate method of transporting the casualty.	_____	_____
3 Transported the casualty.	_____	_____

Performance Measures	GO	NO GO
4 Lifted the casualty onto back	_____	_____
5 Evacuated a casualty using a SKED litter	_____	_____
6 Evacuated a casualty using a Talon litter	_____	_____
7 Made improvised litter(s)	_____	_____
8 Placed the casualty on the improvised litter	_____	_____
9 Transported the casualty	_____	_____

Evaluation Guidance:. Refer to chapter 1, paragraph 1-9e, (1) and (2).

References:
Required: FM 4-25.11 and FM 8-10-6
Related:

081-COM-1007

Perform First Aid for Burns

Conditions: You see a casualty who is suffering from a burn. You will need the casualty's emergency bandage or field dressing and canteen of water.

Standards: Give first aid for a burn without causing further injury to the casualty. Eliminate the source of the burn, if necessary. Apply a dressing lightly over the burn. Ensure that the sides of the dressing are sealed and the dressing does not slip.

Special Condition: None

Special Standards: None

Special Equipment: None

Cue: None

Note: Conditions, standards, performance steps, and performance measures match task as it appears in STP 21-1-SMCT, 2 May 2011.

Performance Steps

1. Eliminate the source of the burn.

CAUTION
Synthetic materials, such as nylon, may melt and cause further injury.

---

a. Thermal burns. Remove the casualty from the source of the burn. If the casualty's clothing is on fire, cover the casualty with a field jacket or any large piece of nonsynthetic material and roll him/her on the ground to put out the flames.

WARNING
Do not touch the casualty or the electrical source with your bare hands. You will be injured too!

High voltage electrical burns from an electrical source or lightning may cause temporary unconsciousness, difficulties in breathing, or difficulties with the heart (irregular heartbeat).

---

b. Electrical burns. If the casualty is in contact with an electrical source, turn the electricity off, if the switch is nearby. If the electricity cannot be turned off, use any nonconductive material (rope, clothing, or dry wood) to drag the casualty away from the source.

WARNING
Blisters caused by a blister agent are actually burns. Do not try to decontaminate skin where blisters have already formed. If blisters have not formed, decontaminate the skin.

---

c. Chemical burns.

(1) Remove liquid chemicals from the burned casualty by flushing with as much water as possible.

(2) Remove dry chemicals by carefully brushing them off with a clean, dry cloth. If large amounts of water are available, flush the area. Otherwise, do not apply water.

(3) Smother burning white phosphorus with water, a wet cloth, or wet mud. Keep the area covered with the wet material.

d. Laser burns. Move the casualty away from the source while avoiding eye contact with the beam source. If possible, wear appropriate laser eye protection.

Note: After the casualty has been removed from the source of the burn, continually monitor the casualty for conditions that may require basic lifesaving measures.

> **WARNING**
>
> Do NOT uncover the wound in a chemical environment. Exposure could cause additional harm.

2. Uncover the burn.

> **WARNING**
>
> Do NOT attempt to remove clothing that is stuck to the wound. Additional harm could result.

   a. Cut clothing covering the burned area.

> **CAUTION**
>
> Do not pull clothing over the burns.

   b. Gently lift away clothing covering the burned area.

   c. If the casualty's hand(s) or wrist(s) have been burned, remove jewelry (rings, watches) and place them in his/her pockets.

3. Apply the casualty's dressing to the burn.

Note: If the burn is caused by white phosphorus, the dressing must be wet.

> **CAUTION**
>
> Do not place the dressing over the face or genital area.
>
> Do not break the blisters.
>
> Do not apply grease or ointments to the burns.

   a. Apply the dressing/pad, white side down, directly over the wound.

   b. Wrap the tails (or the elastic bandage) so that the dressing/pad is covered.

   c. For a field dressing, tie the tails into a nonslip knot over the outer edge of the dressing, not over the wound. For an emergency bandage, secure the hooking ends of the closure bar into the elastic bandage.

   d. Check to ensure that the dressing is applied lightly over the burn but firmly enough to prevent slipping.

Note: Electricity often leaves entry and exit burns. Both burns should be treated.

Note: If the casualty is conscious and not nauseated, give him/her small amounts of water to drink.

4. Watch the casualty closely for life-threatening conditions, check for other injuries (if necessary), and treat for shock. Seek medical aid.

Evaluation Preparation:

Setup: For training and evaluation, use another Soldier to simulate a burn patient.

Brief Soldier: Tell the Soldier the simulated patient requires first aid for his burn to be given.

Performance Measures	GO	NO GO
1 Eliminated the source of the burn.	____	____
2 Uncovered the burn, unless clothing was stuck to the wound or in a chemical environment.	____	____
3 Applied the casualty's dressing.	____	____
4 Watched the casualty closely for life-threatening conditions, checked for other injuries (if necessary), and treated for shock. Sought medical aid.	____	____

Evaluation Guidance:. Refer to chapter 1, paragraph 1-9e, (1) and (2).

References:
Required: FM 4-25.11
Related:

052-192-1270

React to a Possible Improvised Explosive Device (IED)
(UNCLASSIFIED//FOR OFFICIAL USE ONLY) (U//FOUO)

Conditions: This task is identified as FOUO, refer to DTMS or CAR to view.

052-192-1271

Identify visual Indicators of an Implosive Device (IED)
(UNCLASSIFIED//FOR OFFICIAL USE ONLY) (U//FOUO)

Conditions: This task is identified as FOUO, refer to DTMS or CAR to view.

093-89D-1264

Search Suspect Vehicle for Improvised Explosive Device (IED)
Search Suspect Vehicle for Improvised Explosive Device (IED)

Conditions: In a contemporary operational environment (COE), given force protection or any EOD mission that requires the searching of vehicles for IED's using EOD specific tools and equipment; appropriate protective ensembles;

chemical, biological, radioactive, nuclear and explosive (CBRNE) detection and monitoring sets; communication and navigation tracking systems; electronic counter measures (ECM) capability; supporting unit's operation order (OPORD) and standing operating procedures (SOP), maps and overlays; and target site intelligence requirements.

Standards: Identify all suspicious items that can be classified as possible IED's during a vehicle search IAW applicable TM's without error.

Performance Steps

1. Check the area around the vehicle.
2. Ensure vehicle is stabilized and blocked to prevent rocking, tilting or moving.
3. Conduct external search of vehicle to include, but not limited to, underside, bumpers, wheel wells, and grill.
4. Open trunk and engine compartment remotely, if possible, to gain access.
5. Conduct search of trunk and engine compartment.
6. Open interior of vehicle remotely, if possible, to gain access.
7. Conduct search of interior of vehicle.
8. Record and mark the location of any suspect item.
9. Report location of suspect item.
10. Continue search if necessary.
11. Verify all applicable safety precautions are followed.

Evaluation Preparation: Gather all items required in the condition statement (or appropriate substitutions) and ensure all safety requirements are met.

Performance Measures	GO	NO GO
1 Check the area around the vehicle.	_____	_____
2 Ensure vehicle is stabilized and blocked to prevent rocking, tilting or moving.	_____	_____
3 Conduct external search of vehicle to include, but not limited to, underside, bumpers, wheel wells, and grill.	_____	_____
4 Open trunk and engine compartment remotely, if possible, to gain access.	_____	_____

Performance Measures	GO	NO GO
5 Conduct search of trunk and engine compartment.	____	____
6 Open interior of vehicle remotely, if possible, to gain access.	____	____
7 Conduct search of interior of vehicle.	____	____
8 Record and mark the location of any suspect item.	____	____
10 Continue search if necessary.	____	____
11 Verify all applicable safety precautions are followed.	____	____

Evaluation Guidance: Refer to chapter 1, paragraph 1-9e, (1) and (2).

References
Required: TM 60A-1-1-22
Related:
Related:

301-371-1000

Report Intelligence Information

Conditions: You have observed enemy activity and significant terrain and weather features. You must immediately report the activity to your chain of command via radio, wire, cable, or messenger.

Standards: Submit observations in a spot report, using the size, activity, location, unit, time, and equipment observed (SALUTE) format, to your chain of command within 5 minutes of observing enemy activity. Identify in the report the size, activity, location, unit, time, and equipment observed.

Special Condition: None

Special Standards: None

Special Equipment: None

Cue: None

Note: None

Performance Steps

1. Draft message summary information in the SALUTE format.

    a. S-Size. Report the number of personnel, vehicles, aircraft, or size of an object. Make an estimate if necessary.

    b. A-Activity. Report detailed account of the detected element activity. Indicate the activity types or types and an amplifying sub-type if applicable.

        (1) Attacking. (direction from)

        (2) Defending. (direction from)

        (3) Moving. (direction from)

        (4) Stationary.

        (5) Cache.

        (6) Civilian. (criminal acts, unrest, infrastructure damage)

        (7) Personnel recovery. (isolating event, observed signal)

        (8) Other. (Give name and description)

    c. L-Location. Report where you saw the activity. Include grid coordinates with Grid Zone Designator or reference from a known point including the distance and direction from the known point.

    d. U-Unit. Report the detected element unit, organization, or facility. Indicate the type of unit, organization, or facility detected. If it cannot be clearly identified, describe in as much detail as possible, including uniforms, vehicle markings, and other identifying information.

        (1) Conventional.

        (2) Irregular.

        (3) Coalition.

        (4) Host Nation.

        (5) Non-governmental Organization (NGO).

        (6) Civilian.

        (7) Facility.

    e. T-Time. Report the time and date the activity was observed, not the time you report it. Always report local or Zulu time.

    f. E-Equipment. Report all equipment associated with the activity, such as weapons, vehicles, tools. Add a narrative if necessary to clarify, describe, or explain the type of equipment. Provide nomenclature, type, and quantity of all equipment observed. If equipment cannot be clearly identified, describe in as much detail as possible.

    (1) Air Defense Artillery (ADA) (missile (MANPADS), missile (other), gun)

    (2) Artillery (gun (self propelled), gun (towed), missile or rocket, mortar)

    (3) Armored track vehicle (tank, APC, command and control (C2), engineer, transport, other)

    (4) Armored wheel vehicle (gun, APC, C2, engineer, transport, other)

    (5) Wheel vehicle (gun, C2, engineer, transport, other)

    (6) Infantry weapon (anti-armor missile, anti-armor gun, RPG, heavy machinegun, GL, small arms, other)

    (7) Aircraft (RW (attack helicopter (AH)), RW (utility helicopter (UH)), RW (observation helicopter), FW (attack), FW (transport), unmanned aircraft, other)

    (8) Mine or IED (buried, surface, VBIED, PBIED, other)

    (9) CBRN

    (10) Supplies (Class III, Class V, other)

    (11) Civilian

    (12) Other

2. Provide spot report to appropriate authority / chain of command using the available means of communication.

Evaluation Preparation:

Setup: Simulate a situation that requires Soldiers to immediately report intelligence information. You may need two to four personnel (dressed in aggressor uniforms or local attire if available) where they are observable with the naked eye (or binoculars if available). Direct the personnel to perform some type of activity that meets the information requirements. Provide the Soldier with a 1:50,000 scale topographic map of the test area. Provide paper and a pen or pencil for the Soldier to take notes and prepare the report. If you require the Soldier to radio the report to someone else, provide two radios and SOI. Accompany the Soldier being tested to a location where the Soldier can observe the threat.

Brief Soldier: Tell the Soldier he/she is-

    –Performing an offensive or defensive mission.
    –Patrolling in a stability or civil support operation.
    –Manning a checkpoint or roadblock.
    –Occupying an observation post.
    –Passing through an area in a convoy.

Instruct the Soldier to report the activity observed. Once the Soldier completes the report, have the Soldier select a means of transmitting the report to the receiving authority.

Performance Measures	GO	NO GO
1 Drafted message summary information in the SALUTE format.	_____	_____
2 Reported all information to the appropriate authority / chain of command within 5 minutes of the observation.	_____	_____

Evaluation Guidance: Refer to chapter 1, paragraph 1-9e, (1) and (2).

References
Required: FM 2-91.6, FM 3-21.75, and FM 6-99.2
Related:

071-COM-0804

Perform Surveillance without the Aid of Electronic Device

Conditions: You are a member of a squad or team in a defensive position and must conduct surveillance within your assigned sector during both daylight and limited visibility (night).

Standards: Identify potential activity indicators and conduct a visual search of your assigned sector. Submit SALUTE reports, as required.

Special Condition: None

Special Standards: None

Special Equipment:

Cue: None

Note: None

Performance Steps
    1. Identify potential activity indicators in sector (Figure 071-COM-0804-1).

SIGHT Look for--	SOUND Listen for--	TOUCH Feel for--	SMELL Smell for--
• Enemy personnel, vehicles, and aircraft • Sudden or unusual movement • New local inhabitants • Smoke or dust • Unusual movement of farm or wild animals • Unusual activity--or lack of activity--by local inhabitants, especially at times or places that are normally inactive or active • Vehicle or personnel tracks • Movement of local inhabitants along uncleared routes, areas, or paths • Signs that the enemy has occupied the area • Evidence of changing trends in threats • Recently cut foliage • Muzzle flashes, lights, fires, or reflections • Unusual amount (too much or too little) of trash	• Running engines or track sounds • Voices • Metallic sounds • Gunfire, by weapon type • Unusual calm or silence • Dismounted movement • Aircraft	• Warm coals and other materials in a fire • Fresh tracks • Age of food or trash	• Vehicle exhaust • Burning petroleum products • Food cooking • Aged food in trash • Human waste

OTHER CONSIDERATIONS	
Armed Elements	Locations of factional forces, mine fields, and potential threats.
Homes and Buildings	Condition of roofs, doors, windows, lights, power lines, water, sanitation, roads, bridges, crops, and livestock.
Infrastructure	Functioning stores, service stations, and so on.
People	Numbers, gender, age, residence or DPRE status, apparent health, clothing, daily activities, and leadership.
Contrast	Has anything changed? For example, are there new locks on buildings? Are windows boarded up or previously boarded up windows now open, indicating a change in how a building is expected to be used? Have buildings been defaced with graffiti?

Figure 071-COM-0804-1. Potential Indicators.

2. Perform observation techniques of the sector.

   a. Conduct day observation.

      (1) Use rapid scan technique. (Figure 071-COM-0804-2).

Note: The rapid scan technique is used to detect obvious signs of enemy activity. It is usually the first method you will use.

Figure 071-COM-0804-2. Rapid/Slow Scan.

     (a) Search a strip of terrain about 100 meters deep, from left-to-right, pausing at short intervals.

     (b) Search another 100-meter strip farther out, from right-to-left, overlapping the first strip scanned, pausing at short intervals.

     (c) Continue this method until the entire sector of fire has been searched.

     (2) Use slow scan technique.

Note: Slow scan search technique uses the same process as the rapid scan but much more deliberately; this means a slower, side-to-side movement and more frequent pauses.

     (3) Use detailed search technique paying attention to the following: (Figure 071-COM-0804-3).

Note: The detailed search, even more than the rapid or slow scan, depends on breaking a larger sector into smaller sectors to ensure everything is covered in detail and no possible enemy positions are overlooked.

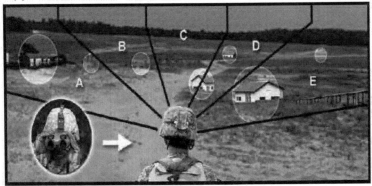

Figure 071-COM-0804-3. Detailed Search.

     (a) Likely enemy positions and suspected vehicle/dismounted avenues of approach.

     (b) Target signatures, such as road junctions, hills, and lone buildings, located near prominent terrain features.

     (c) Areas with cover and concealment, such as tree lines and draws.

   b. Conduct limited visibility observation.

     (1) Use dark adaptation technique.

     (a) Stay in a dark area for about 30 minutes.

     (b) Move into a red-light area for about 20 minutes followed by about 10 minutes in a dark area.

Note: The red-light method may save time by allowing you to get orders, check equipment, or do some other job before moving into darkness.

     (2) Use night vision scan technique (Figure 071-COM-0804-4).

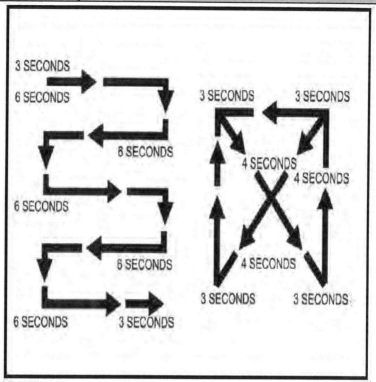

Figure 071-COM-0804-4. Night scanning patterns.

(a) Look from right to left or left to right using a slow, regular scanning movement.

(b) At night avoid looking directly at a faintly visible object when trying to confirm its presence.

(3) Use off center vision technique.

Note: The technique of viewing an object using central vision is ineffective at night due to the night blind spot that exist during low illumination. You must learn to use off-center vision.

(a) View an object by looking 10 degrees above, below, or to either side of it rather than directly at it.

(b) Shift your eyes from one off-center point to another.

(c) Continue to pick-up the object in your peripheral field of vision.

3. Submit SALUTE report (Figure 071-COM-0804-5).

Line No.	Type Info	Description
1	(S)ize/Who	Expressed as a quantity and echelon or size. For example, report "10 enemy Infantrymen" (not "a rifle squad").
If multiple units are involved in the activity you are reporting, you can make multiple entries.		
2	(A)ctivity/What	Relate this line to the PIR being reported. Make it a concise bullet statement. Report what you saw the enemy doing, for example, "emplacing mines in the road."
3	(L)ocation/Where	This is generally a grid coordinate, and should include the 100,000-meter grid zone designator. The entry can also be an address, if appropriate, but still should include an eight-digit grid coordinate. If the reported activity involves movement, for example, advance or withdrawal, then the entry for location will include "from" and "to" entries. The route used goes under "Equipment/How."
4	(U)nit/Who	Identify who is performing the activity described in the "Activity/What" entry. Include the complete designation of a military unit, and give the name and other identifying information or features of civilians or insurgent groups.
5	(T)ime/When	For future events, give the DTG for when the activity will initiate. Report ongoing events as such.

Report the time you saw the enemy activity, not the time you report it. Always report local or Zulu (Z) time. |
| 6 | (E)quipment/How | Clarify, complete, and expand on previous entries. Include information about equipment involved, tactics used, and any other essential elements of information (EEI) not already reported in the previous lines. |

Figure 071-COM-0804-5. SALUTE Format.

Evaluation Preparation:

Setup: Provide the Soldier with the equipment and or materials described in the conditions statement.

Brief Soldier: Tell the Soldier what is expected of him by reviewing the task standards. Stress to the Soldier the importance of observing all cautions, warnings, and dangers to avoid injury to personnel and, if applicable, damage to equipment.

Performance Measures	GO	NO GO
1 Identified potential activity indicators in sector.	____	____
2 Performed observation techniques of the sector.	____	____
3 Submitted SALUTE report.	____	____

Evaluation Guidance: Refer to chapter 1, paragraph 1-9e, (1) and (2).

References
Required:
Related: FM 3-21.75

301-348-1050

Report Information of Potential Intelligence Value

> **WARNING**
> Do not wait until you have complete information to transmit. Even small amounts of information of critical tactical value may provide indicators of the threat's intentions.

Conditions: You are a Soldier with the responsibility to actively observe and provide concise accurate reports while in an area of operations. You are given information requirements, a means of communication (radio, wire, cable, or messenger) as prescribed in the unit's standard operating procedures (SOPs), required mission-specific equipment and a situation which requires you to immediately report information of critical tactical value.

Standards: Transmit information to the receiving authority in size, activity, location, unit, time and equipment (SALUTE) format to include significant terrain and weather conditions via the available means of communication. Information will be reported within 5 minutes after observation with six out of six SALUTE items correctly identified. Note: Your unit SOPs will specify the receiving authority. Examples of receiving authorities are company commander, team commander, company intelligence support team (CoIST), or S2 (Intelligence Officer [U.S. Army]) section.

Special Condition: None

Special Standards: None

Special Equipment:

Cue: None

Note: None

1. Identify information concerning threat activity and significant terrain and weather conditions including-

a. Order of battle factors; for example, threat weapons systems, composition, and direction of movement.

Note: If you cannot identify a weapon system or vehicle by name, include a description of the equipment.

b. Military aspects of terrain; for example, observation and fields of fire, avenues of approach, key and decisive terrain, obstacles, and cover and concealment (OAKOC).

c. Weather factors; for example, severe weather, precipitation, trafficability, surface winds and gusts, and ground visibility.

Note: Use Spot Reports (Level 1 Report) to transmit information of immediate value. Transmit Spot Reports as rapidly and securely as possible. The SALUTE format is an aid for the observer to report the essential reporting elements. (You may precede each message segment of the Spot Report with the meaning of the acronym SALUTE.)

2. Draft message summary information in the SALUTE format.

a. S-Size. Report the number of personnel, vehicles, aircraft, or size of an object. Make an estimate if necessary.

b. A-Activity. Report detailed account of the detected element activity. Indicate the activity types or types and an amplifying sub-type if applicable.

    (1) Attacking. (direction from)

        (a) ADA. (engaging)

        (b) Aircraft. (engaging) (rotary wing (RW), fixed wing (FW))

        (c) Ambush. (improvised explosive device (IED) (exploded), IED (unexploded), Sniper, Anti-armor, Other)

        (d) Indirect fire. (point of impact, point of origin)

        (e) Chemical, biological, radiological, and nuclear (CBRN)

    (2) Defending. (direction from)

    (3) Moving. (direction from)

    (4) Stationary.

    (5) Cache.

    (6) Civilian. (criminal acts, unrest, infrastructure damage)

    (7) Personnel recovery. (isolating event, observed signal)

    (8) Other. (Give name and description)

c. L-Location. Report where you saw the activity. Include grid coordinates with Grid Zone Designator or reference from a known point including the distance and direction from the known point.

d. U-Unit. Report the detected element unit, organization, or facility. Indicate the type of unit, organization, or facility detected. If it cannot be clearly identified, describe in as much detail as possible, including uniforms, vehicle markings, and other identifying information.

(1) Conventional.

(2) Irregular.

(3) Coalition.

(4) Host Nation.

(5) Non-governmental organization (NGO).

(6) Civilian.

(7) Facility.

e. T-Time. Report the time and date the activity was observed, not the time you report it. Always report local or Zulu time.

f. E-Equipment. Report all equipment associated with the activity, such as weapons, vehicles, tools. Add a narrative if necessary to clarify, describe, or explain the type of equipment. Provide nomenclature, type, and quantity of all equipment observed. If equipment cannot be clearly identified, describe in as much detail as possible.

(1) Air Defense Artillery (ADA) (missile (MANPADS), missile (other), gun).

(2) Artillery (gun (self propelled), gun (towed), missile or rocket, mortar).

(3) Armored track vehicle (tank, APC, command and control (C2), engineer, transport, other).

(4) Armored wheel vehicle (gun, APC, C2, engineer, transport, other).

(5) Wheel vehicle (gun, C2, engineer, transport, other).

(6) Infantry weapon (anti-armor missile, anti-armor gun, RPG, heavy machinegun, GL, small arms, other).

(7) Aircraft (RW (attack helicopter (AH)), RW (utility helicopter (UH)), RW (observation helicopter), FW (attack), FW (transport), unmanned aircraft, other).

(8) Mine or IED (buried, surface, VBIED, PBIED, other).

(9) CBRN.

(10) Supplies (Class III, Class V, other).

(11) Civilian.

(12) Other.

3. Select a means of communication; for example, radio, wire, cable, or messenger.

Note: Consider the communications means available and the information's potential significance to your mission. Radio is fast and mobile; yet, normally it is the least secure of the three communications means available at tactical units. Wire is more secure but it is subject to wiretapping and requires more time, personnel and equipment to install. Messenger is very secure but requires more delivery time and is limited by weather, terrain, and threat action.

4. Transmit the message to the receiving authority.

a. If using a messenger, provide the messenger with explicit reporting instructions and a message, preferably written, which is clear, complete, and concise.

b. If using radio, use proper radio/telephone procedures according to unit SOPs. Use the radio only as needed. The enemy may intercept your transmission, exploit the message information, or locate your transmitter for targeting or jamming.

c. If you encounter jamming or interference on your radio net, within 10 minutes of the incident, transmit a meaconing, intrusion, jamming, and interference (MIJI) feeder report, preferably via messenger, wire, or cable to your net control station. Your Signal Operating Instructions (SOI) contains the MIJI format.

Evaluation Preparation: *Setup*: Simulate a situation that requires Soldiers to immediately report information of critical tactical value. You may need two to four personnel (dressed in aggressor uniforms or local attire if available) where they are observable with the naked eye (or binoculars if available). Direct the personnel to perform some type of activity that meets the information requirements. Provide the Soldier with a 1:50,000 scale topographic map of the test area. Provide paper and a pen or pencil for the Soldier to take notes and prepare the report. If you require the Soldier to radio the report to someone else, provide two radios and SOI. Accompany the Soldier being tested to a location where the Soldier can observe the threat.

Brief Soldier: Tell the Soldier he/she is–

Tell the Soldier he/she is-

–Performing an offensive or defensive mission.
–Patrolling in a stability or defense support of civil authorities operation.
–Manning a checkpoint or roadblock.
–Occupying an observation post.
–Passing through an area in a convoy.

Instruct the Soldier to report the activity observed, weather factors, and any significant military aspects of the terrain. Once the Soldier completes the report, have the Soldier select a means of transmitting the report to the receiving authority.

Performance Measures	GO	NO GO
1 Identified information concerning threat activity and significant terrain and weather conditions.	_____	_____
2 Drafted a message in SALUTE format.	_____	_____

Performance Measures	GO	NO GO
3 Selected a means of communication.	_____	_____
4 Transmitted the message to the receiving authority within 5 minutes of the observation.	_____	_____

Evaluation Guidance: Refer to chapter 1, paragraph 1-9e, (1) and (2).

References
Required: FM 3-21.75 and FM 6-99.2
Related: FM 2-91.6

071-COM-0512

React to Man-to-Man Contact

Conditions: You are a member of a dismounted squad conducting operations and you have encountered an unarmed adversary. You may be equipped with personnel protective equipment (PPE).

Standards: Dominate the enemy using the basic fighting strategy by achieving the clinch, gaining a dominant position and finishing the fight.

Special Condition: None

Special Standards: None

Special Equipment:

Cue: None

Note: This task is only a basic introduction to combatives. For advanced combatives, refer to FM 3-25.150, Combatives.

Performance Steps

1. Close the distance.

Note: Controlling a standup fight means controlling the range between fighters. The untrained fighter is primarily dangerous at punching range. The goal is to avoid that range. Even if you are the superior striker, the most dangerous thing you can do is to spend time at the range where the enemy has the highest probability of victory.

    a. Achieve the clinch.

        (1) Face your opponent, and assume the Fighting Stance just outside of kicking range.

        (2) Tuck your chin, and use your arms to cover your head while aggressively closing the distance.

        (3) Drive your head into your opponent's chest.

        (4) Move your cupped hands to your opponent's biceps.

        (5) Aggressively fight for one of the dominant clinch positions.

    b. Achieve the Modified Seatbelt Clinch. (Figure 071-COM-0512-1)

Figure 071-COM-0512-1. Modified Seatbelt Clinch.

    (1) Raise one of his arms.

    (2) Move yourself perpendicular to your opponent.

    (3) Reach around your opponent's waist to grab his opposite-side hip.

    (4) Pull his arm into your chest with your other arm.

    (5) Control his arm at the triceps.

    c. Achieve the Double Under-hooks Clinch. (Figure 071-COM-0512-2)

Figure 071-COM-0512-2. Double Underhooks Clinch.

(1) Drive your overhook hand (with a knife edge) under your opponent's underhook arm.

(2) Clasp your hands in a Wrestler's Grip behind your opponent, while keeping head pressure on his chest.

d. Achieve the Rear Clinch. (Figure 071-COM-0512-3)

Figure 071-COM-0512-3. The Rear Clinch.

(1) Step behind your opponent.

(2) Clasp your hands around your opponent's waist in an Opposing Thumbs Grip.

(3) Place your forehead in the small of his back to avoid strikes.

Note: From this secure position, you can attempt to take the opponent down.

  2. Gain dominant position.

    a. Achieve the Rear Mount. (Figure 071-COM-0512-4)

Figure 071-COM-0512-4. The Rear Mount

(1) Place one arm under your opponent's armpit and the other over his opposite shoulder.

(2) Clasp your hands in an Opposing Thumbs Grip.

WARNING

When in the Rear Mount, DO NOT cross your feet; this would provide the opponent an opportunity for an ankle break.

---

(3) Wrap both legs around your opponent, with your heels hooked inside his legs.

Note: Keep your head tucked to avoid headbutts.

b. Achieve the Mount. (Figure 071-COM-0512-5)

Note: The Mount allows the fighter to strike the opponent with punches, while restricting the opponent's ability to deliver effective return punches. The Mount also provides the leverage to attack the opponent's upper body with chokes and joint attacks.

Figure 071-COM-0512-5. The Mount.

(1) Position your knees as high as possible toward the opponent's armpits.

(2) Place your toes in line with or inside of your ankles to avoid injuring your ankles when your opponent attempts to roll you over.

    c. Achieve the Guard. (Figure 071-COM-0512-6)

Note: A fighter never wants to be under his opponent; the Guard enables him to defend himself and transition off of his back into a more advantageous position. The Guard allows the bottom fighter to exercise a certain amount of control over the range by pushing out or pulling in his opponent with his legs and hips. With skill, the bottom fighter can defend against strikes and even apply joint locks and chokes.

Figure 071-COM-0512-6. The Guard.

(1) Control opponent's arms at the elbows.

(2) Lock your ankles around opponent's torso.

    d. Achieve Side Control. (Figure 071-COM-0512-7)

Figure 071-COM-0512-7. Side Control.

(1) Keep the leg closest to your opponent's head straight.

(2) Bend the other leg so that the knee is near your opponent's hip.

(3) Keep your head turned away to avoid knee strikes.

(4) Place your elbow on the ground in the notch created by the opponent's head and shoulder.

(5) Position your other hand palm down on the ground under the opponent's near-side hip.

3. Finish the Fight.

Note: When dominant body position has been achieved, the fighter can begin attempts to finish the fight secure in the knowledge that if an attempt fails, as long as he maintains dominant position, he may simply try again.

a. Achieve the Rear Naked Choke.(Figure 071-COM-0512-8)

Note: The Rear Naked Choke slows the flow of blood in the carotid arteries, which can eventually cause your opponent to be rendered unconscious for a short period of time.

Figure 071-COM-0512-8. Rear Naked Choke.

(1) Place your bicep along one side of your opponent's neck; take your forearm and roll it around to the other side of neck, his chin will line up with your elbow.

(2) Tighten choke up and grab your shoulder or arm.

(3) Place your opposite hand behind the head as if your combing his hair back.

(4) Tuck your head in to avoid getting hit.

(5) Roll your shoulders back, push chest forward and finish the choke.

b. Achieve the Cross Collar Choke from the Mount and Guard. (Figure 071-COM-0512-9 and 10)

Note: The Cross-Collar Choke is a blood choke that can only be employed when your opponent is wearing a durable shirt. This choke should be performed from either the Mount or Guard.

Figure 071-COM-0512-9. Cross Collar Choke.

Figure 071-COM-0512-10. Cross Collar Choke Continued.

(1) Open your opponent's same-side collar With your non-dominant hand.

(2) Reach across your body, and insert your dominant hand into the collar you just opened.

(3) Relax the dominant hand, and reach all the way behind your opponent's neck.

(4) Grasp his collar with your fingers on the inside and your thumb on the outside.

(5) Release the grip of your non-dominant hand, and move your dominant-side forearm across your opponent's neck under the first arm, clearing his chin.

(6) Reach all the way back untilyour dominant hand meets the other hand using the same grip.

(7) Turn your wrists so that your palms face you, and pull your opponent into you.

(8) Expand your chest,and pinch your shoulders together.

(9) Bring your elbows to your hips to finish the choke.

c. Achieve the Bent Arm Bar from the Mount and Side Control. (Figure 071-COM-0512-11)

Note: The Bent Arm Bar is a joint lock that attacks the shoulder girdle. This technique can be employed from either the Mount or Side Control.

Figure 071-COM-0512-11. Bent Arm Bar.

(1) Drive your opponent's wrist and elbow to the ground with thumbless grip.

(2) Move your elbow to the notch created by your opponent's neck and shoulder.

(3) Keep your head on the back of your hand to protect your face from strikes.

(4) Place your other hand under his elbow.

(5) Grab your own wrist with a Thumbless Grip.

(6) Drag the back of your opponent's hand toward his waistline.

(7) Lift his elbow, and dislocate his shoulder.

    d. Achieve the Straight Arm Bar from the Mount. (Figure 071-COM-0512-12)

Note: The Straight Arm Bar is a joint lock designed to damage the elbow. While this exercise outlines a Straight Arm Bar performed from the Mount, this technique can be performed from any dominant position.

Figure 071-COM-0512-12. Straight Arm Bar from the Mount.

(1) Decide which arm you wish to attack.

(2) Isolate that arm by placing your opposite-side hand in the middle of your opponent's chest, between his arms.

(3) Target the unaffected arm and press down to prevent your opponent from getting off the flat of his back.

(4) Loop your same-side arm around the targeted arm and place that hand in the middle of your opponent's chest, applying greater pressure.

(5) Place all of your weight on your opponent's chest and raise to your feet in a very low squat.

(6) Turn your body 90 degrees to face the targeted arm.

(7) Bring the foot nearest to your opponent's head around his face, and plant it in the crook of his neck on the opposite side of the targeted arm.

(8) Slide your hips down the targeted arm, keeping your buttocks tight to your opponent's shoulder.

(9) Secure your opponent's wrist with both of your hands in Thumb Grips.

(10) Keep his thumb pointed skyward to achieve the correct angle.

(11) Pull your heels tight to your buttocks, and pinch your knees together tightly with the upper arm trapped between your knees, not resting on your groin.

(12) Apply steady pressure by trapping your opponent's wrist on your chest, and arching your hips skyward.

e. Achieve the Straight Arm Bar from the Guard. (Figure 071-COM-0512-13)

Note: Fighting from your back can be very dangerous. When your opponent attempts to strike and apply chokes from within your Guard, use the Straight Arm Bar from the Guard, a joint lock designed to damage the elbow.

Figure 071-COM-0512-13. Straight Arm Bar from the Guard.

(1) Secure the arm at or above the elbow when your opponent presents a straight arm.

(2) Hold your opponent's elbow for the remainder of the move.

(3) Insert your other hand under the opponent's thigh on the side opposite the targeted arm.

Note: The hand should be palm up.

(4) Open your Guard, and bring your legs up, while curling your back to limit the friction.

(5) Contort your body by pulling with the hand that is on the back of your opponent's thigh.

(6) Bring your head to his knee.

(7) Place your leg over his head.

(8) Grab your opponent, and pull him down by pulling your heels to your buttocks and pinching your knees together with your leg.

(9) Move the hand that was behind your opponent's thigh to grasp the wrist that you secured at the elbow with a Thumb Grip.

(10) Curl your calf downward and push up with your hips to break your opponent's arm.

f. Achieve the Guillotine Choke. (Figure 071-COM-0512-14 and Figure 071-COM-0512-15)

Figure 071-COM-0512-14. Guillotine Choke.

Figure 071-COM-0512-15. Guillotine Choke Continued.

(1) Direct your opponent's head underneath one of your arms, and take a step back when your opponent charges your legs.

(2) Wrap your arm around your opponent's head and under his neck.

(3) Grasp the first hand where a watch would be with your other hand, ensuring that you have not reached around your opponent's arm.

(4) Cinch the choke by bringing your arm further around your opponent's head, improving your grip.

(5) Cinch up the choke and sit down to place him in your guard.

Note: Your palm should be facing your own chest.

(6) Sit Down.

(7) Place your opponent within your Guard.

(8) Finish the choke by pulling with your arms and pushing with your legs.

Evaluation Preparation:

Setup: Provide the Soldier with the equipment and or materials described in the conditions statement.

Brief Soldier: Tell the Soldier what is expected of him by reviewing the task standards. Stress to the Soldier the importance of observing all cautions, warnings, and dangers to avoid injury to personnel and, if applicable, damage to equipment.

Performance Measures	GO	NO GO
1 Achieved the Clinch.	_____	_____
2 Gained a dominant position.	_____	_____
3 Finished the Fight.	_____	_____

Evaluation Guidance: Refer to chapter 1, paragraph 1-9e, (1) and (2).

References
Required:
Related: FM 3-25.150

Subject Area 5: Adapt

171-COM-0011

Employ Progressive Levels of Individual Force When Confronting Civilians

---

WARNING
During the assessment ensure that biological threats associated with close contact/combat are taken into consideration and protective measures are taken to prevent exposure.

Conditions: You are a member of a section or team that is securing a critical area or defusing a civil disturbance and you are approached/confronted by one or more hostile civilians. You have your individual weapon, personal protection equipment (PPE), and the rules of engagement (ROE).

Standards: Assess and immediately report threats situations to your leadership. Protect yourself against hazards. Isolate hostile civilians, if required. Control the situation using the least amount of force possible.

Special Condition: None

Special Standards: None

Special Equipment:

Cue: None

Note: The operational environment must be considered at all times during this task. All Army elements must be prepared to enter any environment and perform their missions while simultaneously dealing with a wide range of unexpected threats and other influences. Units must be ready to counter these threats and influences and, at the same time, be prepared to deal with various third-party actors, such as international humanitarian relief agencies, news media, refugees, and civilians on the battlefield. These groups may or may not be hostile to us, but they can potentially affect the unit's ability to accomplish its mission.

Performance Steps

1. Assess the situation by identifying the level of hostile civilian threat.
    a. Verbal.
    b. Physical without weapons (touching, pushing).
    c. Physical with weapons (rocks, clubs, spitting).
    d. Physical with firearms shown.
    e. Physical with firearms used.
2. Report the situation immediately to the section or team leader.
3. Protect yourself against physical and other hazards.
    a. Use full - face shields.
    b. Use double layer latex gloves.
Note: Any exposure incident must be reported to the chain of command.
4. Isolate hostile civilian(s), if required.
    a. Identify hostile group(s) sphere of influence.
    b. Remove the individual with the most influence of the crowd.
    c. Use the 5S's (Search, Silence, Segregate, Safeguard, Speed to the rear).
5. Employ no more force than is necessary to control the situation using graduated response measures.
Note: Soldiers should employ the lowest level of force necessary to address a threat but may use any level, even deadly force, without performing earlier steps, if the circumstances or threat do not allow for the use of graduated levels of force.
    a. Avoid confrontation if possible.
    b. Do not deliberately instigate, threaten, provoke, or bluff.
    c. Speak sternly to the civilian and state the peaceful intent of your mission.
    d. Tell the civilian to "STAND BACK" and warn them that you may have to use force.
    e. If a civilian places his or her hands on your body, brush them back with hand or availble PPE.
    f. If a civilian attempts to inflict bodily harm, use any authorized materials (such as water hoses, chemical gases) to impede movement.
    g. Use your individual weapon, if necessary, as prescribed by the established ROE.

6. Establish and maintain control of the situation.

a. Comply with the ROE, any host-nation requirements, applicable international treaties and operational agreements.

Note: ROE are directives issued by competent military authority that delineate the circumstances and the limitations under which United States forces will initiate and/or continue combat engagement with other forces encountered. ROE help commanders accomplish the mission by regulating the rules of the use of force. Everyone must understand the ROE and be prepared to execute them properly in every possible confrontation.

b. Minimize casualties and damage.

c. Maintain professional demeanor and appearance.

Evaluation Preparation:

Setup: Provide the Soldier with the equipment and or materials described in the conditions statement.

Brief Soldier: Tell the Soldier what is expected of him by reviewing the task standards. Stress to the Soldier the importance of observing all cautions, warnings, and dangers to avoid injury to personnel and, if applicable, damage to equipment.

Performance Measures	GO	NO GO
1 Assessed the situation by identifying the level of hostile civilian threat.	_____	_____
2 Reported the situation immediately to the section or team leader.	_____	_____
3 Protected yourself against physical and other hazards.	_____	_____
4 Isolated hostile civilian(s), as required.	_____	_____
5 Employed no more force than was necessary to control the situation.	_____	_____
6 Established and maintained control of the situation.	_____	_____

Evaluation Guidance: Refer to chapter 1, paragraph 1-9e, (1) and (2).

References
Required:
Related: FM 27-10, FM 3-22.40, and TC 7-98-1

181-105-1001

Conduct Operations According to the Law of War

Conditions: You are a Soldier assigned to a deployed unit which has a mission that requires you to be actively involved in operations that are governed by the law of war. As a Soldier, you are responsible for identifying, understanding, and complying with the provisions of the law of war, including the Geneva and Hague Conventions and the 10 Soldier's rules. You are also responsible for identifying necessary actions to prevent law of war violations from occurring.

Standards: Identify, understand, and comply with the law of war. Identify problems or situations that violate the policies and take appropriate action, including notifying appropriate authorities, so that expedient action may be taken to correct the problem or situation.

Special Condition: None

Special Standards: None

Special Equipment:

Cue: None

Note: None

Performance Steps

1. Identify the key elements of the law of war.
   a. Describe how the Hague Convention and Geneva Conventions pertain to combat operations.
   b. Describe international customary law of war.
2. Describe the responsibilities of U.S. Soldiers to obey the law of war.
3. Identify the basic principles of the law of war.
   a. Define military necessity.
      (1) Describe a legitimate military target.
   b. Define unnecessary suffering.

   c. Define discrimination and distinction.
   d. Define proportionality.

4. Identify the "10 Soldier's Rules".
 a. Soldiers only fight enemy combatants.
 b. Soldiers treat humanely all who surrender or are captured.
 c. Soldiers do not kill or torture detained personnel.
  (1) List the 5 S's and T.
  (2) Describe humane treatment.
  (3) Describe respect and protect.
 d. Soldiers collect and care for the wounded.
 e. Soldiers do not attack protected places or persons.
  (1) Identify protected persons.
  (2) Identify protected places.
 f. Soldiers do not attack medical personnel, facilities or equipment.
 g. Soldiers destroy no more than the mission requires.
 h. Soldiers treat civilians and noncombatants humanely.
 i. Soldiers do not steal. Soldiers respect private property and possessions.
 j. Soldiers should do their best to prevent violations of the law of war.
 k. Soldiers report all violations of the law of war to their superior.
5. Identify actions to prevent law of war violations.
 a. List actions to protect civilians/noncombatants.
 b. List actions to protect prisoners of war, retained persons and detainees.
 c. List actions to protect medical transports and facilities.
 d. List actions to prevent engagement of unlawful targets.
 e. List actions to prevent excessive use of force.
 f. List actions to prevent the unauthorized use of medical service symbols,
flag of truce, national emblems, and enemy insignia/uniforms.
 g. List actions to prevent unnecessary destruction and seizure of property.
 h. List actions to prevent unnecessary suffering and harm.
 i. List actions to enforce the rights and responsibilities of EPWs, and
detainees.

Evaluation Preparation:

Setup: Evaluate this task at the end of law of war training.

Brief Soldier: Tell the Soldier that he or she will be evaluated on his or her ability
to identify, understand, and comply with the law of war, including the Geneva and
Hague Conventions and the 10 Soldier's Rules. Tell the Soldier that he or she will
also be evaluated on his or her ability to identify problems or situations that
violate the law of war and take appropriate action to prevent law of war violations
do not occur.

Performance Measures	GO	NO GO
1 Identified the key elements of the law of war.	_____	_____
2 Described the responsibilities of U.S. Soldiers to obey the law of war.	_____	_____
3 Identified the basic principles of the law of war.	_____	_____
4 Identified the "10 Soldier's Rules."	_____	_____
5 Identified actions to prevent law of war violations.	_____	_____

Evaluation Guidance: Refer to chapter 1, paragraph 1-9e, (1) and (2).

References
Required: AR 27-1 and FM 27-10
Related:

191-376-5148

Search an Individual

Conditions: You are given a subject who needs to be searched, and you have authorization to search. The subject may or may not have weapons or contraband concealed on his person.

Standards: Conduct a search of the selected subject, locating weapons and contraband on the subject. Maintain control of the subject throughout the search. Determine the final course of action based on the situation and the result of the search.

Special Condition: None

Special Standards: None

Special Equipment:

Cue: None

Note: None

1. Determine which type of search to perform based on the situation.
Note: A full search of a person's body should be done by members of the same sex, but this should not prevent you from conducting a pat-down search for your safety if you suspect weapons may be involved.
2. Conduct a stand-up search with handcuffs.
    a. Direct the subject to—
        (1) Turn and face away from you.
        (2) Spread his feet until you say "Stop."
        (3) Point his toes outward.
        (4) Bring his hands behind his back with palms out and thumbs upward.
        (5) Stand still.
    b. Ensure that the assisting military police Soldier, if available, is in the correct position. The assistant military police Soldier should stand in front of the subject and to one side at a 45° angle, out of the subject's reach.
Note: You may or may not have an assistant when searching. You should always try to get another military police Soldier to assist, but you should be prepared to search without one if the situation dictates.
    c. Approach the subject cautiously, apply handcuffs, and maintain positive control of the subject throughout the search.
    d. Position yourself behind the subject and remain balanced, with your front foot forward and rear foot to the outside of the subject's feet.
    e. Search the subject's headgear.
        (1) Remove the headgear carefully.
        (2) Bend the seams of the headgear before crushing to detect hidden razor blades or similar items.
        (3) Complete the search of the headgear, and place it on the ground.
    f. Search the subject using the pat-and-crush method in the following sequence:
Note: Mentally divide the body into two parts, and repeat the search for both sides in the same sequence, overlapping areas in the center.
        (1) The head and hair.
        (2) The selected side from arm to shoulder.
        (3) The neck and collar. Bring neckwear worn by the subject to the back, and carefully look for weapons or contraband.
        (4) The selected side of the back to the waist.
        (5) The selected side of the chest to the waist.
Note: When searching females, check the bra by pulling out the center far enough to allow concealed weapons or contraband to fall out.
        (6) The waistband, from the front to the middle of the back.
            (a) Bend the material and then crush it to detect razor blades.
            (b) Check between the belt and the pants, the pants and the undergarment, and the undergarment and the skin.
        (7) The selected side of the buttocks.
Note: Squat when searching the lower half of the subject's body so you are not placed in an unbalanced position.

(8) The selected side hip, abdomen, and crotch.

(9) The selected side leg from the crotch to the top of the shoe.

(10) The selected side shoe. Check the top edge of the boot or shoe by carefully inserting a finger in the top edge to feel for weapons.

g. Reverse the position of your feet, and search the opposite side.

3. Conduct a stand-up search without handcuffs.

Note: The decision to place handcuffs on the subject before searching must be based on the situation and according to the local provost marshal office (PMO) policy. It is always safer to have the subject restrained before searching, but in some instances, you may not be authorized. Obtain guidance from your local PMO if you are unsure.

a. Direct the subject to —

(1) Raise his arms above his head, lock his elbows, and spread his fingers with palms facing you.

(2) Turn so that his back is toward you.

(3) Spread his feet apart (more than shoulder width), with his toes pointed out.

(4) Interlock his fingers and place his hands on the crown of his head.

b. Perform step 2b.

c. Position yourself for the search. Perform step 2d.

d. Search the headgear.

(1) Direct the subject to raise his interlocked hands off his head.

(2) Remove the headgear.

(3) Direct the subject to return his interlocked hands to his head.

(4) Perform step 2e(2) and step 2e(3).

e. Search the subject.

(1) Grasp two fingers of the subject's right hand, or both of the interlocked hands with your left hand. Apply pressure, and pull the subject slightly backward to keep the subject off balance.

(2) Search the subject by performing step 2f.

f. Reverse the search to the subject's opposite side.

(1) Grasp two fingers of the subject's left hand with your opposite hand or grasp the interlocked hands with both hands without releasing the subject's right fingers.

(2) Reverse the position of your feet.

(3) Search the opposite side of the subject's body in the same manner as the right side.

4. Conduct a frisk search.

a. Position the subject. Perform step 3a.

b. Perform step 2b.

c. Conduct the frisk similar to the stand-up search, except use the massaging method rather than the crushing method to locate weapons.

Note: Although the main intent of a frisk is to ensure that the subject is not carrying a weapon, other contraband found can still be used against the subject. However, be prepared to justify your actions in legal proceedings that result from the search.

(1) Conduct the frisk by searching the outside of the garments only.

(2) Do not search the subject's pockets or waistband unless the pat down suggests the presence of a weapon.

(3) Ask permission to search items that the subject is carrying, such as a purse or backpack. If given permission, search the items in a manner consistent with looking for weapons. If the subject refuses permission to search the items, or if you are unsure if you are authorized to search these items, contact the military police desk sergeant for further guidance.

(4) Stop the search if a weapon is found, and take whatever measures necessary for your safety before continuing the search.

5. Conduct a prone search.

a. Position the subject.

(1) Command the subject to face you, to raise his arms above his head, lock his elbows, and spread his fingers with the palms facing you.

(2) Visually check the subject's hands for evidence of weapons.

(3) Order the subject to turn around and drop to his knees.

(4) Search the back of the subject's hands for evidence of weapons.

(5) Direct the subject to lie on his stomach, extend his arms straight out to the sides with the palms up, and place his forehead on the ground.

(6) Tell the subject to spread his/her legs as far as possible, turn his/her feet outward, and keep his/her heels in contact with the ground.

Note: Positioning the subject as described is dependent upon the subject following your directions. If the subject refuses, you may have to take his/her to the ground using physical force or whatever alternate use of force is authorized by your PMO.

b. Ensure that the assistant, if available, is in front of and to one side of the subject, opposite the side that is to be searched first.

c. Apply the handcuffs.

(1) Approach the front of the subject at about a 45° angle.

(2) Squat and place your knee that is nearest the subject between his/her shoulder blades.

(3) Direct the subject to put the arm nearest you, behind him/her, with the palm facing up.

(4) Grasp the subject's hand in a handshake hold and put the first handcuff on it.

(5) Hold the handcuff chain along with the belt or waistband of the subject's trousers, direct the subject to put his other hand behind him, with the palm facing out, and apply the other handcuff.

d. Search the subject.

Note: Refer to the note of step 1 in reference to searching members of the opposite sex.

(1) Hold the chain between the handcuffs, and lift the subject's arms slightly. Search the area in the small of the back and any area the subject can reach. Release the chain and stand.

(2) Move to the area of the subject's waist and face the subject's head. Squat, but do not rest your knee on the ground or on the subject. Pivot, if required to conduct the rest of the search.

(3) Remove the subject's headgear.

(a) Bend the seams before crushing to determine if razor blades or similar devices are hidden.

(b) Place the headgear on the floor or ground.

(4) Search the subject's head and hair.

(5) Search the subject from fingers to shoulders. Search the collar and neck area (pull any neckwear to the subject's back), and remove anything that could be used as a weapon.

(6) Search the subject's back from shoulder to waist on the side nearest you.

(7) Grasp the inside of the subject's closest elbow, and pull the subject toward his side, just high enough to search the front without the subject being completely placed on his side. Then, search the front from shoulder to waist. Check the bra area on female subjects.

(8) Switch hands while controlling the subject's elbow without changing position.

(9) Search the subject from waist to knee, including the crotch.

(10) Return the subject to the facedown position, and release the elbow. Remind the subject to keep his feet spread and his heels on the floor.

(11) Tell the subject to raise his foot by bending at the knee.

(12) Grasp the subject's foot, and search from the knee up. Check the top of the footwear by inserting a finger in the top edge and feeling for evidence of weapons. You must also check the edges and soles.

(13) Tell the subject to put his foot back down.

(14) Stand and move to the subject's unsearched side. Move around the subject's head, but do not walk between the subject and the assistant military police Soldier.

(15) Ensure that the assistant moves to the side opposite of the side being searched.

(16) Squat beside the subject, with your body facing the same direction as the subject's head.

(17) Complete the search of the unsearched side using the same method.

(18) Help the subject stand once the search is complete by turning him onto his side facing away from you. Have him bring his knees up to his chest. Grasp his arms, and assist the subject to his knees and then to his feet.

6. Determine the next course of action based on the situation, the result of the search, and/or directions given by the military police desk sergeant or your supervisor.

Evaluation Preparation:

Setup: Provide the Soldier with the items listed in the conditions. Provide a scenario that requires a subject to be searched. Have a role player play the part of the subject. Provide weapons and/or contraband for the role player to conceal on his person. Provide a role player to act as an assistant (not required to test the task).

Brief Soldier: Tell the Soldier to determine the type of search to perform based on the scenario given or directions from the evaluator. Tell the Soldier to perform all of the steps of the search unless otherwise directed. Tell the role players to follow all directions given by the Soldier.

Performance Measures	GO	NO GO
1 Determined which type of search to perform based on the situation.	_____	_____
2 Conducted a stand-up search with handcuffs.	_____	_____
3 Conducted a stand-up search without handcuffs.	_____	_____
4 Conducted a frisk search.	_____	_____
5 Conducted a prone search.	_____	_____
6 Determined the next course of action based on the situation, the result of the search, and/or directions given by the military police desk sergeant or the supervisor.	_____	_____

Evaluation Guidance: Refer to chapter 1, paragraph 1-9e, (1) and (2).

References
Required: FM 3-19.13
Related:

301-CAT-1001

See Yourself Culturally

Conditions: In an operational environment, where a Soldier is required to determine their own cultural motivators.

Standards: Identify the cultural motivators that affect their interactions and understanding of others.

Special Condition: None

Special Standards: None

Special Equipment:

Cue: None

Note: None

Performance Steps

1. State the key concepts within the definition of culture.

Note: Members of a culture often do not question their culture; instead, it just "is." Understanding what culture is and who you are is very important to operating in today's world. Culture is a system of rules and regulations that guide our lives, both personally and publicly. The Army defines culture as "The set of distinctive features of a society or group, including but not limited to values, beliefs, and norms that ties togther memberrs of that society or group and that drives action and behavior."

Addtional aspects or characteristics of culture are:

(1) Culture is shared; there is no "culture of one."

(2) Culture is patterned, meaning that people in a group or society live and think in ways forming definitive, repeating patterns.

(3) Culture is changeable, through social interactions between people and groups.

(4) Culture is internalized, in the sense that it is habitual, taken for granted, and perceived as "natural" by people within the group or society.

(5) Culture is learned.

(6) The distinctive features that describe a particular culture include its myths and legends.

2. Identify domains that shape culture.

Note: When defining culture, it is important for a Soldier to remember that culture is not static. There are many factors that will influence and shape a culture. Understanding these factors will allow you to gain understanding of a culture-who they are and what they care about. You can integrate this information into military mission planning, build a greater rapport with the people in your area of operations, and improve decision-making. By fully understanding how family/kinship, religion/sprituality, sex/gender, politics/social relations, economics/resources, time/space, language/communication, technology/material culture, history/myth, aesthetics/recreation/sustenance, and learning/knowledge affect the people, we can ensure that we have a full understanding of the culture.

3. Identify effect of bias on interpersonal interactions.

Note: Effective communications between individuals, even between cultures, relies on the communicants knowing the answer to these three questions: How do I see me? How do I see you? and How do you see me? In cross-cultural communications, the third question is much more important than the other two. A Soldier's bias effects how they communicate.

4. Identify cultural considerations effecting communication.

Note: The characteristics of a culture can influence a great many things. When we are dealing with other cultures, the characteristics of our culture AND their culture will surely influence how we and they think, our interactions, communication styles and objectives.

Evaluation Preparation:

None

Performance Measures	GO	NO GO
1 Stated the key concepts within the definition of culture.	_____	_____
2 Identified domains that shape culture.	_____	_____
3 Identified effects of bias on interpersonal interactions.	_____	_____
4 Identified cultural considerations effecting communications.	_____	_____

Evaluation Guidance: None

References
Required: ADP 3-0, FM 3-06, FM 3-07, FM 3-24, and ADP 7-0
Related:

150-SRT-0001

Develop Professionally

Conditions: While serving on or off duty in a military organization.

Standards: Develop professionally throughout your career and daily activities.

Special Condition: None

Special Standards: None

Special Equipment: None

Cue: None

Note: None

1. Continue to inculcate the Army Values and Warrior Ethos.

Explanation: Army Values are the basic building blocks of a Soldier's character. They help Soldiers judge what is right or wrong in any situation. Army Values form the very identity of the Army, the solid rock on which everything else stands, especially in combat. They are the glue that binds together the members of a noble profession. The Warrior Ethos describes the frame of mind of the professional Soldier. It proclaims the selfless commitment to the Nation, mission, unit, and fellow Soldiers that all Soldiers espouse. When internalized, it produces the will to win. The Army Values and Warrior Ethos are mutually dependent. A Soldier cannot follow one while ignoring the other. Together they guide the personal conduct of every Soldier.

2. Live the Soldier's Creed.

Explanation: The Soldier's Creed captures the spirit of being a Soldier and the dedication Soldiers feel to something greater than themselves. It outlines the fundamental obligations of Soldiers to their fellow Soldiers, their unit, and the Army. In fact, the Soldier's Creed extends beyond service as a Soldier; it includes commitment to Family and society. It begins with an affirmation of who Soldiers are and what they do. The Creed also entails the four tenets of the Warrior Ethos.

The Soldier's Creed

I am an American Soldier.
I am a Warrior and a member of a team. I serve the people
of the United States and live the Army Values.
I will always place the mission first.
I will never accept defeat.
I will never quit.
I will never leave a fallen comrade.
I am disciplined, physically and mentally tough, trained, and
proficient in my warrior tasks and drills.
I always maintain my arms, my equipment, and myself.
I am an expert and I am a professional.
I stand ready to deploy, engage, and destroy
The enemies of the United States of America in close combat.
I am a guardian of freedom and the American way of life.
I am an American Soldier.

3. Develop and expand moral character with each new experience and assignment.

Explanation: Members of the Army must continually evaluate and develop their moral qualities throughout their career. A Soldier's character is made up from the seven core values of loyalty, duty, respect, selfless service, honor, integrity, and personal courage. Becoming a person of character is a career long process involving day-to-day experience, education, self-development, developmental counseling, coaching, and mentoring. Soldiers should always remember that doing the right thing is critical. Doing the right thing for the right reason and with the right motive is even better.

4. Strive for excellence within your specialty as you increase in rank and responsibility.

Explanation: Soldiers are expected to be students of their military occupational specialty. The aforementioned is accomplished in part by; attending formal military and civilian schooling throughout your career; seeking additional responsibility; and assisting peers and subordinates without being asked. Soldiers show their commitment to the Army and their specialty by willingly performing their duties at all times and subordinating their personal welfare to that of others without expecting reward or recognition. Interpersonal, conceptual, technical, and tactical skills constitute what a leader must KNOW. Army leadership demands competence in a diverse range of human activities that expand in complexity in positions of greater responsibility.

Evaluation Preparation:

None

Performance Measures	GO	NO GO
1 Continued to inculcate the Army Values and Warrior Ethos.	_____	_____
2 Know and lives the Soldier's Creed.	_____	_____
3 Developed and expanded their moral character with each new experience and assignment.	_____	_____
4 Strived for excellence within their specialty and as he/she increased in rank and responsibility.	_____	_____

Evaluation Guidance: None

References
Required:
Related:

150-SRT-0002

Develop in the five Dimensions of Comprehensive Soldier Fitness

Conditions: You are a Soldier in a military organization serving both on and off duty. You have AKO access for the GAT and Comprehensive Resilience Modules, a unit Resilience training program, a unit Physical Readiness Training (PRT) program, and AR 350-1, TC 3-22.20, and AR 600-9.

Standards: Develop in the five dimensions of comprehensive Soldier fitness: Physical, Emotional, Social, Spiritual, and Family (Build Resilience).

Special Condition: None

Special Standards: None

Special Equipment: None

Cue: None

Note: None

Performance Steps

1. Physical. Maintain physical readiness; excel in physical activities that require strength, endurance, and mobility.
   a. Participate in collective or individual PRT sessions for 60-90 minutes, four to five times per week IAW AR 350-1 and TC 3-22.20.
   b. Pass the APFT and strive to achieve the Army Physical Fitness Badge (APFB) with a score of 270 points or higher.
   c. Meet Army HT/WT and/or body composition standards IAW AR 600-9.
   d. Participate in off-duty leisure/recreational activities that enhance physical readiness.
   e. Strive to maintain a healthy diet by employing appropriate Soldier fueling practices.
2. Emotional: Approach challenges in a positive, optimistic way.
   a. Complete mandatory on-line comprehensive resilience modules on the Emotional dimension based on GAT performance.
   b. Actively participate in unit resilience training.
   c. Keep an optimistic mental approach.
   d. Decrease anxiety by learning to put it in perspective; avoid catastrophic thinking and, don't dwell on irrational, worst-case outcomes of a situation.
   e. Learn to maintain composure and increase effectiveness in challenging

situations through the use of real-time resilience.

3. Social: Build and maintain trusted and valued relationships.

a. Complete mandatory on-line comprehensive resilience modules on the social dimension based on GAT performance.

b. Actively participate in unit resilience training.

c. Communicate effectively with peers, family members, and leaders through the use of assertive communication.

d. Build connection by developing active constructive responding skills; show authentic interest and ask your family, friends, and battle buddies to elaborate on their positive experiences. Avoid passive constructive, active Destructive, and passive destructive responses.

e. Share positive experiences with family, friends, and battle buddies.

4. Spiritual: Strengthen beliefs, principals, and values that sustain a person beyond Family, institutional, and societal sources of strength.

a. Complete mandatory on-line comprehensive resilience modules on the spiritual dimension based on GAT performance.

b. Actively participate in unit resilience training.

c. Hunt the good stuff; learn to look for the positive experiences and not dwell on the negative.

d. Develop gratitude: notice and appreciate something you receive and express thanks for it.

e. Know what matters; what is meaningful and important in your life.

f. Believe in a higher purpose; something that transcends your family, career, and society; and gives your life meaning.

g. Build spiritual resilience through exercising your faith on a daily basis.

h. Develop positive relationships and be part of a community.

i. Practice relaxation and energy management through deep breathing, prayer, or meditation.

5. Family: Grow daily as part of the Army and supportive family unit: identify issues and help other Soldiers as needed.

a. Complete mandatory on-line comprehensive resilience modules on the family dimension based on GAT performance.

b. Actively participate in unit resilience training.

c. Develop effective communication skills; become an assertive communicator; and remain confident, calm, clear and controlled in all conversations. Refrain from using an aggressive or passive communication style.

d. Learn to deal with trust and insecurity issues with family, friends, and battle buddies. Employ the gentle start-up method to improve communication: talk about what you feel, describe the situation in neutral terms, and talk about what you need.

e. Develop conflict resolution skills: work to remain calm and logical during disagreements, respect and value yourself and your spouse, learn to compromise, focus on the positive, ask for what you want, and learn to let go.

f. Spend quality time and develop strong emotional connections with Family, friends, and battle buddies.

g. Actively participate in your unit family readiness group (FRG) and installation Family and Morale, Welfare and Recreation (FMWR) and Better Opportunities for Single Soldiers (BOSS) programs as appropriate.

h. Go to your local Army Community Service (ACS) office to obtain access to additional services as needed.

Evaluation Preparation:

None

Performance Measures	GO	NO GO
1 Maintained physical readiness	___	___
2 Approached challenges in a positive, optimistic way	___	___
3 Built and maintain trusted, valued relationships	___	___
4 Strengthened beliefs, principles, and values	___	___
5 Grew daily as part of the Army and supportive Family unit; identified issues and helped other Soldiers as needed	___	___

Evaluation Guidance: None

References
Required: AR 350-1, AR 600-9, and TC 3-22.20
Related:

071-COM-0801

Challenge Persons Entering Your Area

Conditions: You are a member of a squad or team providing security for your unit in a field environment. You have your assigned weapon, individual protective equipment, and the current challenge and password. An unknown person or persons is approaching your area.

Standards: Detect and challenge all approaching personnel; prevent compromise of password; allow personnel positively identified as friendly to pass; and disarm, detain and report personnel not positively identified.

Special Condition: None

Special Standards: None

Special Equipment:

Cue: None

Note: None

Performance Steps

1. Detect all personnel entering your area.
2. Challenge an individual that enters your area.
   a. Cover the individual with your weapon without disclosing your position.
   b. Command the individual to "HALT" before they are close enough to pose a threat.
Note: Commands and questions must be loud enough to be heard by the individual but not loud enough that others outside of the immediate area can hear. Commands should be repeated as necessary.
   c. Ask "WHO IS THERE?" just loud enough for the individual to hear.
Note: The individual should reply with an answer that best describes them, example "Sergeant Jones."
   d. Order the individual to "ADVANCE TO BE RECOGNIZED."
   e. Continue to keep individual covered without exposing yourself.
   f. Order the individual to "HALT" when they are is within 2 to 3 meters from your position.
Note: The individual should be halted at a location that provides protection to you and prevents them from escaping if they are deemed unfriendly.
   g. Issue the challenge in a low voice.
Note: The challenge should only be heard by the individual challenged to prevent all others from overhearing. You may also ask the individual questions that only a friendly person should be able answer correctly.
   h. Determine if the individual is friendly based upon their return of the correct password and your own situational awareness.
      (1) Allow the individual to pass if the individual returns the correct password and you are convinced the individual is friendly.
      (2) Detain an individual if they return an incorrect password or cannot be positively identified as friendly.
         (a) Direct the individual to disarm.
         (b) Notify your chain of command.

(c) Await instruction from your command.

3. Challenge a group that enters your area.

Note: These procedure and precautions are similar to those for challenging a single person.

a. Cover the group with your weapon without disclosing your position.

b. Order the group to halt before they are close enough to pose a threat to you.

c. Command "WHO IS THERE?" just loud enough to be heard by the group.

d. Wait for reply from group.

Note: Reply should clearly identify group, example "Friendly Patrol."

e. Order the leader of the group to "ADVANCE TO BE RECOGNIZED".

f. Continue to keep group leader covered without exposing yourself.

g. Order the group leader to "HALT" when the individual is within 2 to 3 meters from your position.

Note: The group leader should be halted at a location that provides protection to you and prevents the leader from escaping if they are deemed unfriendly.

h. Issue the challenge to only the group leader.

Note: You may also ask questions that only a friendly person should be able to answer correctly.

i. Determine if the group leader is friendly based upon their return of the correct password and your own situational awareness.

(1) Direct the group leader to remain with you to assist in identifying group members, if you determine he/she is friendly.

(a) Direct the group leader to vouch for or positively identify each member of his group as they pass to your flank.

(b) Detain any individual in the group not recognized by the group leader by disarming them, and having them wait until your chain of command provides additional instructions.

(2) Detain the group leader, if not positively identified as friendly.

(a) Direct the individual to disarm.

(b) Direct him/her to inform their group to wait.

(c) Notify your chain of command.

(d) Await instruction from your chain of command.

Evaluation Preparation:

Setup: Provide the Soldier with the equipment and or materials described in the conditions statement.

Brief Soldier: Tell the Soldier what is expected of him by reviewing the task standards. Stress to the Soldier the importance of observing all cautions, warnings, and dangers to avoid injury to personnel and, if applicable, damage to equipment.

Performance Measures	GO	NO GO
1 Detected all personnel entering your area.	_____	_____
2 Challenged all individuals that entered your area.	_____	_____
3 Challenged all groups that entered your area.	_____	_____

Evaluation Guidance: None

References
Required:
Related: FM 22-6 and FM 3-21.75

071-COM-0815

Practice Noise, Light, and Litter Discipline

Conditions: You are member of a mounted or dismounted element conducting a tactical mission and have been directed to comply with noise, light and litter discipline. Enemy elements are in your area of operation.

Standards: Prevent enemy from locating your element by exercising noise, light, and litter discipline at all times.

Special Condition: None

Special Standards: None

Special Equipment:

Cue: None

Note: None

Performance Steps

    1. Exercise noise discipline.

       a. Avoid all unnecessary vehicular and foot movement.

       b. Secure (with tape or other materials) metal parts (for example, weapon slings, canteen cups, identification [ID] tags) to prevent them from making noise during movement.

Note: Do not obstruct the moving parts of weapons or vehicles.

    c. Avoid all unnecessary talk.

    d. Use radio only when necessary.

    e. Set radio volume low so that only you can hear.

    f. Use visual techniques to communicate.

  2. Exercise light discipline.

    a. Do not smoke.

Note: The smoking of cigarettes, cigars, etc., can be seen and smelled by the enemy.

    b. Conceal flashlights and other light sources so that the light is filtered (for example, under a poncho).

    c. Cover or blacken anything that reflects light (for example, metal surfaces, vehicles, glass).

    d. Conceal vehicles and equipment with available natural camouflage.

  3. Exercise litter discipline.

    a. Establish a litter collection point (empty food containers, empty ammunition cans or boxes, old camouflage) when occupying a position.

    b. Verify all litter has been collected in preparation to leaving a position.

    c. Take all litter with you when leaving a position.

Evaluation Preparation:

Setup: Provide the Soldier with the equipment and or materials described in the conditions statement.

Brief Soldier: Tell the Soldier what is expected of him by reviewing the task standards. Stress to the Soldier the importance of observing all cautions, warnings, and dangers to avoid injury to personnel and, if applicable, damage to equipment.

Performance Measures	GO	NO GO
1 Exercised noise discipline.	_____	_____
2 Exercised light discipline.	_____	_____
3 Exercised litter discipline.	_____	_____

Evaluation Guidance: None

References
Required:
Related: ATTP 3-34.39

191-376-5216

Search a Vehicle for Explosive Devices or Prohibited Items at an Installation Access Control Point

Conditions: You are on duty at the vehicle search lane of an installation access control point. You are given a vehicle to search in a well-lit area, a search mirror, a flashlight, a reflective vest, the local standing operating procedure (SOP), personnel in the vehicles, possible explosive devices and/or prohibited items, and a directive to search the identified vehicle for suspected explosive devices or prohibited items. Some iterations of this task should be performed in MOPP.

Standards: Search the identified vehicle interior, exterior, and undercarriage finding all explosive devices and/or prohibited items or clearing the vehicle.

Special Condition: None

Special Standards: None

Special Equipment:

Cue: None

Note: None

Performance Steps

    1. Stop the vehicle by using hand-and-arm signals.

DANGER

Always position yourself so that you are highly visible to traffic, and wear a reflective vest. Never step into the path of an approaching vehicle to direct movement or to stop a vehicle. Failure to comply may cause permanent injury or death.

    2. Direct the driver to turn off the engine and apply the parking brake.

    3. Interview the driver and vehicle occupants.

       a. Identify yourself to the driver and occupants.

       b. Inform the driver that the vehicle must be searched as a condition for entry onto the installation.

c. Identify each occupant by physically taking possession of and looking at a military or Department of Defense (DOD) identification (ID) card, state driver's license, or other form of state or federal government-issued photo ID; and compare the photo to the person.

Note: Notify the supervisor and the military police if the photo does not match the person being identified or if the ID shows signs of tampering.

d. Request to see the—

(1) Vehicle registration.

(2) Proof of vehicle insurance.

Note: Notify the supervisor and the military police if the documentation you are being shown is not valid.

(3) Logbook or itinerary and the manifest, shipping papers, or bill of lading for commercial vehicles.

e. Determine why the driver and occupants need access to the installation. Ask questions such as—

(1) Where are you going?

(2) Who are you going to meet?

(3) Do you drive this vehicle most of the time?

(4) Are there contraband or prohibited items in this vehicle?

(5) Has this vehicle been repaired recently? If so, what was repaired?

(6) What is the cargo being transported? Did you watch it being loaded? Do you normally operate this particular vehicle?

f. Maintain eye contact with the driver throughout the interview, and report suspicious behavior to the supervisor.

g. Notify the supervisor and the military police if the driver appears to be impaired from alcohol or drug use or if suspected prohibited items are in plain view during the interview.

4. Direct occupants to exit the vehicle.

a. Direct the driver to open interior compartment doors, the hood, the trunk, and rear doors.

b. Direct occupants to move to a designated safe area (about 5 meters from the vehicle and out of the flow of traffic) where they can be observed.

5. Identify the type of commercial vehicle being searched if applicable.

Note: There are numerous types of commercial vehicles. For example, a tractor trailer and a garbage truck are different and have different characteristics. Each type of commercial vehicle has its own unique "hot spots" or areas that need to be checked.

6. Search the undercarriage of the vehicle.

a. Use a flashlight and a mirror to carefully inspect under the vehicle.

b. Check for new frame welds, items taped or attached to the frame, an unusual-looking muffler, a fresh undercoating, or signs of recent component installations (fuel tanks, mufflers, other items).

7. Search the exterior of the vehicle.

a. Check for explosive devices or prohibited items while searching the exterior of the vehicle. Look for—

(1) Anything unusual in factory-built compartments.

(2) New or shiny bolts and screws.

(3) Unusual scratches, possibly made by screwdrivers, wrenches, or similar tools.

(4) Signs of tampering, such as broken parts or bent sheet metal.

(5) Unusually clean or dirty components and areas.

(6) Wire or tape stored in the vehicle.

(7) New or broken welds.

(8) Greasy or oily fingerprints in otherwise clean areas.

(9) Fresh bodywork (fresh fiberglass, fresh paint).

(10) Fresh wiring and electrical tape.

(11) New caulk.

(12) A missing or altered vehicle identification number.

(13) False compartments that are not part of the vehicle design.

DANGER

Remove rings, necklaces, other jewelry, and loose clothing. Ensure that the engine is off and the parking brake is set before beginning the inspection. Failure to comply may cause permanent injury or death.

b. Check the exterior front. Look for—

(1) Nonoperational headlights.

(2) A modified front grill or false compartment.

(3) No access to the front bumper cavity.

c. Check exterior sides. Look for—

(1) Compartments, new welds, taped items, or fresh paint on the front fender wells.

(2) Doors that feel heavy when swung.

(3) Foreign items in the gas tank tube.

Note: The driver opens the gas tank for inspection.

DANGER

Do not inhale toxic agents while searching vehicle gas tank tubes. Failure to comply may cause permanent injury or death.

d. Check tires. Look for—

(1) New tires.

(2) Tires with a solid sound.

(3) Strange odors from air valves.

(4) Unusually clean or dirty lug nuts or hubcaps.

e. Check the exterior rear. Look for—

(1) Nonoperational taillights.

(2) No access to the rear bumper cavity.

f. Check the tailgate if applicable. Look for—

(1) An unusually heavy tailgate.

(2) Fresh paint or body filler.

(3) Inconsistent or nonhollow sounds when tapped.

g. Check the pickup bed if applicable. Look for—

(1) Inconsistent or nonhollow sounds when tapped.

(2) Fresh paint or body filler.

(3) An unusually thick floor.

    (4) Unusual welds or seams.

    (5) Caulk.

  h. Check the cargo area if applicable. Look for—

    (1) Fresh paint or body filler.

    (2) An inconsistent or nonhollow sound when tapped.

    (3) An unusually thick floor.

    (4) A false ceiling.

    (5) Caulk or glue.

    (6) A strange smell.

8. Search the engine compartment. Check for—

  a. A large battery box or extra battery.

  b. Odd or clean wires.

  c. Larger components (air cleaners, fan blade shrouds).

WARNING

Do not place your hands near the fan blades while conducting a search. Some vehicles are equipped with an automatic cooling system that may cause the fan blades to start operating after the ignition switch is turned off. Failure to comply may cause personal injury.

---

  d. Unusual odors which indicate that containers may contain fuel.

  e. Foreign objects in the air filter cavity.

  f. Freshly painted areas, new welds, shiny bolts, or sheet metal work on firewalls.

  g. A clean engine in a dirty car.

  h. A hood that feels heavy when it is opened and closed. (Instruct the driver to open the hood, but move the hood up and down yourself.)

  i. A false wall or modified fender compartment.

  j. Clean or wiped areas.

9. Search the trunk compartment if applicable. Check for—

  a. A new trunk mat or carpet.

  b. Caulk, glue, or strange smells.

  c. A trunk lid that feels heavy when it is opened and closed.

  d. A raised floor.

  e. Strange odors from the spare tire.

  f. Nonhollow or inconsistent sounds in the walls.

  g. An unusual space between the back seat and trunk wall.

  h. A spare tire that is not flush with the floor.

10. Search the interior of the vehicle.

  a. Search the dash. Look for—

    (1) Nonworking electrical components. Check to see if the light-emitting diode is on when the vehicle power is off.

    (2) New, damaged, or scratched screws.

    (3) Plugged air vents.

    (4) Broken or missing blowers.

  b. Look for a false compartment in the glove box.

  c. Look for unusual lumps or bulges in the front and rear seats.

   d. Feel for rigid front and rear seats.

   e. Look for a false or modified ceiling.

   f. Look for an unusually thick floor.

   g. Look for stress cracks in the windshield.

11. Take action when the search reveals suspected explosive devices or other prohibited items in the vehicle.

   a. Search for explosive devices.

      (1) Do not attempt to handle or disarm suspected explosive devices.

      (2) Suspend radio and cellular telephone traffic for 100 meters around the vehicle.

      (3) Secure the driver and occupants of the vehicle, and notify the supervisor and military police.

      (4) Immediately evacuate the surrounding area.

      (5) Secure the scene until it is cleared by explosive ordnance disposal (EOD) personnel or until you are properly relieved.

      (6) Release the driver, occupants, and collected documentation and identification to the supervisor or military police.

   b. Search for prohibited items.

      (1) Do not handle prohibited items unless you are ordered to do so by the supervisor or military police.

      (2) Notify the supervisor and military police.

      (3) Secure the driver and occupants of the vehicle.

      (4) Secure the scene until it is cleared by the supervisor or until you are properly relieved.

      (5) Release the driver, occupants, and collected documentation and identification to the supervisor or military police.

12. Release the driver and occupants if no explosive devices or other prohibited items are found or if suspected items are cleared by the military police or EOD personnel.

   a. Give ID cards and gathered documentation to the driver.

   b. Help the driver safely enter the flow of traffic.

Evaluation Preparation: *Setup*: Provide the Soldier with the items listed in the conditions. Identify role players as a driver and an occupant for the vehicle. Ensure that role players are authorized to operate the vehicle before beginning the task. Instruct role players to comply with instructions given by the Soldier searching the vehicle. Have role players place a dummy explosive device or dummy prohibited item somewhere in, under, or on the vehicle to be searched before the Soldiers arrive to test. The dummy explosive device or dummy prohibited item can be handmade. It should not be so large that it gains immediate discovery or so small that it cannot be detected by a highly motivated Soldier conducting a reasonable search.

Brief Soldier: Tell the Soldier that an armed partner is pulling overwatch security through the duration of the task. The tester will act as the supervisor and the military police. Identify the vehicle that you want the Soldier to search, and tell the Soldier to conduct the task according to the performance steps. Tell the Soldier that the vehicle has a role player driver and a role player occupant and that both role players will respond to his instructions.

Performance Measures	GO	NO GO
1 Stopped the vehicle by using hand-and-arm signals.	_____	_____
2 Directed the driver to turn off the engine and apply the parking brake.	_____	_____
3 Interviewed the driver and vehicle occupants.	_____	_____
4 Directed occupants to exit the vehicle.	_____	_____
5 Identified the type of commercial vehicle being searched if applicable.	_____	_____
6 Searched the undercarriage of the vehicle.	_____	_____
7 Searched the exterior of the vehicle.	_____	_____
8 Searched the engine compartment.	_____	_____
9 Searched the trunk compartment if applicable.	_____	_____
10 Searched the interior of the vehicle.	_____	_____
11 Took action when the search revealed suspected explosive devices or prohibited items in the vehicle.	_____	_____

Performance Measures	GO	NO GO
12 Released the driver and occupants if no explosive devices or other prohibited items were found or if suspected items were cleared by military police or EOD personnel.	_____	_____

Evaluation Guidance: Evaluation Guidance: None

References
Required:
Related: AR 190-13, AR 525-13, ATTP 3-39.10, and ATTP 3-39.32

191-405-0087

Search a Vehicle

Conditions: You have probable cause or have been directed to search a vehicle. You are given a locally produced "consent-to-search" waiver; Department of the Army (DA) Forms 2823 (Sworn Statement), 3975 (Military Police Report), and 4137 (Evidence/Property Custody Document); an occupied vehicle; and an improvised mirror device.

Standards: Perform all steps to conduct a lawful search of a vehicle, identify and collect all contraband and/or evidence, and ensure the proper disposition of the individuals.

Special Condition: None

Special Standards: None

Special Equipment: None

Cue: None

Note: None

Performance Steps
1. Stop the vehicle.
2. Inform the occupants of the reason for the search.
3. Request a consent to search, if needed.
   a. Prepare a "consent-to-search" waiver and have the driver sign it.
   b. Identify the occupants by looking at their driver's licenses or identification (ID) cards.

    c. Ask the occupants to get out of the vehicle.

    d. Direct the occupants to move to a place about 5 meters from the vehicle and out of the flow of traffic where they can be watched.

  4. Search the vehicle.

    a. Search the inside of the vehicle to include--

      (1) Behind and under the seat.

      (2) Under the dashboard.

      (3) The glove and tool compartment.

      (4) Above the sun visor.

    b. Search the exterior of the vehicle, in sequence, to include--

      (1) The left front-fender well and behind the wheel.

      (2) Under the front bumper and behind and underneath the grill.

      (3) Under the hood. Raise the hood and check all areas behind the radiator and around the engine.

      (4) The right front-fender well and behind the wheel.

      (5) Underneath the right side of the body, back to and including the right rear-fender well, and behind the wheel.

      (6) Inside cargo areas and trunk.

      (7) Under and behind the rear bumper.

      (8) The left rear-fender well and behind the wheel.

      (9) Underneath the left side of the body, back to left front-fender well.

      (10) The top of the vehicle.

Note: Use an improvised mirror device to search the undercarriage as well as areas that are difficult to see.

  5. Use a mirror device to search underneath the vehicle. Refer to Figure 191-405-0087-1.

  6. Performed the following procedures when--

    a. A consent to search was needed, but was not given.

      (1) Repeat steps 3b through 3d.

      (2) Have the driver move the vehicle so that it does not block the flow of traffic and lock it.

      (3) Contact the desk sergeant who will call the military magistrate's judge's office for authority to search.

      (4) Release the vehicle to the driver, and thank him for cooperating if authority to search the vehicle is not obtained. Help the driver reenter the flow of traffic.

    b. Authority to search the vehicle is obtained. Return to the vehicle and search it according to step 4.

  7. Release the vehicle to the driver and help him to reenter the flow of traffic if prohibited items are not found in the vehicle.

  8. Apprehend the offender, and transport him to the military police (MP) station when prohibited items are found in the vehicle and the offender is military.

  9. Apprehend the offender, transport him to the MP station, and notify civilian authorities when prohibited items are found in the vehicle and the offender is not military.

10. Complete DA Form 3975 Military Police Report and DA Form 4137 Evidence/Property Custody Document.
11. Advise the offender of his rights before questioning him.
12. Take the offender's statement on DA Form 2823, Sworn Statement.
13. Dispose of prohibited items as directed by your supervisor.

Evaluation Preparation:

Setup: Provide a vehicle and someone to act as a driver.

Brief soldier: Remind the soldier of the necessity to use interpersonal communications skills. Tell him to be firm, but courteous.

Performance Measures	GO	NO GO
1 Stopped the vehicle.	_____	_____
2 Informed the occupants of the reason for the search.	_____	_____
3 Received a consent to search.	_____	_____
4 Searched the vehicle.	_____	_____
5 Used a mirror device to search underneath the vehicle.	_____	_____
6 Performed the required procedures when a consent to search a vehicle was needed, but was not given and when the authority to search a vehicle was obtained.	_____	_____
7 Released the vehicle to the driver and helped him to reenter the flow of traffic if prohibited items were not found in the vehicle.	_____	_____
8 Apprehended the offender and transported him to the MP station when prohibited items were found in the vehicle and the offender was military.	_____	_____

Performance Measures	GO	NO GO
9 Apprehended the offender, transported him to the MP station, and notified civilian authorities when prohibited items were found in the vehicle and the offender was not military.	____	____
10 Completed DA Form 3975 Military Police Report and DA Form 4137 Evidence/Property/Custody Document.	____	____
11 Advised the offender of his rights before questioning him.	____	____
12 Took the offender's statement on DA Form 2823 Sworn Statement.	____	____
13 Disposed of prohibited items as directed by your supervisor.	____	____

Evaluation Guidance: Evaluation Guidance: Evaluation Guidance: None

References
Required: ATTP 3-39.10, DA Form 2823, DA Form 3975, and DA Form 4137
Related:

APPENDIX A

Battle Drills

React to Contact:

071-COM-0502 Move Under Direct Fire
071-100-0030 Engage Targets with an M16 Series Rifle/M4 Series Carbine
071-326-0608 Use Visual Signaling Techniques
113-571-1022 Perform Voice Communications
071-326-0503 Move Over, Through, or Around Obstacles (Except Minefields)
071-COM-0510 React to Indirect Fire while Dismounted
071-326-3002 React to Indirect Fire while Mounted
071-410-0002 React to direct Fire while Mounted
071-326-0513 Select Temporary Fighting Positions
071-COM-0501 Move as a Member of a Fire Team
071-COM-4407 Employ Hand Grenades

Establish Security:

071-COM-0801 Challenge Persons Entering your Area (Moved to Survive)
071-COM-1004 Perform Duty as a Guard (Moved to Survive)
191-376-4114 Control Entry to and from a Restricted Area
191-376-5140 Search a Vehicle for Explosive Devices or Prohibited Items as an Installation Access Control Point
071-COM-0815 Practice Noise and Light Discipline (moved to survive)
191-376-5151 Control Access to a Military Installation
113-587-2070 Operate SINCGARS Single-Channel (SC)
113-571-1022 Perform Voice Communications
171-COM-4079 Send a Situation Report (SITREP)
071-COM-4080 Send a Spot Report (SPOTREP)
071-326-0513 Select Temporary Fighting Positions
071-326-0608 Use Visual Signaling Techniques

Perform Actions as a Member of a Convoy:

551-001-1042 Dismount a Vehicle
551-001-1043 React to Vehicle Rollover
551-001-1041 Establish Security while Mounted
551-001-1040 Perform 5/25/200 Meter Scan
551-88M-1658 Prepare Vehicle for Convoy Operations
113-571-1022 Perform Voice Communications

Evacuate a Casualty:

081-COM-0101 Request Medical Evacuation
081-COM-1003 Perform First Aid to Clear an Object stuck in the Throat of a Conscious Casualty
081-COM-1005 Perform First Aid to Prevent or Control Shock
081-COM-1023 Perform First Aid to Restore Breathing and/or Pulse
081-COM-1032 Perform First Aid for Bleeding and/or Severed Extremity
081-831-1051 Transport a Casualty using a Military Vehicle
081-COM-1046 Transport a Causality
081-COM-1007 Perform First Aid for Burns
113-571-1022 Perform Voice Communications

React to Ambush:

Near-

052-192-1271 Identify Visual Indicators of an IED
052-192-1270 React to an IED Attack
071-COM-0006 React to Man-To-Man Contact
071-COM-0030 Engage Targets with M4/M16 Rifle
071-COM-4407 Employ Hand Grenades
071-COM-0501 Move as a Member of a Team
071-COM-0502 Move Under Direct Fire
071-COM-0513 Select Temporary Fighting Positions
071-326-0608 Use Visual Signal Techniques
113-571-1022 Perform Voice Communications

Far-

052-192-3261 React to an IED Attack
071-COM-0501 Move as a Member of a Team
071-COM-0513 Select Temporary Fighting Positions
113-571-1022 Perform Voice Communications
071-326-0608 Use Visual Signal Techniques
071-COM-0510 React to Indirect Fire Dismounted
071-COM-0608 Use Visual Signaling Techniques
113-571-1022 Perform Voice Communications
071-326-3002 React to Indirect Fire while Mounted

React to Indirect Fire

071-COM-0510 React to Indirect Fire Dismounted
071-326-0608 Use Visual Signaling Techniques
113-571-1022 Perform Voice Communications
071-326-3002 React to Indirect Fire while Mounted
071-COM-0501 Move as a Member of a Team

APPENDIX B

Proponent School or Agency Codes

The first three digits of the task number identify the proponent school or agency responsible for the task. Record any comments or questions regarding the task summaries contained in this manual on a DA Form 2028 (*Recommended Changes to Publications and Blank Forms*) and send it to the proponent school with an information copy to:

> Commander, U.S. Army Training Support Center
> ATTN: ATIC-ITSC-CM
> Fort Eustis, VA 23604-5166.

Table B-1. Proponent School or Agency Codes	
School Code	**Command**
MSCoE CM **031**	U.S. Army Chemical School Directorate of Training/Training Development 464 MANSCEN Loop, Suite 2617 Fort Leonard Wood, MO 65473-8929
MSCoE EN **052**	Commandant, U.S. Army Engineer School ATTN: ATSE-DT (Individual Training Division) 320 MANSCEN Loop, Suite 370 Fort Leonard Wood, MO 65473
FCoE **061**	Directorate of Training and Doctrine U.S. Army Field Artillery School ATTN: ATSF-D Fort Sill, OK 73503-5000
MCoE **071**	Commandant, U.S. Army Infantry School ATTN: ATSH-OTSS Fort Benning, GA 31905-5593
AHS **081**	Department of Training Support ATTN: MCCS-HTI 1750 Greeley Rd, Ste 135 Fort Sam Houston, TX 78234-5078
SCoE	U.S. Army Combined Arms Support

Table B-1. Proponent School or Agency Codes	
School Code	Command
091 (OMMS) 093 (OMEMS)	Command (CASCOM) Training Directorate USACASCOM, ATTN: ATCL-TD 2221 Adams Avenue., Suite 2018 Fort Lee, VA 23801-1809
SCoE 101	Commander, US Army Quartermaster Center and School ATTN: ATSM-MA Fort Lee, VA 23801-5000
SCoE 113	Commander, USA Signal Center & School ATTN: ATZH-DTM-U Fort Gordon, GA 30905-5074
MCoE 171	Commander, USA Armor Center and School ATTN: ATZK-TDT-TD 204 1ST Cavalry Regiment Road Fort Knox, KY 40121-5123
JAG 181	Commandant, Judge Advocate General Legal Center and School ATTN: JAGS-TDD 600 Massie Road Charlottesville, VA 22903-1781
MSCoE MP 191	Commandant, United States Army Military Police School ATTN: ATSJ-Z 401 MANSCEN Loop, Suite 1068 Fort Leonard Wood, MO 65473-8926

Table B-1. Proponent School or Agency Codes

School Code	Command
APAC **224**	Director, Army Public Affairs Center 6 ACR Road, Bldg 8607 ATTN: SAPA-PA Fort Meade, MD 20755-5650
ICoE **301**	Commander, USA Intelligence Center & Fort Huachuca 550 Cibeque Street, Suite 168 ATTN: ATZS-TDS-I Fort Huachuca, AZ 85613-7002
JFK **331**	U.S. Army JFK Special Warfare Center and School Fort Bragg, NC 28310-5000
SCoE **551**	U.S. Army Combined Arms Support Command (CASCOM) Training Directorate USACASCOM, ATTN: ATCL-A 2221 Adams Avenue Fort Lee, VA 23801-2102
Fort Jackson **SRT**	U.S. Army Training Center, Fort Jackson Director of Basic Combat Training (DBCT), Doctrine and Training Development, ATTN: (ATZJ-DTD) 4325 Jackson Blvd. Fort Jackson, SC 29207-5315

This page intentionally left blank.

GLOSSARY

Section I
Acronyms & Abbreviations

5-Cs	confirm, clear, call, cordon, and control
AAL	additional authorization list
ACE	air combat element (NATO);analysis and control element;armored combat earthmover;assistant corps engineer;aviation combat element (USMC); Avenger Control Electronics
ADA	air defense artillery; audio distribution amplifier; American Dietetic Association
AO	area of operations
APC	armored personnel carrier; activity processing code
AVPU	alertness, responsiveness to vocal stimuli, responsiveness to painful stimuli, unresponsiveness
BII	basic issue items
BSI	body substance isolation; Base Support Installation
CASEVAC	casualty evacuation
CBRN	chemical, biological, radiological, and nuclear
CPR	cardiopulmonary resuscitation
CSF	cerebrospinal fluid
CWIED	command wire improvised explosive device
DETCORD	detonator cord
EH	explosive hazards
EOF	escalation of force
EPW	enemy prisoner of war
F	frequency; fail; Fahrenheit; full; failed; Feeder; FMC
FM	field manual; frequency modulatedmodulation; flare multiunit; force module
FMC	full mission-capable; field medical card
FMI	field manual-interim; Failure Mode Identifier (indicates type of failure experienced by components. FMI has been adopted from SAE practice of J1587 diagnostics)
FOB	forward operating operationsoperational base; Free on Board
FW	Fixed Wing; Framework
GTA	graphic training aid
HQ	headquarters
IBA	individual ballistic armor
IED	imitative electromagnetic deception;improvised explosive device
JP	joint publication
LACE	liquid, ammunition, casualty, and equipment
LN; ln	local national; lane

MANPADS	man-portable air defense system
MEDEVAC	medical evacuation
METT-TC	A memory aid used in two contexts: (1) In the context of information management, the major subject categories into which relevant information is grouped for military operations: mission, enemy, terrain and weather, troops and support available, time available, civil considerations. (2) In the context of tactics, the major factors considered during mission analysis. [Note: the Marine Corps uses METT-T: mission, enemy, terrain and weather, troops and support available-time available.] (FM 6-0)
MIJI	meaconing, interference, jamming, and intrusion
MOI	message of interest; Material of Interest; memorandum of instruction; mechanism of injury
NBC	nuclear, biological, and chemical
NGO	nongovernmental organization; national government organization
NPA	net pay advice; nasopharyngeal airway
OAKOC	observation and fields of fire, avenues of approach, key terrain, obstacles, and cover and concealment
P	needs practice; pass; passed; barometric pressure; mean radius of curvature; positions; power; Propagated Booster; PMC
PBIED	person-borne improvised explosive device
PIR	priority intelligence requirements; priority information requirements
PZ	pickup zone
RCIED	radio controlled improvised explosive device
ROE	rules of engagement
RPG	rocket-propelled grenade
RTO	radio/telephone operator
RW	rotary wing; readwriter
SALUTE	size, activity, location, unit, time, and equipment
SMCT	Soldier's Manual of Common Tasks
SOI	signal operating/operation instructions
SOP	standing operating procedure
STP	shielded twisted pair; Soldier Training Publication; spanning-tree protocol; Soldier training plan
SURG	surgeon
SVBIED	suicide vehicle-borne improvised explosive device
TC	technical coordinator; training circular; track commander; tank commander; tactical commander; technical configuration
TCCC	tactical combat casualty care
TTP	tactics, techniques, and procedures
US	United States; ultrasound

VBIED	vehicle borne improvised explosive device
VOIED	victim-operated improvised explosive device
cont	continued; continuous; continuous fire; controlled substance
pnt	patient

This page intentionally left blank.

REFERENCES

Required Publications

Required publications are sources that users must read in order to understand or to comply with this publication.

ARMY REGULATIONS

AR 350-1. *Army Training and Leader Development.* 18 December 2009.

AR 600-9. *The Army Weight Control Program.* 27 November 2006.

DEPARTMENT OF THE ARMY FORMS

DA forms are available on the APD Web site (www.apd.army.mil).

DA Form 1594. *Daily Staff Journal or Duty Officer's Log.*

DA Form 2028, *Recommended Changes to Publications and Blank Forms.*

DA Form 2404. *Equipment Inspection and Maintenance Worksheet.*

DA Form 2823. *Sworn Statement.*

DA Form 3975. *Military Police Report.*

DA Form 4137. *Evidence/Property Custody Document.*

DA Form 5164-R. *Hands-on Evaluation.*

DA Form 5165-R. *Field Expedient Squad Book.*

DA Form 5988-E. *Equipment Inspection Maintenance Worksheet (EGA).*

DA Form 7656. *Tactical Combat Casualty Care (TCCC) Card.* (Available through normal forms supply channels.)

DEPARTMENT OF DEFENSE FORMS

DD forms are available on the OSD Web site (www.dtic.mil.whs/directives/infongt/forms/formsprogram.htm).

DD Form 1380. *US Field Medical Card.* (Available through normal forms supply channels.)

FIELD MANUALS

ACP 125 US SUPP-1. *Communications Instructions Radiotelephone Procedures for Use by United States Ground Forces.* 1 October 1985.

ADP 3-0. *Unified Land Operations.* 10 October 2011.

ADP 7-0. *Training Units and Developing Leaders.*
23 August 2012.

ATTP 3-06.11. *Combined Arms Operations in Urban Terrain.*
10 June 2011.

ATTP 3-34.80. *Geospatial Engineering.* 29 July 2010.

ATTP 3-39.10. *Law and Order Operations.* 20 June 2011.

FM 2-91.6. *Soldier Surveillance and Reconnaissance:
Fundamentals of Tactical Information Collection.*
10 October 2007.

FM 3-06. *Urban Operations.* 26 October 2006.

FM 3-07. *Stability Operations.* 6 October 2008.

FM 3-11.3. *Multiservice Tactics, Techniques, and Procedures
for Chemical, Biological, Radiological, and Nuclear
Contamination Avoidance.* 2 February 2006.

FM 3-11.4. *Multiservice Tactics, Techniques, and Procedures
for Nuclear, Biological, and Chemical (NBC) Protection.*
2 June 2003.

FM 3-11.5. *Multiservice Tactics, Techniques, and Procedures
for Chemical, Biological, Radiological, and Nuclear
Decontamination.* 4 April 2006.

FM 3-11.19. *Multiservice Tactics, Techniques, and Procedures
for Nuclear, Biological, and Chemical Reconnaissance.* 30
July 2004.

FM 3-19.13. *Law Enforcement Investigations.* 10 January 2005.

FM 3-21.8. *The Infantry Platoon and Squad.* 28 March 2007.

FM 21-60. *Visual Signals.* 30 September 1987.

FM 3-21.75. *The Warrior Ethos and Soldier Combat Skills.*
28 January 2008.

FM 3-22.9. *Rifle Marksmanship M16-/M4-Series Weapons.*
12 August 2008.

FM 3-24. *Counterinsurgency.* 15 December 2006.

FM 3-34.210. *Explosive Hazards Operations.* 27 March 2007.

FM 3-90.119. *Combined Arms Improvised Explosive Device
Defeat Operations.* 21 September 2007.

FM 4-01.45. *Multi-Service Tactics, Techniques, and Procedures
for Tactical Convoy Operations.* 5 January 2009.

FM 4-02.2. *Medical Evacuation.* 8 May 2007.

FM 4-25.11. *First Aid.* 23 December 2002.

FM 4-30.51. *Unexploded Ordnance (UXO) Procedures.*
13 July 2006.

FM 6-99.2. *US Army Report and Message Formats.*
30 April 2007.

FM 8-10-6. *Medical Evacuation in Theater of Operations
Tactics, Techniques, and Procedures.* 14 April 2000

FM 17-95. *Cavalry Operations.* 24 December 1996.

JP 1-02. *Department of Defense Dictionary of Military and
Associated Terms.*15 April 2012.

PAM 750-8. *The Army Maintenance Management System
(TAMMS) Users Manual.* 22 August 2005.

TB 11-5820-1172-10. *Operator and Maintenance Manual for
Defense Advanced GPS Reciever (DAGR) Satellite Signals
Navigation Set AN/PSN-13 AN/PSN-13 (NSN 5825-01-516-
8038) AN/PSN-13A (NSN 5825-01-526-4783).*
1 March 2005.

TC 3-22.20. *Army Physical Readiness Training.*
20 August 2010.

TC 20-32-5. *Commander's Reference Guide for Land Mine and
Explosive Hazards (IRAQ).* 13 February 2003.

TRCHNICAL MANUAL

TM -4230-229-10   . *Operators Manual for Decontaminating
Kit, Skin: M291, (NSN 4230-01-251-8702).* 2 October 1989.

TM 3-4230-235-10. *Operator's Manual for Decontamination
Kit, Individual Equipment: M295 (NSN 6850-01-357-8456)
(EIC: Y67).* 21 November 2008.

TM 3-4240-279-10. Operator's Manual for Mask, Chemical-
Biological: Field, ABC-M17 (NSN 4240-00-542-4450 –
Small) (4240-00-542-4451 –Medium) (4240-00-542-4452 –
Large); M17A1 (4240-00-926-4199 – Small) (4240-00-926-
4201 – Medium) (4240-00-926-4200 – Large); M17A2
(4240-01-143-2017 – X-Small) (4240-01-143-2018 – Small)
(4240-01-143-2019 – Medium) (4240-01-143-2020 –
Large). 5 October 1987

TM 3-4240-300-10-2. *Operator's Manual for Chemical-
Biological Mask: Combat Vehicle, M42 (4240-01-258-0064
– Small) (4240-01-258-0065 – Medium) (4240-01-258-0066
– Large).* 30 August 1998.

TM 3-4240-312-12&P. *Operator's and Unit Maintenance
Manual (Including Repair Parts and Special Tools List) for
Mask, Chemical-Biological: Aircraft, M43, Type I (NSN
4240-01-208-6966 – Small) (4240-01-208-6967– Medium)*

(4240-01-208-6968 – Large) (4240-01-208-6969 – Extra Large); Type II (4240-01-265-2677 – Small) (4240-01-265-2679 – Medium) (4240-01-265-2678 – Large) (4240-01-265-2680 – Extra Large). 30 June 1988.

TM 3-4240-342-10. *Operator's Manual for Mask, Chemical-Biological, Aircraft: Apache Aviator, M48 (NSN 4240-01-386-0198) Small (4240-01-386-4686) Medium (4240-01-386-0201) Large (4240-01-386-0207) Extra Large.* 13 September 2002.

TM 3-4240-346-10 *Operator's Manual for Chemical-Biological mask: Field, M40A1 (NSN 4240-01-370-3821-Small) (4240-01-370-3822-medium) (4240-01-370-3823-Large); Chemical-Biological Mask: Combat Vehicle, M42A2 (4240-01-4100-Small) (4240-01-413-4101-Medium) (4240-01-413-4102-Large).* 31 August 2010.

TM 3-4240-348-10. *Operator Instructions for Mask, Chemical-Biological: Land Warrior, M45 (NSN 4240-01-447-6989 - Extra Small); (4240-01-447-6987 - Small); (4240-01-447-8967 - medium); and (4240-01-447-6988 - Large).* 21 January 2000.

TM 3-4240-542-13&P. *Operator and Field Maintenance Manual (Including Repair Parts and Special Tools List) for Mask, Chemical-Biological: Joint Service General Purpose, Field, M50 (4240-01-512-4431) Small (4240-01-512-4434) Medium (4240-01-512-4437) Large and Mask, Chemical-Biological: Joint Service General Purpose, Combat Vehicle, M51 (4240-01-512-4429) Small (4240-01-512-4435) Medium (4240-01-512-4436) Large.* 30 May 2008.

TM 3-6505-001-10. *Operator's Manual for Reactive Skin Decontamination Lotion (RSDL) (NSN: 6505-01-507-5074) Training Packet, Reactive Skin Decontamination Lotion (RSDL) (6910-01507-5141).* 17 April 2007.

TM 3-6665-311-10. *Operators Manual for Paper, Chemical Agent Detector: M9 (NSN 6665-01-226-5589).* 31 August 1998.

TM 3-6665-426-10. *Operator's Manual for Detector Kit, Chemical Agent: M256A2 (NSN: 6665-01-563-7473).* 2 November 2009.

TM 3-9905-001-10. *Operator's Manual for Sign Kit, Contamination (NSN 9905-01-346-4716).* 23 August 1982.
TM 3-9905-002. *Technical Manual Operator's Manual for Sign Kit, Contamination: CBRN, M328 (NSN: 9905-01-567-7295).* 10 November 2011.

TM 9-1005-319-10. *Operator`s Manual for Rifle, 5.56 MM, M16A2 W/E (NSN 1005-01-128-9936) (EIC: 4GM); Rifle, 5.56 MM, M16A3 (1005-01-357-5112); Rifle, 5.56 MM, M16A4 (1005-01-383-2872) (EIC: 4F9); Carbine, 5.56 MM, M4 W/E (1005-01-231-0973) (EIC: 4FJ); Carbine, 5.56 MM, M4A1 (1005-01-382-0953) (EIC: 4GC).* 30 June 2010.

TM 9-1330-200-12. *Operators and organizational Maintenance Manual for Grenades.* 17 September 1971.

TM 10-8415-209-10 *Operator's Manual for Individual Chemical Protective Clothing.* 31 March 1993

TM 10-8415-220-10. *Operator Manual for Joint Service Lightweight Integrated Suit technology (JSLIST) Chemical Protective Ensemble.* 28 July 2008.

TM 11-5820-1172-13. *Operator and Maintenance Manual Defense Advanced GPS Receiver (DAGR) Satellite Signals Navigation Set AN/PSN-13 (NSN 5825-01-516-8038) AN/PSN-13A (NSN 5825-01-526-4783).* 1 March 2005.

TM 11-5820-890-10-1 *Operator`s Manual for SINCGARS Ground Combat Net Radio, ICOM Manpack Radio AN/PRC-119A (NSN 5820-01-267-9482) (EIC: L2Q) Short Range Vehicular Radio AN/VRC-87A (5820-01-267-9480) (EIC: L22) SHORT Range Vehicular Radio with Single Radio Mount AN/VRC-87C (5820-01-304-2045) (EIC: GDC) Short Range Vehicular Radio With Dismount AN/VRC-88A (5820-01-267-9481) (EIC: L23) Short Range Vehicular Radio With Dismount and Single Radio Mount AN/VRC-88C (5820-01-304-2044) (EIC: GDD) Short Range/Long Range Vehicular Radio AN/VRC-89A (5820-01-267-9479) (EIC: L24) Long Range Vehicular Radio AN/VRC-90A (5820-01-268-5105) (EIC: L25) Short Range/Long Range Vehicular Radio with Dismount AN/VRC-91A (5820-01-267-9478) (EIC: L26) Long Range/Long Range Vehicular Radio AN/VRC-92A (5820-01-267-9477) (EIC: L27).* 1 September 1992.

TM 11-5820-890-10-3 *Operators Manual for SINCGARS Ground Combat NET Radio, NON-ICOM Manpack Radio AN/PRC-119 (NSN 5820-01-151-9915) (EIC: L2A) Short Range Vehicular RadioAN/VRC-87 (5820-01-151-9916) (EIC: L2T) Short Range Vehicular Radio (with Single Radio Mount) AN/VRC-87D (5820-01-351-5259) (EIC: TBD) Short Range Vehicular Radio with Dismount AN/VRC-88 (5820-01-151-9917) (EIC: L2U) Short Range Vehicular Radio with Dismount (with Single Radio Mount) AN/VRC-88D (5820-01-352-1694) (EIC: TDB) Short Range/Long*

*Range Vehicular Radio AN/VRC-89 (5820-01-151-9918)
(EIC: L2V) Long Range Vehicular Radio AN/VRC-90
(5820-01-151-9919) (EIC: L2W) Short Range/Long Range
Vehicular Radio with Dismount AN/VRC-91 (5820-01-151-
9920) (EIC: L2X) Long Range/Long Range Vehicular Radio
AN/VRC-92 (5820-01-151-9921) (EIC: L2Y).* 1 September
1992.

YTM 11-5820-890-10-8 *Operator's Manual for SINCGARS
Ground Combat Net Radio, AN/PRC-119A (NSN 5820-01-
267-9482) (EIC: L2Q), AN/PRC-119D (NSN 5820-01-421-
0801) (EIC: GC9), AN/PRC-119F (NSN 5820-01-451-8252)
(EIC: GA4), AN/VRC-87A (NSN 5820-01-267-9480) (EIC:
L22), AN/VRC-87C (NSN 5820-01-304-2045) (EIC: GDC),
AN/VRC-87D (NSN 5820-01-351-5259) (EIC: GAR),
AN/VRC-87F (NSN 5820-01-451-8248) (EIC: GA5),
AN/VRC-87G (NSN 5820-01-555-7674) (EIC: N/A),
AN/VRC-88A (NSN 5820-01-267-9481) (EIC: L23),
AN/VRC-88D (NSN 5820-01-352-1694) (EIC: GAS),
AN/VRC-88F (NSN 5820-01-452-8435) (EIC: GA3),
AN/VRC-89A (NSN 5820-01-267-9479) (EIC: L24),
AN/VRC-89D (NSN 5820-01-420-6619) (EIC: GD8),
AN/VRC-89F (NSN 5820-01-451-8247) (EIC: GAY),
AN/VRC-90A (NSN 5820-01-268-5105) (EIC: L25),
AN/VRC-90D (NSN 5820-01-420-6618) (EIC: GD9),
AN/VRC-90F (NSN 5820-01-451-8246) (EIC: GA2),
AN/VRC-90G (NSN 5820-01-555-7371) (EIC: N/A),
AN/VRC-91A (NSN 5820-01-267-9478) (EIC: L26),
AN/VRC-91D (NSN 5820-01-420-6621) (EIC: GDG),
AN/VRC-91F (NSN 5820-01-451-8249) (EIC: GA8),
AN/VRC-92A (NSN 5820-01-267-9477) (EIC: L27),
AN/VRC-92D (NSN 5820-01-421-2605) (EIC: GDH),
AN/VRC-92F (NSN 5820-01-451-8250) (EIC: GM2), Used
with Automated Net Control Device (ANCD) AN/CYZ-10
Simple Key Loader (SKL) AN/PYQ-10 Precision
Lightweight GPS Receiver (PLGR) AN/PSN-11 Secure
Telephone Unit (STU) Frequency Hopping Multiplexer
(FHMUX) TD-1456/VRC.* 1 December 1998.

RELATED PUBLICATIONS

Related publications are sources of additional information; they
are not required to understand this publication.

ARMY REGULATIONS

AR 27-1. *Legal Services, Judge Advocate Legal Services.*
30 September 1996.

AR 190-13. *The Army Physical Security Program.*
25 February 2011.

AR 525-13. Antiterrorism. 11 September 2008.

FIELD MANUALS

ATTP 3-34.39. *Camouflage, Concealment, and Decoys.*
26 November 2010.

ATTP 3-39.22. *Physical Security.* 3 August 2010.

FM 22-6. *Guard Duty.* 17 September 1971.

FM 27-10. *The Law of Land Warfare.* 18 July 1956.

FM 3-22.40. *Multiserivce Tactics, Techniques, and Procedures
(MTTP) for Tactical Employment of Nonlethal Weapons
(NLW).* 24 October 2007.

FM 3-22.9. *Rifle Marksmanship M16-/M4-Series Weapons.*
12 August 2008.

FM 3-23.30. *Grenades and Pyrotechnics Signals.*
15 October 2009.

FM 3-25.26. *Map Reading and Land Navigation.*
18 January 2005.

FM 3-25.150. *Combatives.* 1 April 2009.

TC 7-98-1. *Stability and Support Operations Training Support
Package.* 5 June 997.

This page intentionally left blank.

STP 21-1-SMCT
11 September 2012

By Order of the Secretary of the Army:

RAYMOND T. ODIERNO
General, United States Army
Chief of Staff

Official:

Joyce E. Morrow

JOYCE E. MORROW
Administrative Assistant to the
Secretary of the Army
1103303

DISTRIBUTION:
*Active Army, Army National Guard, and United States Army
Reserve:* Distribute in accordance with the initial distribution
number IDN 111447, requirements for STP 21-1-SMCT.

This page intentionally left blank.

WARRIOR ETHOS

The Warrior Ethos forms the foundation for the American Soldier's spirit and total commitment to victory, in peace and war, always exemplifying the ethical behavior and Army Values. Soldiers put the mission first, refuse to accept defeat, never quit, and never leave behind a fellow American. Their absolute faith in themselves and their comrades makes the United States Army invariably persuasive in peace and invincible in war.